I0014023

Managing Operational Enterprise Resource Planning Applications

Richard Fulford

Managing Operational Enterprise Resource Planning Applications

An investigation into the effective management and evaluation of operational enterprise resource planning applications

VDM Verlag Dr. Müller

Impressum/Imprint (nur für Deutschland/ only for Germany)

Bibliografische Information der Deutschen Nationalbibliothek: Die Deutsche Nationalbibliothek verzeichnet diese Publikation in der Deutschen Nationalbibliografie; detaillierte bibliografische Daten sind im Internet über http://dnb.d-nb.de abrufbar.

Alle in diesem Buch genannten Marken und Produktnamen unterliegen warenzeichen-, marken- oder patentrechtlichem Schutz bzw. sind Warenzeichen oder eingetragene Warenzeichen der jeweiligen Inhaber. Die Wiedergabe von Marken, Produktnamen, Gebrauchsnamen, Handelsnamen, Warenbezeichnungen u.s.w. in diesem Werk berechtigt auch ohne besondere Kennzeichnung nicht zu der Annahme, dass solche Namen im Sinne der Warenzeichen- und Markenschutzgesetzgebung als frei zu betrachten wären und daher von jedermann benutzt werden dürften.

Coverbild: www.purestockx.com

Verlag: VDM Verlag Dr. Müller Aktiengesellschaft & Co. KG
Dudweiler Landstr. 99, 66123 Saarbrücken, Deutschland
Telefon +49 681 9100-698, Telefax +49 681 9100-988, Email: info@vdm-verlag.de
Zugl.: Edith Cowan University, Perth,WA

Herstellung in Deutschland:
Schaltungsdienst Lange o.H.G., Berlin
Books on Demand GmbH, Norderstedt
Reha GmbH, Saarbrücken
Amazon Distribution GmbH, Leipzig
ISBN: 978-3-639-13983-9

Imprint (only for USA, GB)

Bibliographic information published by the Deutsche Nationalbibliothek: The Deutsche Nationalbibliothek lists this publication in the Deutsche Nationalbibliografie; detailed bibliographic data are available in the Internet at http://dnb.d-nb.de.

Any brand names and product names mentioned in this book are subject to trademark, brand or patent protection and are trademarks or registered trademarks of their respective holders. The use of brand names, product names, common names, trade names, product descriptions etc. even without a particular marking in this works is in no way to be construed to mean that such names may be regarded as unrestricted in respect of trademark and brand protection legislation and could thus be used by anyone.

Cover image: www.purestockx.com

Publisher:
VDM Verlag Dr. Müller Aktiengesellschaft & Co. KG
Dudweiler Landstr. 99, 66123 Saarbrücken, Germany
Phone +49 681 9100-698, Fax +49 681 9100-988, Email: info@vdm-publishing.com
Edith Cowan University, Perth,WA

Printed in the U.S.A.
Printed in the U.K. by (see last page)
ISBN: 978-3-639-13983-9

This work is dedicated to my daughters Hannah, Molly and Georgina (Georgie).

Table of Contents

List of Figures

List of Tables

Abbreviation of Terms

Au$	Australian Dollar
B2C	Business to Consumer
BI	Business Intelligence
BPR	Business Process Reengineering
CBA	Cost Benefit Analysis
CEO	Chief Executive Officer
CFO	Chief Finance Officer
CIO	Chief Information Officer
CRM	Customer Relationship Management (application)
DB	Database
ERP	Enterprise Resource Planning (application)
ES	Enterprise Systems (ERP and possibly CRM)
Functional Upgrade	An upgrade that merges the functionality of a new version with customisations made to a previous version
IS	Information Systems
IT	Information Technology
KM	Knowledge Management
MRPII	Materials Resource Planning
NPV	Net Present Value
OLAP	Online Analytical Processing
OIPT	Organisational Information Processing Theory
PDA	Personal Digital Assistant
PM	Project Manager
RFID	Radio Frequency Identification
ROI	Return On Investment
ROE	Return On Employee
SBU	Strategic Business Unit
SCM	Supply Chain Management
SISP	Strategic Information Systems Planning
SME	Small and Medium Enterprise
SWOT	Strengths Weakness Opportunities and Threats
TAM	Technology Acceptance Model

Technical Upgrade	An upgrade that advances the application kernel version but does not implement the functionality of the new version
TOC	Total Ownership Cost
TCO	Total Cost Of Ownership
US$	United States of America Dollar
VAR	Value Added Reseller
XML	eXtensible Markup Language

Chapter One - Introduction

The child is a newcomer in a complex system, in a system of her world: she is born in a
family, she then enters a school, later a workplace. She tries to understand the system:
"what makes it tick?" What moves the system? What are the mechanisms, its
interconnections?(...) It is a question of solving the puzzle, of letting it gradually take
shape, of understanding what its structural features and the motives functioning within it.
(Aebli,1988,p.151 cited Engestrom et al, 1999 p. 23) .

This chapter outlines and explains the research problem and rationale. It sets the scene by articulating the broad aims of the research and the significance for academia and practice. The epistemology and associated methods are explained along with a definition of the research boundaries. Next comes a brief description of the field study and research methods used, and finally the book structure is described.

1.1   Research Context and Motivation

ERP systems are not projects that someday will end, but rather, they are a way of life
(Esteves and Pastor, 1999, p.2).

Organisations have probably changed more rapidly in the last 15 years than ever before. Johnson, Scholes and Whittigham (2008) explain that the intensifying of industry dynamics is largely due to the influence of improvements in IT. However, over the same period the major software component of IT, information systems (IS), has, in many respects, changed less than previously. This is because organisations have been deploying IS with upgrade paths that, arguably, keep the applications up-to-date but means that the IS is not replaced and married to changed business requirements.

Early in this 15 year period IS underwent a change from bespoke or small parochial systems to large proprietary applications that are similar or the same across organisations (Brown, Vessey, & Powell, 2000; Melville, Kraemer, & Gurbaxani, 2004). It is now common for a single application to be used by virtually every company in an industry (Davenport, 1998). The most prevalent and largest information systems are enterprise resource planning applications, hereinafter referred to as ERP. Markus, Axline, Petrie, & Tanis (2000) define ERP as "commercial software packages that enable the integration of transaction-orientated data and business processes throughout an organisation" (p.23). The deployment of these technologies throughout the 1990s and this century has altered the very fabric of IS management and evaluation that, to a large extent, is only just becoming recognised by practitioners and academics.

Traditionally, evaluation and management of IS focused on portfolios of projects with each project having a lifecycle of feasibility study, purchase, implement, operate, and replace (Remenyi, 2000). Applications tended to last a few years, for instance the maximum time allowed for depreciation of an IS asset in Australia is five years. This iterative process of implementation and abandonment of IS applications created a process of constant renewal, enabling IT initiatives to be congruent with business initiatives.

Milford & Stewart (2000) propose that ERP implementations are significantly different to other large systems, in terms of both complexity and magnitude. An important aspect is that "ERP systems implementations do not end when the systems are up and running. Users need on-going support, and organisations face a variety of issues such as fixing problems, upgrading to new versions of the software, and managing organisational performance with the system to achieve desired benefits" (Eriksen, Axline, Markus, & Ducker, 1999, p.42). This was confirmed by Davenport et al (2004) when studying the manner in which organisations were dealing with process change post-ERP implementation, they undertook quantitative research of 163 organisations as well as qualitative studies of 28 organisations, they "didn't find a single company that reported it was totally finished implementing ES [ERP] across all business processes" (p. 17).

As the lifespan of IS increases, an organisation must ensure the system continues to meet the organisation's needs and that it does not stifle exploration and innovation (Kallinikos, 2004). However, Phelan, Zrimsek & Frey (2002) of the Gartner Group identified that continuous improvement has not yet been applied to these large-scale IS, and that enterprises find themselves with ongoing suboptimal implementations resulting in lower return on investment and increased total cost of ownership. Phelan et al (2002) suggests that to remedy this, enterprises should work to improve their established ERP implementations.

In 2003, Microsoft assured potential purchasers of their three ERP applications that the company would maintain upgrades for a minimum of 10 years (Microsoft Open Letter, 2003), and an ERP application may "well last 20 years or more" (Markus & Tanis, 2000, p. 177). Four primary reasons are proposed for the lengthening of the ERP lifecycle. First, the large investment that an organisation has made and the potential cost of another implementation preclude abandonment. Second, the extent that an organisation becomes dependent upon the ERP for its underlying business processes means that the organisation cannot countenance the potential disruption to operations. Third, the social fabric of the organisation becomes interwoven with the application and staff resist change. Finally, the vendor's desire to maintain an ongoing relationship with an organisation means the organisation is persuaded to continue with the application.

Markus and Tanis (2000) identify the four phases of ERP maturity shown diagrammatically in Figure 1.

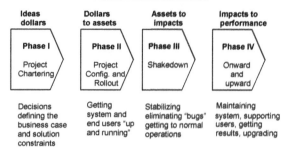

Figure 1.   Enterprise System Lifecycle (Markus & Tanis 2000, p.189)

The four phases are described as follows: the charter phase is concerned with the business case for the initial justification of system and solution definition; the project phase is concerned with the implementation of system and end user training; the shakedown phase is about coming to grips with the systems; and the onward and upward phase is the normal operation where the benefits should occur. Markus and Tanis (2000) propose that the onward and upward phase should include ongoing continuous business improvement and user skill building.

Esteves and Pastor (1999), in a similar vein, identify six stages of maturity of the ERP applications lifecycle: acquisition decision, acquisition, implementation, use and maintenance, evolution and retirement. The use and maintenance phase focuses on achieving the expected benefits of the system and upgrading the system for future improvements; the evolution stage is concerned with incorporating new activities and creating additional benefits; and the proposed maintenance and evolution stages are very similar to the Markus and Tanis (2000) shakedown and onward and upward stages; where the application is managed so as to achieve business benefits over time.

Bannister (2001) identified that the benefits and costs of systems decrease to a point where they cease to have a value for an organisation. Figure 2 depicts this application decay graphically.

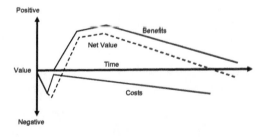

Figure 2.   Systems Net Value Over time (Bannister 2001, p.73)

There is little dispute that this is the likely scenario but an ERP application might be utilised for decades prior to abandonment. The graphical depiction in Figure 3 shows how the extended lifecycle of ERP has led to the largely accepted view of benefits and costs being ongoing or continuous. This is consistent with what Orlikowoski and Iacono (2001) describe as a 'tool' view of ERP: one that assumes that they are "stable, settled artefacts" (p. 123).

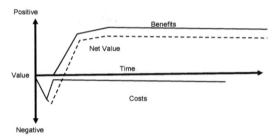

Figure 3.   Normalised ERP Value Over time (Fulford 2006, 3)

In fact, this proposal is unlikely to be the case as the value of an ERP will change over the extended lifecycle in relation to environmental dynamics, IT developments, and an organisation's ability to utilise and harness the functions within the current release of the application. The net value of an ERP is therefore likely to alter throughout the lifecycle. Figure 4 illustrates a possible scenario of the net value of an ERP changing over its lifespan, as costs and benefits vary year by year, thereby supporting the proposal that ERP value needs to be managed throughout the application's life.

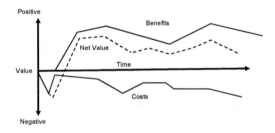

Figure 4.   Posited ERP Value (Fulford 2006,p.3)

The benefits of an ERP investment depends on the interaction of both technology and people over this extended period of time (Boonstrap (2004). Bannister, McCabe, and Remenyi (2001) observed that if re-engineering of an ERP was a continuous process, benefits could be maintained. Markus, Axline, Petrie, and Tanis (2000) explain that this might be difficult to achieve as the knowledgeable personnel who implemented the ERP are often lost to the organisation and the organisation may consequently be unable or unwilling to undertake further reviews or upgrades.

Consequently, much complexity and uncertainty exists concerning the management and evaluation of operational ERP. Remarkably few studies of operational ERP have been undertaken and it is therefore, very important that theory and practice better understand how the benefits and costs of ERP can be managed throughout the life of an application. There being no accepted framework of evaluation theory for ongoing management of the value of ERP, it is necessary to establish appropriate evaluation practices for applications and they should reasonably be ongoing processes. As Deloitte similarly argue:

> *Until now, conventional wisdom saw going live as the end. In sharp contrast to this view our study uncovers at least two distinct waves of ERP-enabled enterprise transformation. The First Wave refers to the changes to an organisation that include and accompany going live with ERP. The Second Wave, on the other hand, refers to the actions that are taken after going live that help organisations achieve the full capabilities and benefits of ERP-enabled processes. (Deloitte Consulting, 1999 cited Seddon et al, 2003, p.84).*

1.2 Significance of the research

Over the last decade many calls have been made in IS theory for research into the phenomenon of ongoing ERP management. Gable, Heever, Scott, and Erlank in 1997 recognised the increase in large-scale packaged applications, and, highlighting a scarcity in academic literature, called for research into ERP. Davenport, in 1998, proposed that ERP was reaching saturation in the market place, with many of its implementations ending in a 'nightmare' for organisations. Davenport identified many challenges, pointing out the "biggest problems were business problems" and that they needed to be better understood. In a study by Deloitte (1999), 49% of a large sample of CIOs considered that "an ERP implementation is a continuous process".

Markus and Tanis (2000), when proposing the ERP lifecycle model shown in figure 1, identified that "an especially interesting part of the model is what happens after 'normal operation' is achieved. When, how and why does the organisation decide to keep things as they are, making the enterprise system of today into the legacy system of tomorrow? When, how and why do organisations upgrade? Is it better to upgrade frequently so as not to risk big conversions? Do organisations really perceive themselves to be locked into a particular vendor? How does this influence their subsequent behaviour?" (p.203). Klaus, Rosemann, and Gable (2000) identified that most large, and a growing number of medium organisations, had already adopted ERP, and those that have not already done so are finding it a competitive necessity and proposed that the subject is "under researched". Chung and Snyder (2000) suggested that "both IT practitioners and researchers need to understand ERP systems better. MIS researchers especially should find a framework useful for adopting ERP systems in firms ... a series of case studies and empirical tests on ERP are suggested for corporations with various stages" (p. 31).

Research by Esteves and Pastor (2001) sought to identify areas of ERP that had been investigated, they found only 12 of 189 articles that were concerned with operational ERP. The 12 articles were seen to be "mainly technology-oriented, such as development of interfaces with other systems, the integration of customer relationship management modules, and use of web technologies" (p. 17). A CSC study conducted in 2001 which surveyed 1009 IS managers from around the world, identified 'optimising enterprise wide systems' as their main priority and that that organisations were wrestling with the complexities involved (Stein, Hawkings, & Foster, 2003, p.1). Dong, Neufeld and Higgins, (2002) reviewed 44 ERP research articles and could not identify any that were longitudinal studies or focused upon ongoing benefit and cost management. They contend that ERP literature is similar to an iceberg in that only a small proportion of the phenomenon is revealed Gable Chan, and Tan (2003) similarly argue:

> *Unlike implementation issues, however, issues related to the ongoing support, modification,*
> *and enhancement of ERP after its implementation have received little attention. Only a*
> *relatively small amount of mostly practitioner and some academic literature exists in this*
> *area. As mentioned above, the system life cycle of ERP is distinct from conceptions*
> *underlying earlier software maintenance research, suggesting that we question the*
> *generalizability of results from past research on software maintenance across all situations*
> *and their transferability into the ERP context. We believe that the significance of the*
> *installed base poses new challenges for practice and opens new opportunities for research*
> *(Gable et al, 2003, p.221).*

ERP success factors all seem to be limited to the implementation cycle and cross-sectional studies are needed to improve understanding of its impacts on organisations (Abdinnour-Helm & Lengnick-Hall, 2005). Gosain (2004) suggested that "very few [ERP] studies have gone beyond looking at implementation to tackle issues looking at longer-term usage and the impact of these technologies on organisations" (p. 152). Bendoly and Jacobs (2005) report ERP "research still seems preoccupied with discussions of implementation and adoption. Only a handful of studies has focused on the actual "use" of ERP" (p. 1). Sarkis and Sundarraj (2005) point out that "one of the major concerns in ensuring success in ERP implementations and extensions is that of the post-implementation audit and evaluation of these systems 'in-use'" (p.190). As recently as 2005 Dowlatshai stated, "Enterprise resource planning (ERP) has gained popularity among many organisations that seek to increase efficiency and productivity as well as to streamline their operations. ERP systems are a well-known concept. The available holistic literature and theory in ERP are, however, scarce" (p. 3745).

El Amrani et al (2006) argues that future ERP research should take both the ERP strategy and organisational context into account. Esteves and Bohorquez (2007) reviewed ERP system research publications from 2001-2005, following the similar process instituted by Esteves and Pastor (2001) and found that "publications within the information systems community on ERP are scant compared to the business that they have generated" (p.419) and that "this study shows that ERP researchers still focus on the implementation phase of the ERP lifecycle" (p.420). After reviewing literature of what they term the 'Use and Maintenance' phase of ERP, they identified the need for research that looks "at the post implementation period of ERP systems to determine how and why business benefits evolve over time" (p.412). In what they term the evolution phase, in which new technology is released from ERP authors, they propose a need for research into how to integrate these technologies with the existing IS, and the subsequent impact on organisations.

This research will provide a greater understanding of management and operational performance methods for operational ERP applications. This will be achieved by examining the management of ERP vis-à-vis the prevalent theory of management and evaluation of IS. Where possible the study will be augmented by a macro perspective of social, historical and political influences. Moreover, the research aims to determine how macro and micro techniques can best be incorporated in order to manage an ERP application during its operational life. In doing so, the research will have significance for both academics and practitioners, providing a richer understanding of the required management processes. The outcomes will inform and support the administration of enterprise applications and reduce the likelihood of their failing to meet organisational needs.

1.3 Researcher's Background and Motivation

The researcher has a commercial background that includes 5 years as a senior business manager of an ERP consultancy organisation and 17 years as a commercial IT professional. He has been involved in multi-site and multi-national IT management, a managing director of an IBM business partner providing ERP software, and systems and managing director of a subsidiary of a 1300 employee public company providing mainly ERP solutions. His technical knowledge includes experience in programming, database design, ERP and CRM implementations. Management experience includes project and program management, as well as operational and executive functions.

He has completed two research dissertations concerning strategic business management and the relationship between IT planning and strategic management. He is now a tenured lecturer at Edith Cowan University in the School of Management, educating in ERP, IS strategies, business strategy and IT evaluation. Understanding of the processes employed to implement ERP, along with the time that an application might last, have caused the researcher to be very interested in the ongoing management of applications and their consequence for businesses over time.

1.4   Research Question and Objectives

The call in IS literature for further research into operational ERP and the researchers interests have given rise to the following research question.

How should the ongoing value of ERP be managed and evaluated?

The specific aim of the research is to develop a theoretical model that will provide guidance for further academic research into the key factors relevant to management and evaluation of operational ERP, and identify a set of guidelines that will assist practitioners in the effective administration of ERP.

1.5   Defining Enterprise Systems and Enterprise Resource Planning Applications

Some of the cited quotations in this book use the term Enterprise Systems (ES) rather than ERP. Davenport (1998) indicated that enterprise systems and ERP are synonymous, and he suggests that enterprise systems are commonly referred to as ERP. Lorenzo and Kawalek (2005) also state that ERP are also known as ES. However, from approximately 1998 to 2005, customer relationship management (CRM) applications were also referred to as ES. Seddon et al (2003) propose that ES includes other applications such as CRM, supply chain management (SCM), Product Lifecycle Management (PLM) and Enterprise Application Integration (EAI). They do, however, recognise ERP as the master class of ES. This document uses the term ES synonymously with ERP, when the term ES is directly cited from publications. The citations have been validated to ensure that they infer ERP rather than a broader meaning for ES.

1.6   Document Structure

Chapter one outlines and explains why the research is significant and the research rationale.

Chapter two presents the theory used to develop the initial conceptual model. The literature review is very broad as would be expected in a study that includes organisations, management and evaluation. The constructs are explained and a conceptual framework of the phenomenon elucidated.

Chapter three explains the ontological and epistemological assumptions for the research. These assumptions and the constructs developed in Chapter 2 are used to develop and explain the research methodology. Limitations of the proposed methodology are also clarified.

Chapter four analysis each of the five case studies in terms of the constructs previously developed. The pilot case gave rise to two further constructs that are also incorporated in the study. Conclusions and a conceptual overview concerning the management and evaluation of ERP are made for each of the case studies.

Chapter five evaluates the constructs in terms of each of the cases and, where possible, identifies commonalities and proposes why these may have occurred. The analysis explains what is happening in the case organisations with regard to management and evaluation of ERP and incorporates these findings with recent theory. The chapter concludes with the design of a potential framework for the management and evaluation of ERP.

Chapter six provides the conclusion of the study, including contribution and implications for theory and practice.

Chapter One – Introduction

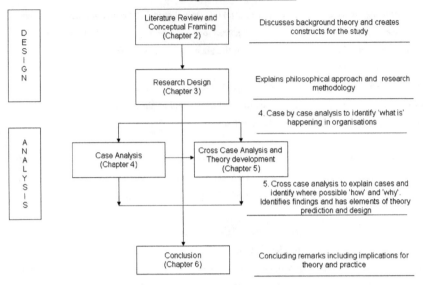

Figure 5.   Book design - chapter 1

Chapter Two - Conceptual Framing

Knowledge is based on a synthesis of a concept (understanding) and experience   Kant (cited Hirschheim, 1985, p.16).

The purpose of this chapter is to review the relevant literature regarding management and evaluation of information systems in organisations. Specifically, the intention is to build an underpinning for the theory building research from the relevant literature which then assists to identify the constructs of the investigation (Eisenhardt, 1989) and an initial conceptual model. The conceptual model has been informed by existing theory, the experiences of the researcher, and the general objective of the research (Miles & Huberman 1994). The theory discussion in this chapter is very much aimed at creating this pre-understanding and, there is more targeted application of theory in the case explanation and theory building discussion in Chapter 5.

The chapter is organised into four sections. First, the capabilities of 2nd generation ERP are identified and the value system of the ERP industry is discussed. Second, management process and governance with regard to IS are reviewed. Third, evaluation theory is examined. Finally, a conceptual framework for the study is explained. The literature review links with Chapter 3, where the constructs developed in this chapter form the basis of the research design, and chapters 4 and 5 where the constructs are verified, amended and used to present the case analysis.

2.1   Enterprise Resource Planning Applications

Enterprise Resource Planning (ERP) programs are core software used by companies to coordinate information in every area of business. ERP programs help to manage company-wide business processes, using common database and shared management reporting tools (Monk & Wagner, 2006, p. 1).

The salient and identifying characteristic of ERP systems is their ability to integrate business processes by standardising data, storing it in a common, shared database, and ensuring that this data is accessible to whoever needs it on a real time basis (Davenport, 1998; Klaus et al, 2000; Shanks and Seddon, 2000 cited Strong, Volkoff, & Elmes, 2003, p. 500). The breadth of ERP means that is envisaged differently by organisations: it can be seen ERP as a data management system; as a group of interconnected modules; as a collection of rules and procedures used for planning and reporting; as well as a communication tool. Organisations often adjust their way of working to fit the package (Markus, et al., 2000b) and, therefore, ERP tends to impose its own logic on a company's strategy, culture and organisation (Davenport, 1998).

Chapter Two - Conceptual Framing

This process takes time and it may well be many years before ERP enables benefits in an organisation (Markus et al., 2000b).

The current level of ERP is often referred to as ERPII which seeks to integrate customers or client facing-solutions, such as CRM/B2C, with back office transactional services such as SCM (Sharif, Irani, & Love, 2005). Seddon et al (2003, p.2) propose that ERP "is a generic 'semi-finished' product with tables and parameters that client organisations and their implementation partners must configure, customize, and integrate with other computer-based information systems to meet their business needs". Brown et al. (2000) postulate three reasons for purchasing ERP: the desire to replace ageing mainframe systems with enterprise-wide architecture; replacement of legacy systems that no longer meet an organisation's needs; and the desire to reduce costs by buying rather than building software.

Nevertheless, an ERP system is a major investment: Klaus et al (2000) estimating an implementation to cost between $50,000 and $100,000,000+; and, Monk and Wagner (2006) believe a large implementation of more than 1,000 employees is likely to cost between US$50 million and US$500 million. Monk and Wagner (2006) also suggest that much of the cost is for consultancy rather than the application itself, citing an example, admittedly in a complex situation, of US$30 million for the application and US$200 million of consultancy fees. Scheer and Habermann (2000) confirm that the cost of implementing ERP might be many times the cost of the application and Doane (1997 cited Brown and Vessey, 1999) that third-party consultants are most often used as implementation partners at two to 10 times the cost of the ERP application. There are also the associated costs of hardware and training.

"By 1998, most of the Fortune 500 companies had installed ERP systems, so ERP vendors refocused their marketing efforts on midsize companies" (Monk & Wagner, 2006, p.30). ERP is also an expensive proposition for mid-sized organisations. According to Monk and Wagner (2006, p.32), "a midsize company might spend US$10 million to US$20 million in total implementation costs and have its ERP system up and running in about two years". Malbert, Soni, and Venkatraman (2001), referring to industry experts, assert that ERP costs between 1 and 6 percent of total revenue. Gosain (2004), citing precise analysis by the Meta Group, proposed that the average implementation costs across all sizes of organisations was US$10.6 million, taking 23 months to complete and having maintenance costs of US$2.1m during the ensuing two year period.

Market saturation has now been reached in capital-intensive manufacturing industries (Fub, Gmeiner, Schiereck, & Strahringer, 2007); nevertheless, AMR Research (2005) predicts a growth in the ERP market from US$47.88bn 2004 to US$64.8bn in 2009. They propose that the 8% annual growth will be from expansion into additional enterprise application segments and selling to a much wider set of vertical industries, company sizes, and geographic markets.

2.1.1 ERP Functions

ERP purports to support all business functions but it especially supports procurement, material management, production, logistics, maintenance, sales, distribution, financial accounting and asset management (Klaus et al., 2000). These functions have been provided as part of ERP for the past 15 years. The competition in the market place has meant that the major products are not significantly differentiated and these core features are similar in the major applications. Additional capabilities are being continually added and the applications now include customer relationship management (CRM), supply chain management (SCM), strategic enterprise management (SEM), internet connectivity and business intelligence (BI). Esteves and Bohorquez (2007) classify these developments as evolution upward and evolution outward. The upward enhancements are to increase the functionality and include BI tools; the enhancement outwards increase connectivity and include, amongst others, the CRM components.

The capabilities of current ERP are illustrated in Figure 6.

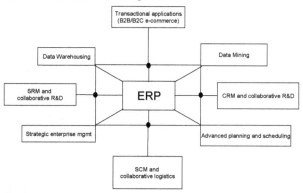

Figure 6. The enabling position of ERP Architecture (Bendoly and Jacobs 2005, p.42)

2.1.1.1 ERP and Business Intelligence

Business intelligence includes a broad category of applications and techniques for gathering, storing, analysing and providing access to data, helping enterprise users make better business and strategic decisions.

ERP applications often include the activities of query and reporting, online analytical processing (OLAP), data mining, forecasting and statistical analysis.

Microsoft Dynamics AX implements BI via maintain OLAP cubes that can be established by simply entering the cube dimensions into the application. The cubes can then be interrogated by the application, Excel and other packages. Interestingly, Microsoft now has a 21% share of the business analytics market, and is rapidly taking further market share (Watson, 2006). SAP's solution to BI is to provide a data warehouse for each major module whereby, "analytics query the warehouse rather than the transaction database" (Monk & Wagner, 2006, p.124). Oracle has traditionally been a database and analytics provider, having an array of options for warehousing and analytics. The Oracle analytics products are apparently in decline (Watson, 2006), but the ERP is still viewed as a leader in the area of BI.

"The on-line, real-time operational data that ERP systems provide enable managers to make better decisions and improve responsiveness to customer needs" (Ross, Vitale and Willcocks, 2002 cited Summer, 2005, p.2). These analytical tools aim to extend second generation ERP beyond transaction processors, and for them to be executive information and decision support systems.

2.1.1.2 ERP and e-business

The Internet's rapid development since the mid-1990s has been a threat to ERP software authors (Monk & Wagner, 2006, p.39). In response ERP authors have been incorporating e-business functions into their applications. SAP has been Internet enabled since the late 1990s with SAP ITS providing Internet access and SAP Business Connector providing information exchange using XML (Ash & Burn, 2003). Microsoft Dynamics AX is supplied with 5 corporate portals embedded in the application and an option to purchase further portals. The application also has XML capability, reports can be automatically published on the Internet and transactional documents can be sent via email. The Oracle ERP, which is named Oracle e-Business suite, has a reputation for being the most comprehensive e-business system.

All of the applications can now provide remote access to functions via the Internet, while Dynamics AX also provides seamless access via mobile technology. Today, "what makes this technology more appealing to organisations is its increasing capability to integrate with the most advanced electronic and mobile commerce technologies" (Al-Mashari, 2003, p.1). Esteves and Bohorquez (2007) see this evolution 'outward' as a major component of the 'new' benefits of ERP applications.

2.1.1.3 Customisation of ERP

It is not the mere fact that ERP can be customised that distinguishes ERP from other packages. It is the rich potential for customisation that distinguishes ERP (Klaus et al., 2000, p.41).

ERP can be customised to meet organisations' requirements. The major ERP products can all be purchased with program source code, these include ERP applications from SAP, Oracle and Microsoft. However, in some instances a charge is levied for the programs.

The customisations are generally made by either consultants or the end user IT department. This quite often occurs pre and post live. Customisations made to a version of ERP software application need to be applied to subsequent releases of the application. This re-implementation of the customisations can take much time and requires thorough testing. ERP applications have tools that aid the processes but these are often found to be over simplistic, particularly for object orientated languages.

2.1.1.4 Potential ERP Benefits

Evaluation of IS is discussed later in this chapter, this section simply aims to identify the specific benefits of ERP.

ERP can eliminate redundant effort and duplicated data, resulting in reduced personnel needs (Markus & Tanis, 2000). They can produce goods and services more quickly resulting in a potential increase in sales (Lawrence, Jennings, & Reynolds, 2005), and produce timely and accurate information (Sumner, 2005). They can also enhance relationships with customers and suppliers (Lawrence et al., 2005).

Poston and Grabski (2000) see the following as tangible benefits from ERP implementations:

- o Inventory Reduction
- o Personnel Reduction
- o Order management improvement
- o Financial close cost reductions
- o Technology cost reduction
- o Procurement cost reduction
- o Cash management improvement
- o Revenue/profit increase
- o On time delivery improvement

Poston and Grabski identify intangible returns as follows:

- o   Information Visibility
- o   Improved processes
- o   Customer responsiveness
- o   Integration
- o   Standardisation
- o   Flexibility

2.1.2 Value Providers of ERP

The ERP value system has three major components: the Software Author who develops the application - SAP, Microsoft and Oracle being examples of Software Author organisations;   Software Resellers, usually referred to as value added resellers (VARS), who apply the technology to organisations largely through consultancy services; and the End User being the organisation that utilises the software. Figure 7 shows the value system.

Figure 7. ERP Value Chain (adopted from Fulford 2003, p.3)

2.1.2.1 Software Authors

The Software Author market is becoming a global oligopoly, and is very profitable for the three dominant players which have almost 40% market share between them (SAP Annual Report, 2006). In 2006, SAP had 24% of the software sales market, Oracle 9% and Microsoft 5% (SAP Annual Report, 2006). As will be discussed later, software sales are made up of new business and maintenance. SAP have the largest installed base, and the maintenance agreements by existing customers accounts for a large proportion of their revenue. Microsoft have the largest penetration of the market, particularly in the fastest growing sector of medium sized organisation (Monk & Wagner, 2006) which is also know as tier 2.

Market saturation at the turn of the century led to a serious decline in sales (Gartner Report, 2002). Since 2000 there has been a number of acquisitions, mergers and insolvencies (Eschender, 2003). Microsft entered the ERP market in the late 1990s with its acquisition of Great Plains and extended that in 2002 with an acquisition of Navision. Oracle has recently broadened its ERP portfolio with acquisitions of two ERP

Software Authors: Peoplesoft and J.D.Edwards. Peoplesoft first bought J.D.Edwards only to be acquired themselves by Oracle in a hostile take-over in 2005.

Generally, Software Authors do not capitalise their product development, therefore having to maintain sales to sustain cost of product enhancements. This is aided greatly by an annual fee for maintenance or upgrade paid by the end-user. This fee can vary from author to author, but is generally between 15% and 25% of the application's value; SAP's maintenance cost starts at 15%, increasing over time and being dependent upon how far in arrears of the current release an organisation becomes. Microsoft Dynamics AX charges 25% of the application cost.

SAP's Annual Report for 2002 identified SAP as deriving 51% of annual product revenue from maintenance contracts. In 2006 SAP achieved 33% of total revenue from new software sales and 37% from maintenance agreements (SAP Annual Report, 2006). This maintenance income significantly buffers the Software Author against the affects of market downturns. A major focus for Software Authors is, therefore, to maintain the relationship with the end user for as long as possible (Swift, 2001).

Microsoft's acquisition of Navision Software in 2001 for a reported US$1.2 billion represented a very forceful move into the ERP Software Author market in what was a time of new sales market decline. One of the major factors was the significant revenue stream that can be maintained from the estimated 35,000 installations of the Navision Software. Navision had a gross operating profit of 84% and net profit of 21% before amortisation of goodwill in fiscal 2001/2002 (Navision Annual Report, 2002). It also achieved a Revenue per Employee (ROE) of approximately Au$370,000. This relatively high ROE is due to the Software Author not requiring a large number of staff for its core activity of software development and channel management. These results were accomplished in what was the worst year for ERP sales in almost a decade, this performance contrasting heavily with the software reseller environment in the same period.

2.1.2.2 Software Reseller

Software resellers or value added resellers (VAR) are a fundamental feature of the value chain; they apply the technology to organisations. The software resellers have extremely high requirements of knowledge both of the applications they sell and the business processes supported by the applications.

The VAR is generally coerced by the Software Author to identify and focus on niche markets, particularly in the SME market place. Klaus et al (2000) suggest that these templates are tailored to specific industries or companies of a certain size. These industry sectors may be broad - manufacturing, warehousing, project services, etc., or narrower - capital goods manufacturer, made to order, plastics extrusion, etc. These standardised components are easy to copy and acquire (Abdinnour-Helm & Lengnick-Hall, 2005) thus minimising the advantage to the reseller. Much of the niche marketing and lead generation costs are the responsibility of the VAR, with branding and broad marketing being the responsibility of the Software Author.

The large Software Authors such as SAP and Oracle often operate directly with end users, but this activity is almost wholly restricted to very large corporate customers. It is reported that SAP will not directly engage with an organisation that has less than US$1 billion revenue. This creates a premise that penetration of the market is largely dependent upon VAR sales initiatives. The VAR lacks power within the value system and is being squeezed by both the end-user and the Software Author (Fulford & Love 2004). The latter's power is derived from the large number of resellers.

The reseller retains a percentage of the maintenance fee, the majority of which is retained by the author to cover the cost of developing future product releases. Software Authors have increased the cost of maintenance over the last decade by as much as 100% (Fulford, 2003). In addition to the maintenance agreement, the reseller must provide product support, usually in the form of a help desk. This is also charged on an annual basis. The imposed increase in maintenance costs has forced resellers to heavily discount or provide the support activity free of charge to maintain sales (Fulford and Love, 2004). It is often this post-sales support that maintains the relationship with the customer and therefore, needs to operate efficiently to maintain profitability for the value system.

The Statement of Financial Position (or balance sheet) is traditionally very weak for Resellers. Project activity may be capitalised during the project but otherwise these companies have relatively low asset value. When software sales slow the Software Reseller is affected almost immediately, particularly as these organisations have substantial payroll costs due to the level of expertise that is required to deploy ERP solutions.

The applications are becoming increasingly complex and diverse in terms of functionality and technology, requiring staff to be constantly re-skilled and technical specialists employed. In times of low activity, staff utilisation reduces considerably. In contrast to Navision, whose revenue per employee was Au$370, 000 (see above), the largest reseller of Navision software during the same period achieved just Au$170, 000 per employee (Columbus IT Partner AS Annual report, 2002). This organisation had to maintain substantial infrastructure in 27 locations around the world, making a loss of approximately $30m (Columbus IT Partner

AS Annual report, 2002) whilst in 2001/2002 Navision made a profit of $48m (Navision Annual Report, 2002).

2.1.2.3 End User and Service Dissemination

The large corporations have generally already implemented ERP applications and the focus for the Software Authors has turned to the medium and small enterprise (Monk & Wagner, 2006, p.30). Love, Irnai, Standing, Lin and Burn (2004) found SMEs to have varied IT budgets and much less predictable motivations for purchasing technology than larger organisations. The desperation of the reseller to utilise personnel provides an opportunity for the end-user. For SMEs there are many 'off the shelf' applications that are commodity priced, for example, Mind Your Own Business (MYOB), whilst larger or more complex organisations have invested, or are seeking to purchase, an highly functional ERP applications possessing a sustainable upgrade path. These organisations choose from a number of software resellers to provide support and consultancy services. This competitiveness in the reseller environment can significantly reduce implementation costs for end-users. To some extent the end-user can be described as the 'prey' that has become the 'predator' (Fulford, 2003).

2.1.2.4 ERP Value System

The key components of the application sales value chain are shown in Figure 8.

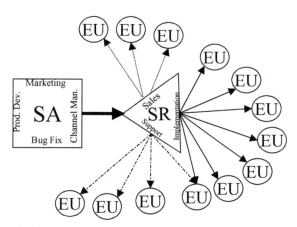

SA: Software Author
SR: Software Reseller
EU: End-user

Figure 8. Key components of the application sales value chain (Fulford 2003,p.6).

The Software Author maintains the product by increasing the number and depth of functionality of application modules. The author also creates service releases or bug fixes to overcome major problems with a previous release. Marketing consists of branding and product information. SAP markets strongly which is probably a major factor for their dominant position. The other major activity with regard to sales generation is channel management, which the recruitment and management of software resellers.

The software reseller is generally responsible for lead generation and sales activity, the major activity being implementation of the application in the form of project services. The other customer-focusing activity is that of post-implementation support of the installed application at the end-user site. The type of arrow in Figure 8 above indicates the level of revenue generated at each stage of the relationship with the end-user. There is little revenue in the sales activity other than perhaps some chargeable identification of the end-user's needs. The major component of revenue is derived from the implementation of the applications during the project lifecycle. The post- implementation stage does generate some revenue, of which the Software Author takes an increasing percentage.

2.1.3 ERP Applications Implications for Research

The Software Authors appear to have considerable power in the value system and may be able to assert pressure upon an organisation. The regular release of new functionality and technology makes it interesting to observe the extent of the Author's influence on decisions related to upgrades and other expenditure. The VAR is a pivotal component of the ERP supply chain and is likely to impact the success of the implementation through consultancy and training. These processes and their outcomes will also need to be understood.

Whether the ERP implementation is viewed as being successful or not is likely to impact the ongoing management and evaluation of the application, particularly if remedial activity is required. Organisations may also have upgraded or re-implemented. Therefore ensuring it is important for the research to understand the antecedents of the implementation, and how management and evaluation might have changed over time. Figure 9 shows possible influences on the ongoing management of ERP of these external factors and the past events.

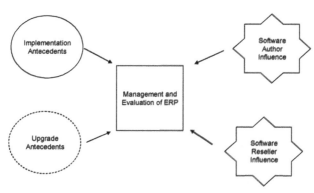

Figure 9. ERP product implications for research

2.2 ERP and Organisational Management

The development and retention of new competitive advantages drawn from these [ERP] systems require a steady watch for appropriate and advantageous use and an organisational diligence that encourages novel applications of the system in problem solving, regulation, and innovation (Bendoly and Jabobs 2005, p.5).

This section discusses the three primary component influences and interfaces between an organisation and an ERP application: ERP and strategic management; ERP and governance; and ERP and organisational structures. This influences are seen as particularly necessary because, as Grant (2003) points out, the most overlooked area of an ERP is the implications for business strategy and organisational structure.

2.2.1 ERP and Strategic Management

An important aspect of management in an organisation is strategic management which in turn has, implications for IS and IT management. As Ward and Peppard (2000, p.34) point out, "management and evaluation of IT is directly related to the strategy of an organisation". Strategic benefits from ERP are likely to accrue only to organisations which treat ERP implementation as a business process rather than an IT project (Davenport 1998, 2000; Markus and Tannis 2000; Somers and Nelson 2000; Bendoly and Kaefer 2004 cited Abdinnour-Helm and Lengnick-Hall 2005). Esteves and Pastor (1999, p.2) identify ERP to "require a high degree of alignment between business strategies, information technology strategies and organisational processes". Davenport (1998) also suggests that all companies struggle with the cost and complexities of ERP applications, but that those having the most trouble install the applications without thinking through the business implications. Davenport (1998, p.2) points out that "if a company rushes to install an enterprise system [ERP] without first having a clear understanding of the business implications, the dream of integration can quickly become a nightmare". It is, therefore, important to understand how business strategy and the communication of that strategy inform the acquisition of ERP and ongoing management of the application.

> *The contribution of large-scale IS deployment to superior business performance is*
> *predicted on the dynamic alignment of business and information technology (IT)*
> *strategies and the underlying architectures and systems that support the strategy*
> *execution" (Grant, 200, p.163) .*

From its beginnings, strategic management has sought to answer the fundamental question of how firms achieve sustainable competitive advantage (Herrmann, 2005). The aim of strategic information systems' planning (SISP) is to align information technology and systems with strategic management. Much theory has been dedicated to aligning IT and business planning, the overriding principle being that IT must be implemented in such a way that its technical, economic and strategic affects are in line with corporate strategy (Potter, 1987; Venktraman, 1994, Porter, 1988; Zuboff, 1988; Earl, 1989; Agnell & Smithson, 1990; Bjornsson & Lundegard, 1992;, Scott-Morton, 1991; Kanter, 1992, Benjamin & Levinson, 1993, Wilcocks et al, 1997). The foregoing premise is that the ability to realise value from IS stems partly from the relationship between business and IS strategy (Potter, 1987, Peppard & Breu, 2003). Importantly, linkages between IT strategy and business strategy are not concerned with linking business strategy with IT strategy per-se, but with the strategy processes (Scott-Morton, 1991).

Venkatraman (1994) identified the four core domains of IT in the corporate context: organisational infrastructure and process; business strategy: information systems infrastructure and process; and information technology strategy. The strategic alignment process produced by Scott-Morton (1991, pp. 162) depicted in Figure 10, is proposed here to be broadly representative of alignment models, establishing the core issues of IT and Strategy in the 1990s.

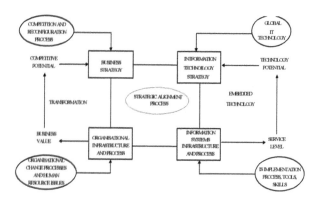

Figure 10. Strategic Alignment Process (Scott-Morton 1991,p.12)

Clear business objectives are a prerequisite to alignment models as they are used to establish the IT mission (Kanter, 1992; Scott-Morton, 1991; Agnell and Smithson, 1990).

A major finding of the MIT 1990 project, which reviewed issues of IT and management, claimed there was no evidence that IT provides organisations with long-term sustainable competitive advantage; and that the real benefits of IT were derived from the constructive combination of IT with organisation structure. Since that time there has been an emphasis on the enabling capabilities of IT to create a focus on organisational structures; thus the core issue of IT strategy became restructuring. These findings produced a keyword 'enabler' in the IT lexicon, IT being an 'enabler' of organisational objectives, particularly in the area of organisational structure (Hammer, 1990; Scott-Morton, 1991; Kanter, 1992; Venkatraman, 1994b). It was therefore important when creating IT strategy not only to understand the structure of the organisation, but also what its future might be (Scott-Morton, 1991).

Latterly this emphasis has increased to ensuring that IT can provide for whatever the structure may become, as organisations are facing increased uncertainty, and therefore, plan for multiple scenarios (Evans, 2003, p.6). Efstathiou (2002) concludes this is because the very nature of IT is changing and reacting to the creation of corporate agendas is a cost-centred mentality. The evolving role of the IT department is then changing to one of a profit driver, this change is referred to as the occurrence of "technological discontinuities or breakthroughs that depart dramatically from the norm of continuous incremental innovations" (Herrmann, 2005, p. 119).

This change of emphasis on the relationship between IT and strategic management can be paralleled with changes in the way organisations are viewed. Strategic management has been emphasised since the 1960s, but it was the beginning of the 1980s when a focus on generic strategies was adopted (Herrmann, 2005). The generic strategy models owe much to Porter's work of that era. The models created by him take an industry view of the competitive environment, focusing on product cost and added value to explain the competitive environment, the dominant models of which are the value chain, SWOT, five forces as well as the generic competitive strategies (Porter, 1980).

The basis of the value chain approach is that the environment, both internally and externally, can be treated as objective realities to be assessed formally and prescriptively (Hackney, Burn, and Dhillon, 2000). The main criticism of this approach is its failure to recognise and acknowledge the diversity and complexity of organisational realities (Hackney et al 2000). The value chain concept categorises IT as a support initiative and as a result reduces the potential of IT to achieve sustainable competitive advantage (Bahn, 2001). The proposed narrowness of the value chain concept has given rise to what is known as resource, competence or knowledge based strategies. Hermann (2005) articulates the evolution of strategic management shown in figure 11.

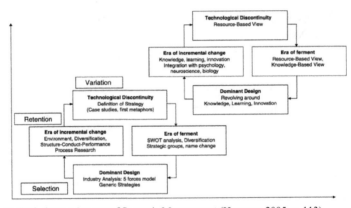

Figure 11. Evolutionary Aspects of Strategic Management (Hermann 2005, p. 113).

The resource based view "rests on the idea that firms create sustainable competitive advantages by developing and applying idiosyncratic firm resources. These firm-specific resources are the basis of competitive advantages when they are costly, rare and non-replicable" (Herrmann, 2005). As Figure 11 illustrates, IT is used in these organisations to increase the span of control of employees and reduce managerial hierarchy by providing information to all areas of the organisation (Lucas, 2000). When trying to identify benefits of IT in this scenario, the wider work systems need to be understood (Alter, 1999).

Deise, Nowikow, King, and Wright (2000) formally categorise organisations into two main types to support this polarity of views - Physcos and Knowcos. Physcos are organisations that compete by adding value to physical products and "require the movement of physical parts around the factory floor, purchasing capital equipment, and managing sizeable inventories of raw materials, work-in-progress and finished goods"(p.84). Knowcos compete by focusing on resources, knowledge and competencies and "focus their core competencies on knowledge of a product or service" (Deise et al., 2000. p.124). The strategy processes will differ in physical and knowledge-based organisations (Johnson and Scholes, 2002). Physical organisations may well continue to utilise the strategy process identified by Porter; Knowcos are proposed to have a competence based strategy that focuses on generating abilities to enable or create possibilities for future strategies. These organisations types are, obviously, at opposite ends of what is a broad spectrum of businesses.

Product based organisations would probably have a value chain perspective as described above by Porter (1980), focusing typically on product cost and adding value. The traditional principle of management of IT in a product based organisations has been that IT must be implemented in such a way that its technical, economic and strategic impact is in line with corporate strategy (Agnell & Smithson, 1990; Benjamin & Levinson, 1993; Bjornsson & Lundegard, 1992; Earl, 1989; Kanter, 1992; Porter, 1988; Potter, 1987; Scott Morton, 1991; Venkatraman, 1994b; Willcocks, Feeny, & Islei, 1987; Zuboff, 1988).

ISP works well with Porter's perspective but less so with an informal approach to management, as Porter's models do not take sufficient account of firms' resources, or competencies, and their ability to improve profitability in organisations that are not product focused (Zack, 1999). With resource based organisations, competitive advantage will be more difficult to define as evaluation of their progress will be based on speed, innovation, service and customisations, as well as volume, scale and low cost (Herrmann, 2005). Organisations following a resource based strategy will probably focus IT on improving or endowing its 'bundle resources within its administrative framework' to achieve a competitive advantage (Melville et al., 2004). The focus is very much on leveraging resources and capabilities across many markets and products (Zack, 1999).

The many types of organisations and industries makes it no longer practical to suggest a standardised approach to the strategic management of IS, although it is accepted, as proposed by Grant (2003), Esteves and Pastor (1999) and Ward and Peppard (2000), that knowledge of strategic emphasis is necessary for ERP management. An important aspect of the research will be to understand the strategy process and how strategies are disseminated so as to impact ERP management.

Johnson and Scholes (2002) identify the three following strategic views or lenses for strategy development:

- o Design lens, wherein strategy is developed through formal planning processes.
- o Experience lens, wherein protagonists make strategic moves based on environmental conditions and their knowledge, strategy is generally termed as emergent.
- o Ideas lens, wherein ideas proliferate from all levels of an organisation and impact strategy.

Co-incidentally, these strategy processes correlate quite well with the organisational types outlined above: design lens with Deise et al's (2000) Physcos; and Ideas lens with Deise et al's Knowcos. McNurlin and Sprague (2004) are helpful in relating the focus of IT expenditure to underlying business focus and strategies. Their use of the terms utility, dependent and enable can be explained briefly as follows:

- o Utility: IT is focused on economies of scale
- o Dependent: IT is focused on supporting current business strategies and programs
- o Enable: IT is focused on creating flexibility to meet future changes in the marketplace

The categorisations of McNurlin and Sprague(2004) and Johnson and Scholes (2002) are used to help to explain the process of strategic management and its relationship with ERP management and evaluation.

2.2.2 ERP and IT Governance

Possibly due to the broadening approaches to strategic management of recent years, governance of both organisations and information technology has come to the fore. Organisational, or corporate, governance identifies how an organisation should function and prioritise activities in support of stakeholders (Johnson & Scholes, 2002). Similarly, "IT Governance is the system by which an organisation's IT portfolio is directed and controlled. IT Governance describes (a) the distribution of IT decision-making rights and responsibilities among different stakeholders in the organisation, and (b) the rules and procedures for making and monitoring decisions on strategic IT concerns" (Peterson 2004, p.4). Peterson (2004) describes IT governance as a new form of old school IT management and strategic planning. It aims to effectively manage the structures, processes and relationships of IT and how they support an organisations goals (De Haes and Van Grembergen, 2005). This section of the investigation aims to establish how IT governance models might support ongoing management of ERP.

IT governance is the responsibility of the Board of Directors and Executive Management and is an integral part of organisational governance (Governance Institute Whitepaper, 2003). It should specify the decision rights and accountability framework to encourage desirable behaviour in the use of IT (Weill & Woodham, 2002). Numerous governance models have been produced that have both similar and contrasting aims and components. The governance frameworks shown in Figure 12 are the predominant models in use today, with the most common being Control Objectives for Information and Related Technology (COBIT), Information Technology Infrastructure Library (ITIL), Val IT, and International Organisation for Standardisation (ISo) 17799 .

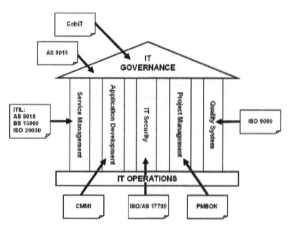

Figure 12. Frameworks relating to IT functions (Ratcliffe 2004, p.86)

In summary: PMBOK is a project management activity used in ICT and other projects, including construction; ISo1799 is a security management framework aimed at protecting the organisations' information, financial and human capital; Capability Maturity Model Integration (CMMI) is used to support software development; ITIL is a broad framework, aimed at both IT service in the form of help desk and support as well as security, and having a level of application management which appears to be concerned with ongoing support; ISO 9001 is a quality management system for IT and other services; and the Australia Standard, Good Governance Principles AS8000 (2003) is based on corporate governance and the relationships between company stakeholders.

Val IT and COBIT have the largest component of strategic and application management. Val IT uses the vision and goals of an organisation to develop the IT goals and is largely focused on investment decisions, evaluation and risk management. While COBIT has an intricate mechanism of translating business objectives into IT activities. The process is one of acquisition of applications to meet business objectives and not one of managing the evolving existing applications as shown in Figure 13.

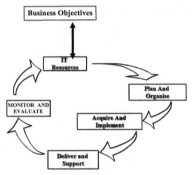

Figure 13. COBIT Framework (COBIT Framework, n.d.).

The COBIT framework identifies the following as the objectives of managing delivery and support (COBIT Framework, nd.)

- o DS1 Define service levels
- o DS2 Manage third-party services
- o DS3 Manage peformance and capacity
- o DS4 Ensure continuous service
- o DS5 Ensure systems security
- o DS6 Identify and attribute costs
- o DS7 Educate and train users
- o DS8 Assist and advise IT customers
- o DS9 Manage the configuration
- o DS10 Manage problems and incidents
- o DS11 Manage data
- o DS12 Manage facilities
- o DS13 Manage operations

These activities seem to imply that the system is relatively stable when it is implemented and that continuous improvement is not necessary. The only aspect that alludes to ongoing management of an application such as an ERP application is 'Manage Configuration'. However, the latter, is defined as, "Ensuring the integrity of hardware and software configurations requires establishment and maintenance of an accurate and complete configuration repository. This process includes collecting initial configuration information, establishing baselines, verifying and auditing configuration information, and updating the configuration repository as needed. Effective configuration management facilitates greater system availability, minimises production issues and resolves issues faster "(COBIT Framework, n.d.,p.8). Which is not the same as the management of ERP envisaged here.

Broadly speaking, the governance frameworks are aimed at strategic control and long term strategies for implementation management of new systems and their evaluation, (Weill & Ross, 2004), as well as quality services (Weill & Woodham, 2002). The frameworks do not appear to have a large focus on ongoing optimisation of IS. It is of interest to understand which if any of these models are being utilised to manage ERP.

2.2.3 ERP and Organisational Structures

Organisational structure impacts the ability to 'fit' an ERP system to an organisation (Morton & Hu, 2004). An organisation's structure is generally dictated by its environmental conditions and strategy. Organisational information process theory (OIPT) states, "in order to prosper, organisations must resolve uncertainty". The number and types of uncertainty vary by organisation and include the stability of the external environment, the predictability of core processes, how tasks are subdivided, and the level of interdependence among those subdivisions. Organisations often take a polarised view aiming to either be controlled or flexible, Newell et al (2007) points out that it is difficult for organisations to be efficient and flexible, to become what they term "ambidextrous". Organisations that wish to be flexible are challenged "when the degree of interconnectivity and interdependency increases the complexity of a given configuration, the degree of flexibility of each element tends to decrease" (Pozzebon and Pinsonneult 2004, p.335). Organisations wishing to be flexible, according to theory, are generally resource based organisations where employees are knowledge workers.

Newell et al (2007, p.164) propose that ERP are the "antithesis of agility because of the demands they make on organisations during adoption and implementation"; and as Bancroft et al (1997 cited, Markus & Tanis, 2000, p.182) point out, "organisations that continually change their organisational structure and business models and particularly those that are not run 'in a very top-down manner' may find enterprise systems unsuitable as corporate solutions." Control organisations do much better with ERP as these organisations are more stable. The 'fit' between ERP and different organisational types was investigated by Morton and Hu (2004), using the organisational types identified by Mintzberg (1979). The outcome of their research is summarised in Table 1.

Table 1.   Fit Between ERP Systems And Organisation Types (Morton and Hu, 2005).

Organisational Type	Structural Dimensions			Degree of ERP Fit	Likelihood of Implementaion Success
	Formalization	Structural Differentiation	Decentralization		
Machine Bureaucracy	High	Medium	Low	High	High
Professional Bureaucracy	Low	High	High	Low	Low
Divisonalized Form	Medium	High	High	Low	Low
Adhocracy	Low	High	High	Low	Low

The table shows that only in a Machine Bureaucracy is ERP likely to be a particularly good fit. Kalinkos (2004) suggests that ERP moves less structured organisations to formally structured organisations, with organisations become procedurised which cuts development from vital sources of knowledge and practice: "They put a premium on control, efficiency and standardisation and inevitably subordinate issues of exploration and innovation in organisations" (p.27). Therefore, organisations having a resource based strategy are probably less likely to have successful ERP implementations. Which is cause for concern for organisations and should presumably be taken into account when selecting and managing ERP.

The basic premise is that the ERP must have consistent objectives, or be segregated and managed in a way that provides for different and perhaps opposing objectives. Therefore, an organisation "must select and deploy the subset of information processing mechanisms that fits particular uncertainties ... ERP's impact depends, at least part on the amount and types of uncertainties at hand" (Gattiker and Goodhue 2005, p.562).

According to Davenport (1998) all companies struggle with the cost and complexities of ERP applications, those having the most trouble are those which install the applications without thinking through the business implications. Many organisations are able to install ERP in the sense of making the system available, but fail in their efforts to diffuse and incorporate the system throughout the organisation's daily practices (Lorenzo and Kawalek 2005). The management practices, organisational structure and management emphasis appear to have a direct impact on the complexity of an implementation and even the applicability of an ERP. This research needs to be cognisant of these factors, and to that end the following questions posed by Davenport (1998) will be used to understand how this process is envisaged in an organisation:

- o How might an ERP strengthen competitive advantage?
- o How might it erode them?
- o What will be the system's effect on organisation and culture?
- o Should the system be used across all functions, or should only certain modules be implemented?

This implies that business managers must exhibit strong leadership with regard to the deployment of IT, requiring they understand the IT resources (Bassellier et al, 2003). However, Willcocks and Sykes (2003), in asserting the management function has been 'asleep at the wheel' with regard to ERP, identify three asleep modes: technological determinism, supplier/consultant driven, and absent relationships and capabilities. Technological determinism occurs when the technology is all encompassing and owned by the IT function, with ERP being regarded as the new software system; supplier/consultant driven implementations arise from executive decisions without the inclusion of the already poorly trained senior IT staff, resulting in consultants selling to senior executives with consequent cost overruns; and absent relationships occurs when the IT function is made responsible for ERP but does not have the capabilities, both technical and management of suppliers, to implement and manage the application.

The research of Willcocks and Sykes (2003) pinpoints management as needing to take more responsibility for ERP and not to devolve responsibility to external providers. However, this creates something of a dilemma for organisations in the early stages of adoption because they do not yet have the expertise in terms of the application to make considered decisions. Figure 14 shows diagrammatically Somers, Nelson, & Ragowsky, (2003) suggestion that ERP benefits may only be achievable when it has been implemented and the application is used to its fullest.

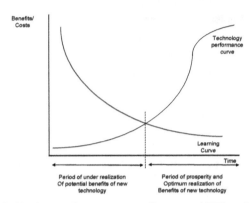

Figure 14. The goal of implementation management (Somers et al 2003, p. 6)

Holland and Light (2001) propose a maturity model for ERP and identify that "After user managers have learnt more about what the software can do, for example, after a year or so, they are often in a much better position to specify what they want to achieve with their software" (Holland and Light 2001, p.4). Orlikowsky (1992 cited Boonstrap, 2004) also proposes that the result of an IT investment depends on the interaction of both technology and people over an extended period of time. The findings of Davenport & Brooks (2004) about achieving more value from ERP has three components, namely:

1. Integrate – unify and harmonize ERP, data and processes with an origination's unique environment, using the system to better connect organisational units and processes, customers and suppliers.
2. Optimise – standardise most processes using the best practice embodied in ERP software; mould and shape processes to fit the unique or strategic needs of the business; and ensure processes flow and fit with the systems themselves
3. Inform – use the organisation to transform work by converting data into context-rich information and knowledge that support the unique business analysis and decision-making needs.

These appear to be a sound basis for ERP management. However, the hiatus between acquiring an application and knowing how to best utilise it is concerning. As this has implications for the uptake of knowledge and the level of control of an implementation that an organisation can undertake.

2.2.4 ERP and Management Implications for Research

The models adopted in the 1990s for strategic alignment are probably no longer or only partially valid for many types of organisations. The governance models that are becoming increasingly popular do not seem to sufficiently address the ongoing management of benefits of IS. Implicit however, is that strategic management of ERP is known to be fundamentally important for providing benefits to organisations, particularly as ERP are often purchased to provide competitive advantage or to preclude competitive disadvantage from a competitor that has already implemented an ERP. This contention is borne out in much of the ERP theory, many studies having identified that ERP projects should be business driven rather than technology driven, and should focus on an organisation's competitive advantage (see for ex. Abdinnour-Helm & Lengnick-Hall (2005).

According to Madupusi and D'Souza (2005), misalignment of ERP systems and international strategy is one of the primary reasons for delayed or failed ERP implementations. Rosemann, Vessey, & Weber (2004) argue that the 'fit' is of paramount importance and the greater, what they term, the 'ontological distance' between the organisation and the system, the more likely there will be fundamental problems with the success of the system. Markus et al (2000b) also explain that, "companies experience problems at all phases of the ERP system life cycle and many of the problems experienced in later phases originated earlier but remained unnoticed or uncorrected " (p.245), the implication being that there might be antecedents that impact the ongoing management of the ERP.

The important aspect of the foregoing for this book is, 1. to understand the strategy processes in organisations and the management foci that prevail, and how they impact ERP, 2. how management gauge the impact of ERP on competitive advantage 3. the length of time between acquiring an ERP and understanding the capabilities of the application, 4. the organisational and environmental variances are likely to preclude a prescriptive theoretical framework , 5. the antecedents of events such as implementation and upgrades and their ongoing impact.

2.3 ERP and Evaluation

The Department of Finance 1994 defined evaluation as "a systematic, objective assessment of appropriateness, effectiveness and/or efficiency of a program or part of a program. Depending upon the purpose of the evaluation and the stage of development of the program, an evaluation may focus on more than one of these issues". The main body of IT evaluation literature is concerned with project evaluation where individual projects are assessed in terms of feasibility and success. An increasing area of discussion is the evaluation of IT infrastructure - those IT investments that underpin an organisation. Industry and e-business evaluations are also major topics. As ERP potentially impacts all of these categories the aim here is to précis the relevant areas of the very broad subject of IT evaluation theory.

2.3.1 Project Evaluation

Project evaluation helps management decide, in a rational way, the true business value of a potential project investment (Keen & Digrius, 2003). Tanaszi (2003) peoposes, "The IT project evaluation and selection process itself has serious implications for an organisation's ability to get the most value from IT investments" (p.24). The methods employed to evaluate IT projects' expenditure are split into two primary domains: ex-ante and ex-post.

2.3.1.1 Ex-ante Domain

"Ex-ante is the predictive evaluation performed to forecast and evaluate the impact of future situations, the purpose being to support systems' justification and often uses financial or other indicators to estimate the outcome" (Remenyi, Sherwood-Smith, & White, 1997, p.55). Much of an ex-ante evaluation focuses on project portfolio management where projects bubble up from the low levels of an organisation and are approved or rejected at a higher level (Keen & Digrius, 2003).

Ex-ante evaluation has two principal domains; tangible and intangible (Irani & Love, 2002). The tangible methods are mainly based on financial analysis such as Return on Investment (Bernroider & Koch, 2001), Cost Benefit Analysis (King & Schrems, 1978) and Return on Management (Strassman, 1997). These tangible techniques primarily identify the cost of an IT acquisition and the expected financial return. They are well suited to the automation of processes where relatively straightforward measures such as headcount and cost reductions are appraised (McKay and Marshal, 2004). These methods match well with the needs of the physical/product based organisation that hopes to improve efficiencies.

The traditional evaluation methods of ROI and NPV appropriate to 1990s are much less appropriate for resource based organisations (Chan & Qi, 2003), because the nature of benefits from IT investments are changing to: enabling competitive advantage through the changing power of players; providing for strategic alliances; and support of decision making (Mckay & Marshall, 2004). Many of today's IS benefits are intangible as they assess effects of the system which cannot be directly measured, valued or related to change (Remenyi, 1997). Remenyi (2001), explains, "Although difficult to be precise about their actual value, especially in financial terms, intangible benefits can make a critical contribution to the success of an organisation"(p.21).

Many techniques aim to consider intangible benefits, for example, Broadbent and Weil (1997) developed an intangible evaluation method called the business maxims model. This model aimed to identify the business context from which corporate executives, business-unit managers and IT executives, create ' IT and business maxims'. These maxims then dictate key areas of IS expenditure. Another prominent model is information economics which assesses IT against the long-term organisational objectives using a scoring model for strategic issues (Parker, Benson, & Trainor, 1988). These intangible techniques predominately attempt to align IT with the strategic focus of an organisation rather than its specific strategies. Therefore they fit well with resource/knowledge focused organisations utilising IT to create strategic opportunities.

Shang and Seddon (2002), also conducting research in this domain, propose tangible benefits for ERP applications under five dimensions: operational, managerial, strategic, IT infrastructure and organisational. Murphy and Simon (2002) recognise the applicability of Shang and Seddon's dimensions but suggest that ERP systems should also be evaluated using intangible benefits. Poston and Grabski (2000), as summarized in Table 2, have identified specific benefits of ERP and whether these are tangible or intangible.

Table 2.   Returns From ERP (Poston & Grabski, 2000)

Hard returns – tangible benefits from ERP implementation		Intangible returns – intangible benefits for ERP implementations	
Return	% of survey respondents	Return	% of survey respondents
Inventory reduction	32	Information/visibility	55
Personnel reduction	27	New/improved processes	24
Productivity improvement	26	Customer responsiveness	22
Order mgmt. improvement	20	Cost reduction	14
Financial close cycle reduction	19	Integration	13
Technology cost reduction	14	Standardisation	12
Procurement cost reduction	12	Flexibility	9
Cash mgmt. improvement	11	Globalisation	9
Revenue/profit increases	11	Year 2000	8
Transportation/logistics cost reduction	9	Business performance	7
Maintenance reduction	7	Supp/demand chain	5
On-time delivery improvement	6		

This research aims to identify whether tangible and/or intangible techniques are being utilised to evaluate acquisition, upgrades and customisation of ERP.

2.3.1.2 Ex-Post Domain

"Post implementation evaluation or ex-post at the highest level is used to examine 'what is' against some previously suggested situation. This is done to confirm the value of the investment and support operational decisions about improvements" (Remenyi, 2000, p.22). Ex-post evaluations are concerned with post-project success and are used to assess the value of existing situations, and to confirm or refute the value of an IT investment (Remenyil, 2001). Banister and Remenyi (2000) found the volume of research of ex-post evaluation to be remarkably small and complex in nature. Two seminal views on IS success are current: a version by De Lone and Mclean 1992 that was updated in 2003; and the other by Seddon, Staples, Patnayakuni, and Bowtell (1999). Delone and McLean produced the model of IS success, shown in 15, reviewing published theory from 1979 to 1989.

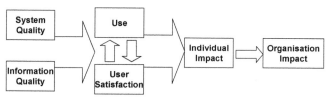

Figure 15. Model of IS Success (Delone and Mclean 1992, p.87)

The 'causal' model posits that organisational outcomes are a consequence of the impact of IT on an individual user and that an individual user will only use IT if he or she is satisfied with the system. Satisfaction in turn is related to the quality of the system and the information it provides. IS success is, therefore, dependent on system and information quality.

Delone and Mclean reviewed the model in 2003, making two major changes. Firstly, a dimension of service quality was added; the service quality or 'ServQual' had been proposed by Pitt et al in 1997, and is the quality of the IT function itself in meeting user demands in terms of service level agreements, training, etc. This addition assumed that use was not only dependent on systems and information, but also on the relationship with the IT function and the support it provides. The second change was due to the increased capability of IT to provide benefits outside the organisation through e-business and other technological advances. The major benefits of e-business are defined by Gide and Soliman (1999) to be improving customer service, reducing costs, providing business intelligence, simplifying processes, generating revenue and enabling faster decisions.

Seddon et al (1999) argued the original Delone and Mclean model as being unduly simplistic because it did not differentiate between types of IT and types of user. Seddon proposed a 6 by 5 matrix of correlation between these two factors and, soon after his paper was published, Alter (1999) reported that the users proposed in Seddon's paper were in turn dependent upon system quality and that this model was too simplistic also. Seddon et al (1999) then produced the model shown in Figure 16.

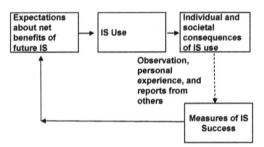

Figure 16. IS Success (Seddon et al 1999, p.10)

The model posits that IT results are dependent on use and the societal impact. It appears to be a good overview of the prevalent theories, and implies that the success of IS is dependent on the quality of systems and, in turn, acceptance by users.

2.3.1.3 Project Evaluation Summary

The evaluation process at the highest level has the following four quadrants.

Table 3.   Ex-ante and ex-post tangible and intangible cost benefit analysis

Tangible	Quantified measure of cost and benefit	Post project cost benefit appraisal, meets expectations of ex-ante costs and benefits
Intangible	Relate IT to business context. Try to identify total cost proposition	User acceptance, impact on individual performance, organisations ability to respond. Identify indirect cost and disbenefits
	Ex-ante domain	Ex-post domain

The primary focus of ERP is upon organisational efficiencies, but ERP can also relate to resource based strategies and a focus on competencies (He, 2004). It is possible that whether the evaluation applied to ERP is tangible or intangible will depend upon the focus of the system or module under review. If the system has been implemented for efficiency gains, tangible techniques would seem to be applicable, but if the aim is for increased effectiveness, intangible measures are likely to be more appropriate. In either case costs are likely to be made up of actual, intangible and 'disbenefits'.

2.3.2 Evaluation of IT Infrastructure

The evaluation of an IT project's capacity to sustain business competitiveness is important, however, there are many aspects of IT considered to be infrastructure. Whether ERP constitutes infrastructure is open to debate, much IS theory suggests that it is, but practitioners generally think of an infrastructure layer as being predominantly part of the network with an application layer supported by that. Broadbent and Weil (1997) claim that IT infrastructure may contain hardware platforms, base software platforms, communications technology, client server technology and other software that provide common handling mechanisms for different data types and methods, standards and tools. Andresen and Gronau (2005) agree with this stance and suggest that ERP largely constitutes infrastructure.

The distinction as to whether ERP is infrastructure or not, is important as the management and evaluation processes differ for infrastructure to that for strategic acquisitions. Hackney et al (2000) point out that strategy is demand oriented, focusing on information requirements, whereas infrastructure is supply oriented being concerned with providing the applications. Broadbent and Weil (1997) suggest that infrastructure is difficult to justify as executives have to make the decision about this aspect prior to deciding the strategies it will support. They claim infrastructure to be dictated by a firm's strategic context, being built up so as to support business maxims identified by senior managers. McNurlin and Sprague (2004) identify three drivers for IT infrastructure:

- o The infrastructure was built as a desire for economies of scale and cost cutting and as such has been dictated by a series of strategic decisions on which these decisions are based.
- o Infrastructure has been decided by accident rather than design.
- o A strategic view has been taken of infrastructure and it has been implemented to support and enable future strategies, whatever they may be.

Markus and Tanis (2000) observe that companies that continually change their organisational structures and business models may find ERP inhibiting. Therefore, the flexibility of infrastructure is important, particularly if the McNurlin and Sprague strategic view of infrastructure is accepted. A major consideration for resource-based organisations in particular questions whether the infrastructure will be sufficiently flexible.

Flexibility is defined as the degree to which the infrastructure can be reused and shared. Flexible infrastructure will enable an organisation to respond quickly to changes in its environment and competitive situation, whilst inflexible infrastructure will inhibit organisational change (Kayworth, Chatterjee, &

Sambamurthy, 2001), and further, "A firm with high infrastructure flexibility could make rapid changes to information systems in support of changing business needs while firms with low flexibility infrastructures will be unable to imitate the IT innovations of its competitors"(p. 8). McNurlin & Sprague, (2004) aver that building in flexibility adds cost and complexity to IS, but that these options may be exercised in the future as organisations in a more volatile market place would be expected to have a more extensive IT infrastructure. This may seem somewhat esoteric, however, as it is apparent from the organisational types discussed above the flexibility of infrastructure, including ERP, may well directly impact potential benefits.

Organisations take different approaches to IT infrastructure investments depending on strategic objectives. These might be costs savings through economies of scale, current strategy needs or longer-term requirements for flexibility. These emphases are likely to, or perhaps should, impact the ERP management process.

2.3.3 e-Business Evaluation

"The greatest value of a Web site is its accessibility. Running a very close second is the fact that your web site can remember everything about the people who decide to visit – when they come, what pages they look at, how long they spend on each page, which products they find most interesting and more" (Cutler & Sterne, 2000). E-business systems in ERP applications may contain a great deal of information of partner usage that may aid evaluation of the application.

The evaluation of e-business becomes more complex as the system becomes more pervasive and the extent of services increases. There is a number of models that gauge the extent of e-business such as: the Stages of Growth of e- business (SOGE) promoted by McKay and Marshall (2004); and the Leveraging the Organisation Through ICT and e-business of Price Waterhouse. These models propose that the impact of e-business on a value system differs depending on the extent of that it is used in the supply chain.

E-business systems can be evaluated using what is known as e-metrics, a mode of operation to enable evaluation and segmentation of customer and prospect profiles (Cutler & Sterne, 2000). E-metrics are used to identify such things as customer loyalty and attrition rates, providing for rapid remedial actions to be taken to improve system performance. The process of e-metrics appears to be very much aligned with product organisations where events are measured against current business emphasis.

Applegate et al (2002) identifies evaluation methodologies of e-business systems in resource-based organisations to include the reduction in time, cost and risk of launching new online business initiatives; expanding the reach of existing IT enabled businesses; and the range of business opportunities that can be pursued. It also provides information to customers, suppliers, and partners so enabling better decision making. This should also enable them to charge a price premium for products and services based on value-added information; launch new information based products and services; increase revenue per user; and add new revenue streams. It will also decrease time to market or just-in-time order replenishment; enable new channels to market; and/or extend the reach and range of existing channels. This resource-based view of Applegate et al (2002) is very different to that of the e-metrics process which focuses on the current activity. For the case examples the approach above prompts a need to ascertain the prevalent uses of e-business components of ERP and to understand how they are or might be evaluated.

2.3.4 ERP and Evaluation Implications for Research

Davenport, Harris, and Cantrell (2004) note that with adopters of ERP there is ongoing process and application changes. Markus and Tanis (2000) categorise this as the onward and upward phase and suggest it should include continuous business improvement and user skill building. Stefanou (2001) agrees and proposes that it should incorporate decisions concerning new releases and extending the application to include new modules. The decisions to upgrade, use additional areas of an application or even re-address implemented areas are discrete decisions that should reasonably undergo a feasibility and evaluation study. Figure 17 delineates the theoretical process of evaluation.

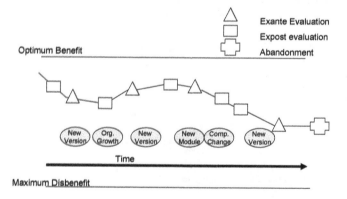

Figure 17. Proposed framework of evaluation.

Khoo and Robey (2007) identified three reasons to upgrade an ERP these were business needs, IT policy and mitigation of software risks. The decision to apply an upgrade or additional functionality would seem to require a rigorous ex-ante evaluation. Also, ERP itself appears to require ongoing evaluation to ascertain if an organisation's competitive environment is changing or the organisation is changing substantially, in order to ascertain if the ERP fits the new business model. Indeed, the move to a long-term commitment to ERP that require an infrastructure of IT to enable them to operate efficiently has led to a need for ongoing ex-post evaluation.

Whether the evaluation is tangible or intangible would seem to depend upon the focus of the system or module under review. If the system has been implemented for efficiency gains, tangible techniques are likely to be most applicable; however, if the aim is to be more effective, then intangible measures are likely to be more appropriate. In either case, costs will comprise actual, indirect and Bannister's (2001) 'disbenefits'. The frequency of the ERP evaluation is likely to depend upon market volatility, rate of technology change and underlying management practices. The evaluation outcomes could be customise, re-implement, upgrade, do nothing or abandon the ERP.

In this post-live stage, the benefits and costs of the ERP are shown to change in line with an organisation's ability to implement new features, re-implement existing modules to meet changing needs, and vary the use of the ERP to meet the requirements of the environment. It is recommended that at some time in the future (organisations have indicated that it might be as long as 25 years), the benefits will decline and/or costs will increase leading to abandonment. The constant renewal through subsequent releases could be depicted as in Figure 18 , using a revised life cycle model of Markus & Tanis (2000).

Figure 18. Cyclic model of ERP management

The adapted model supports the view expressed by Markus & Tanis (2000), that "Organisations recycle through the phases when they undertake major upgrades" (p.178). ERP evaluation should then feasibly occur continuously or at intervals throughout the ERP lifecycle.

2.4 Social Considerations

The IS disciple, being hybrid and dealing with socio-technical hybrids, is hard to classify as a natural or a human science. The very definition of information systems as a set of technical (scientific) and human resources devoted to the management of information in organizations spells out the composite nature of the field (Ciborra 2002, p.15).

Keen (1980, p.10, cited Weber, 1997) describes management information systems as a fusion of behavioural, technical and managerial issues. IS concepts are related to efficiency and rationality, in practice they function in diverse ways related to social and political processes that exist (Doolin,2004). Orlikowoski and Iacono (2001) propose that to successfully implement IS applications an 'ensemble' view of technology is required, where the activity is perceived as socio-economic. Lim et al (2004) explain that ERP adoption is a sequence of progressive phases, marked by corresponding transitions in system perceptions and beliefs by users; in this way it is evolutionary.

Gosain (2004) found that individuals embedded in an actor network find it difficult to use technology differently to the ways others expect and that they produce greater stability in work practice. Gattiker and Goodhue (2005) when researching ERP benefits in sub-units of large organisation found that the greater the level of differentiation of sub units the lower the benefits of ERP. Similarly, Morton and Hu (2005) found that ERP applications were most appropriate for machine bureaucracies. Melin (2003) explains that this is because "the use of IS can institutionalize operating procedures and certain patterns of communication and coordination, restricting reorgnizing activities and changes in control and power structures" (p. 10).

When researching multi-national ERP roll outs Carton and Adam (2003) found that local managers are given too little scope and time to adequately adapt to the ERP template for their site with the risk of short-term productivity loss. They concluded that mechanisms should be put in place to better understand how to accommodate local specifications whilst enforcing the required level of standardisation. Foucault (1982) identifies that power operates by structuring the field of possible actions. That management is concerned with, failure or success, and that this is not an IT matter, but a matter of management and culture. Ward, Hemingway, & Daniel (2005) assert that ultimately an ERP implementation will require negotiation and 'detailed contracts on all aspects of benefits, resources and changes and the sooner the organisation arrives at that point the more immediate and apparent the benefits. Abdinnour-Helm and Lengnick-Hall (2005) identify that ERP can be implemented in many other types of organisations and propose that they could be effective in flexible organisations with a cultural change.

IS systems render social phenomenon visible (Doolin, 2004), and this research will strive to understand the social aspects of organisations that impact upon the management and evaluation of ERP.

2.5 Conceptual Framework

Yin (2003b) advocates the construction of a conceptual model of existing theory prior to designing the methodology. The framework expresses the pre-understanding for the research as part of the hermeneutic cycle (Gummeson, 1999) as "a conceptual framework helps to graphically or normatively identify the key factors, constructs or variables and the presumed relationships between them (Miles and Huberman 1994, p.18).

The conceptual framework for ongoing ERP evaluation, illustrated in Figure 19 identifies the important aspects that have been identified from the theory review. The framework shows that the success of the initial evaluation and previous upgrades are likely to influence the evaluation and the perspective of IS in the organisation. The perspective of IS, the business strategy process and the financial position are all proposed to be factors. Such external elements as competitors, industry norms, IT developments and possibly the media are also considered to be relevant. These are justified in the following discussion.

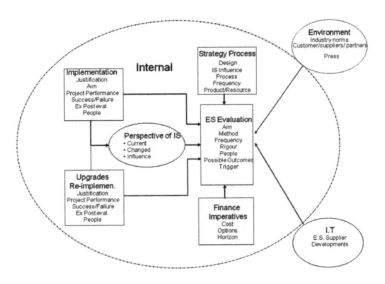

Figure 19. Influencing factors of ERP management and evaluation

---

El Amrani et al (2006) believed future ERP research should take into account the ERP strategy and organisational context. Organisational strategy, as discussed in this chapter, is likely to be a major factor in the evaluation process in terms of the process, method and outcomes.

Ward, Brown, & Massey (2005) postulated that prior to a system being in use, the perceived organisational benefits and the opinions of both peers and IS consultants exert influence on attitudes towards IS; and that this initial attitude can determine later attitudes. Bannister (2002) proposes, when discussing IS, that a view of history provides valuable perspective. The success or otherwise of the initial implementation and upgrades has the potential to impact the evaluation of ERP for many reasons. Firstly, the consequence of the implementation will have affected user satisfaction and the general perception of IS in the organization, and, as was described in the ex-post section, this will impact the benefits that the application can provide. Secondly, Orlikowski and Robey (1991) identified technology as being a social process. This social process creating the norms of the system within an organisation (Karahanna, Straub, & Chervany, 1999). Jasperson, Carter, and Zmud (2005) explain that the norms of the organisation become highly relevant for ex-post evaluation as "political and learning models better explain post-adoptive behaviours" (p. 531). Thirdly, the original implementation or upgrades may have created an imperative to improve the application. Fourthly, Farbey, Land, & Targett (1996) found that those responsible for implementing IT in organisations become totally committed towards the 'success' of the IT investment and Staples, Wong, and Seddon (2002) identified users with a realistic post implementation expectation to rate systems higher.

Bhattacherjee and Premkumar (2004) also found that users' perspectives change over time with regard to IT usefulness; and that the change is more prevalent at the initial and long term stages.
It is likely then, that the discreet evaluation processes, if indeed formal processes exist, will be affected by the assumptions of the evaluators, particularly with regard to the success of the original implementation, the evaluators involvement in the original evaluation, their perspective of IS and the success or otherwise of upgrades. This research seeks to understand, at a macro level, the perception of IS in terms of the degree to which it is perceived as being fundamental for an organisation; how ERP is perceived; and how the perception may have changed over the life of the application.

The financial position of the organisation is likely to significantly impact the evaluation process. For instance, the evaluation process is likely to have more possible outcomes if the company is highly profitable. Similarly, if the ERP is fully depreciated or not is likely to have an impact; as an organization would presumably be more likely to abandon a fully depreciated ERP than one that has a high asset value.

The organisation's wider environment through competitor initiatives and industry norms are also likely to be relevant. Sammon et al. (2003) identify strong vendor hype as influential, whereby organisations appear "to have little choice but to jump on the bandwagon"(p.155). Similarly, Markus and Tanis (2000) warn that vendors assert pressure on adopting organisations and it is important to understand how this happens. These and the influences of Software Authors and VARs discussed earlier will be analysed. In addition, the press and media will possibly impact the evaluation process, particularly if abandonment is contemplated.

To suggest a prescriptive theory aimed at organisations that operate in different industries, with different structures, strategies and approaches to management would be naïve. What can perhaps be achieved is to identify key issues that an organisation needs to consider and some important guidelines that might be employed in the process of managing and evaluating an ERP. Therefore, for a theory to be valid it must be a formative model that is moulded to fit the factors experienced by an organisation.

Some of the constructs are events and others organisational or environmental factors. Layder (1993) categorises constructs as 'typologies', he identifies two types; action typologies which are performed activities; and structural typologies which relate to setting and context. Many of the constructs discussed here are structural typologies, these might influence the management of ERP, but they are not actual events. There are only three events: the strategy and management process of the organisation; management and evaluation of the ERP; and the outcomes produced. Figure 20 depicts the typologies used in this research.

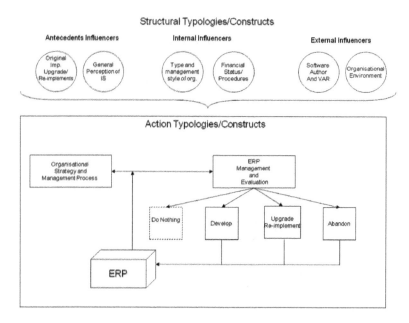

Figure 20. Conceptual model of structure and constructs

Little prior theory has emerged about the process of management and evaluation of ERP, but there is a plenitude of theory concerning the structural typologies and their impact on strategy. It is known there are many approaches to strategy, see for example Johnson and Scholes (2002) who identify a myriad of strategies and strategic choices; and environmental conditions that vary depending on industry and sector dynamics.

Furthermore realistic presumptions are that the frequency of the ERP evaluation should depend upon the market volatility, rate of technology change and underlying management practices. Ultimately, the highest level of evaluation may result in outcomes to customise, re-implement, upgrade, do nothing or abandon the ERP. The conceptual framework delineated above is used as the basis for the research methodology and has been adapted throughout the data gathering exercise as finer grained information emerged.

2.6 Conclusion

This chapter has detailed various facets of second generation ERP applications and has reviewed theory concerning ERP management and evaluation. This has identified broad constructs that will underpin the analysis into this scarcely researched phenomenon of management and evaluation of operational ERP.

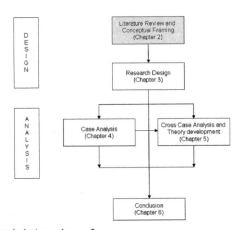

Figure 21.   Book design - chapter 2

The constructs form the basis of the research design presented in Chapter 3, and are used extensively in the case analysis explained in Chapters 4 and 5.

Chapter 3 - Research Design

Research begins with a problem that is to be solved or some question of interest. The theory that is developed should depend on the nature of this problem and the questions that are addressed (Gregor, 2006, p. 619).

The aim of this chapter is to describe the research design and method. Whether the research design should start with the method or epistemology is open to debate. Crotty (1998) proposes that the method should be first identified and subsequently the relevant epistemology. Others, such as Heidegger (1962) and Gadamer (1976), suggest that our beliefs and assumptions are fundamental to our being able to make sense of the world and need to be a priori for research. Weber (1997) agrees and points out that when we try to understand some phenomenon we are already operating within an existing set of beliefs and assumptions. The process adopted here is to discuss the possible approaches to epistemology, given the researchers subjective or objective orientation, for the questions to be addressed. The overriding principle is to create a rigorous platform for relevant research.

There is currently some debate over the domain of IS research. The debate relates to the phenomena that IS research should be concerned with. This matter is obviously important to this reserach, so this chapter first identifies the implications of the debate. Next, the major epistemological approaches that have been and are being utilised in IS research are described. The discussion then addresses the research objectives and how they relate to the philosophical approaches. These aspects are used as the basis for identifying the epistemology and methodology.

3.1 What is "Information Systems" Research

IS research, like all research in other fields, has significance when it advances our theoretical, conceptual, and practical understanding of critical issues and phenomena around the IS field. The more the research makes an impact and critical difference to stakeholders and the domain that it serves, the greater its significance (El Sawy, Galliers, & Watson, 2006, p.63).

This aim of this section is to discuss the theoretical backdrop to the research by describing the circumstance of IS theory.

The IS subject matter is very broad being concerned with machines and human behaviour, and the phenomena of how the two interact (Baskerville & Myers, 2002; Gregor, 2006; Orlikowoski, Barley, & Robey, 2001). The diversity of the IS subject has caused researchers to lean heavily on other disciplines to explain the phenomena (Baskerville & Myers, 2002). In recent times a call has been made for an IS identity, for IS to be a reference discipline, with a focus on the "IT artefact" (Agarwal & Lucas Jr, 2005; Baskerville & Myers, 2002; Benbasat & Zmud, 2003; Boland Jr & Lyytinen, 2004; Boudreau, Gefen, & Straub, 2001; Mingers, 2001; Orlikowoski et al., 2001; Orlikowoski & Iacono, 2001; Vessey, Ramesh, & Glass, 2002).

Unfortunately, the call for IS to be a reference discipline seems to have created more questions than answers and the implications need to be brought to the fore prior to the research methodology being discussed. In 2001, Orlikowoski and Iacono, suggested that the IT artefact had not been apparent in IS research and called for a focus on the conceptualisation of IT. They identified five premises for theorizing the IT artefact. Firstly, that IT artefacts are "not natural, neutral, universal or given", which, presumably, indicates IT not to be part of the natural sciences. They further suggest that IT artefacts are "always embedded in some time, place, discourse, and community", identifying that the transitive nature of IT will not allow the development of enduring laws, and that it is open to interpretation. Thirdly, these researchers say IT artefacts are "usually made up of a multiplicity of often fragile and fragmentary components, whose interconnections are often partial and provisional and which require bridging, integration, and articulation in order for them to work together". This fourth premise obviously highlights issues with the conceptualisation and boundaries of the IT phenomena. Finally, IT artefacts "emerge from ongoing social and economic practices ... coexisting and coevolving with multiple generations of the same or new technologies at various points in time", thereby explaining that the phenomena is changing with the possibility of multi-occurrences or at least multiple states. They suggest these broad terms should form the boundary of IT research.

Benbasat and Zmud (2003) agreed that there is an identity crisis in IT but, citing Orliwoski and Iacono (2001), propose that too often elements of behaviours lodged deeply within IT development activities, and both forward and reverse causation, are seemingly absent from IS scholarship. They ask for a broader perspective, than that proposed by Orliwoski and Iacono, one that may rely on other reference disciplines as long as there is a focus on IT/IS. They particularly highlight the potential problems of inclusion and exclusion of certain factors in the IT discipline as proposed by Orliwoski and Iacono.

Galliers (2003) in a direct response to Benbasat and Zmud, "seriously contend" their points. Central to Galliers' arguments is the belief that, as IS and organisations change, so should the discipline. However, they also position IS as "quintessentially trans-disciplinary in nature". In particular they call for a focus on human activity as well as IT, and that neither the "boundary nor the locus of the field should be confined to a pre-established set".

Fichman (2004), proposes that the dominant paradigm of IT research may be reaching the point of diminishing returns as a "framework for making ground breaking research" and urges researchers to go beyond the dominant paradigm. His dominant paradigm is concerned, in summary, with adoption and diffusion, and its resultant impact on an organisation. Fichman further proposes a focus on Innovation Configurations, Social Contagion, Management Fashion, Innovation Mindfulness, Technology Destiny, Quality of Innovation and Performance Impacts. These are a very different set of foci to those proposed by Orlikowoski and Iacono (2001).

Agarwal and Lucas Jr (2005) present what they term an alternate view to that of Benbasat and Zmud (2003), and whilst they "agree with many of their observations" they propose that a considerable portion of effort should be upon macro studies of the transformational impact of IT. Agarwal and Lucas discuss impacts that are much broader, for instance, customer service, structure of organisations, and national and global economics.

There is perhaps a need to address the perception of IS research as, according to Benbasat and Zmud (1999a), it has taken the brunt of much criticism. They cite examples such as "80% of IS management research may be irrelevant", it is "pretentious", and it lacks recognition by IS practitioners. There is agreement that an identity crisis exists in the IT discipline, however, there seems little agreement of the IT artefact . The debate about what constitutes the discipline has highlighted a major problem - that the discipline, being so very broad, might feasibly include numerous macro and micro approaches to research from many disciplines. This lack of consensus about this changing, ubiquitous phenomenon is perhaps unsurprising, but leaves the rigour of research into the 'discipline' open to interpretation and perhaps debate.

This inestigation is conceivably typical of IS research in that it strives to understand a ubiquitous set of applications which are implemented in a vast number of organisations operating in diverse industries around the globe. The approach taken here is s very practical one and one that was advocated by Hirschheim (1985), specifically that IS are social rather than technical systems, and the scientific paradigm adopted by the natural sciences is appropriate to IS only insofar as it is appropriate for the social sciences. This research examines IS and humans in an organisational context and the interaction of the two, and in so doing views IS as a social, transitive, phenomena.

The approach follows the lead of Hirscheim (1985) and defines knowledge in the fashion, where knowledge is only 'asserted'. It is supported by evidence and knowledge claims are conceived of in a probabilistic sense. Knowledge is therefore not infallible but conditional; it is a societal convention and is relative to both time and place. This largely agrees with the definition of Orlikowoski and Iacono (2001). However, this definition is very broad, leaving the research open to multi-various techniques and methods that again bring into question the rigour of the approach. Hirschheim (1985) sees this as the very nature of science, suggesting the following:

> *Science is a convention, related to societal norms, expectations, values, etc. In its most conceptual sense, it is nothing more than the search for understanding. It would use whatever tools, techniques and approaches that are considered appropriate for the particular subject matter under study. The consequence of this conception of science is that virtually any 'scholarly' attempt at acquiring knowledge could be construed to be 'science' (p112).*

A myriad of techniques and methods could be utilised; this research adopts an approach that seems applicable to the phenomenon to be examined, without suggesting it to be the only approach.

3.2 Philosophical Foundations of the Research

There are probably as many approaches as researchers (Eisenhardt, 1989).

The purpose of this section is to discuss the philosophical paradigms used in IS research and applicable for this study.

It is not surprising given the complexity and lack of uniformity of IS theory that its philosophic underpinnings are also indefinite; this obviously being common with many disciplines. Much variability is also apparent in the use of philosophical terms in the IS literature. As it is in social science texts (Crotty, 1998). To help clarify the discussions, the terms and definitions from Burrell and Morgan (1979, p.3.), shown in Figure 22, have been used to indicate meaning in this section. The proposal by Burrell and Morgan (1979) is that there are two approaches to social science, one being subjective, the other being objective. These give rise to the two primary ontological perspectives of nominalism and realism. Similarly, epistemology has the two extremes of anti-positivism and positivism, while human nature is voluntaristic or deterministic, and the methodology is primarily either ideographic or nomothetic.

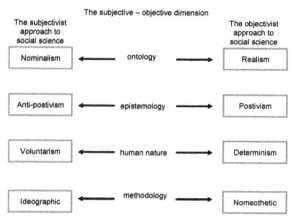

Figure 22.   A scheme for analysing assumptions about the nature of social science
(Burrel & Morgan 1979, p. 3)

The Burrel and Morgan (1979) use of the ontological paradigms of nomonalism and realism are by no means
universally accepted. Fitzgerald and Howcroft (1998) propose that the two ontology perspectives are
relativist and realist. The realist perspective is consistent between the parties Fitzgerald and Howcroft
(1998) and Burrel and Morgan (1979). However, Fitzgerald and Howcroft (1998) suggest relativists
believe socially-transmitted terms direct how reality is perceived and this varies across different languages.
Burrel and Morgan (1979) use nomanilism because a subjective view of the 'world' does not have any
substantive social structures, and therefore an ontological would be pointless nomenclature. In the following,
where Fitzgerald and Howcroft's view of ontology is seen as more relevant, the term relativist is used instead
of nominalist.

The debate between realists and relativists/nominalists has been termed the "quarrel of the Universals"
dating back to at least the Middle Ages (Monod, 2004, p. 124). The debate concerning philosophy continues
in the IS literature with many researchers becoming aligned with one or other approaches. Traditionally, as
seen by Orlikowski and Baroudi (1991), positivism was the predominant paradigm. Through the 1990s anti-
positivists' research became increasingly popular (Walsham, 1995). In recent years an increasingly
vociferous call for a critical perspective is heard (Abdinnour-Helm,2005; Carlsson, 2003; Daellenbach,2001;
Dobson, 2001, 2003, 2007; Myles, & Jackson, 2007; Doolin, 1998; Heap, Hollis, Lyons, Sugden, & Weale,
1992, Kilby, 2004; Klecun and Cronford,2005; McGrath,2005; Pozzebon, 2004; and Walsham,2005).
According to Orlikowoski and Baroudi (1991), the three distinct philosophical approaches to IS research are

positivist, anti-positivists and critical. These are broad positions that imply particular ontological and epistemological orientations, a positivist approach approximating being objective, and an anti-positivist approach, subjective in terms of Burrel and Morgan (1979). Put simply, the critical realist has an epistemology of anti-positivism and an ontology of realism.

There are underlying differences to these three approaches. Hirschheim (1985) outlined the development of these philosophies from positivism to anti-positivism to critical. The development of the philosophical assumptions will not be discussed at length here, with the will focus being the differences in the philosophical perspectives.

The positivists' name originated from Auguste Comte (1798 – 1857) who believed that social order transitioned through three states - theological, metaphysical and positive. The positive state of mind has given up the vain search after absolute notions, the origin and destination of the universe and the causes for phenomena, and applies itself to the study of laws. The underlying principle of early positivism is causality and objectivity, wherein causality is the belief of determination, and objectivity is the belief of existence of an external reality that can be described directly (Monod, 2004). The suggestion is that only one description of a phenomenon exists (Monod, 2004), and that one cannot be proved to be wrong with further tests (Orliwoski and Baroudi, 1991). As William Shakespeare puts it:

Truth is truth, to the end of reckoning (William Shakespeare, Measure for Measure)

At the very fundamental level, positivism is about positing a conclusion (Crotty, 1998), one that is seen to be a truth. There is confidence that scientific knowledge is accurate and verifiable rather than comprising opinions, beliefs, feelings or assumptions (Crotty, 1998). With positivisim there is a separation between the world and the self, between object and subject, between objectivity and subjectivity (Monod, 2004). Hirscheim (1985) explains that positivism relies on the unity of scientific method and is, therefore, valid for all forms of inquiry, "it does not matter whether the domain of study is animate or inanimate objects; human, animal or plant life; physical or non-physical phenomena". He avers logic, and more generally, mathematics, provide the foundation of this science. It is proposed here that traditional positivism views the world objectively, in Burrel and Morgan (1979) parlance, and is primarily and in turn, realist, positivist, determinist and nomethetic. While positivism has its background in natural sciences where laws are sought, it is now used extensively in social science. One of its first uses in social science concerned the predictive nature of Darwin's famous Theory of Evolution (Hirschheim, 1985).

Chapter Three - Research Design

The traditional view of positivism is now very much in doubt and the term "positivism" has largely been revised and is now referred to as "logical-positivism": "the move to physicalism signalled the end of the classic claim that knowledge had to be indubitable. It was now acknowledged that intersubjective agreement provided sufficient justification for knowledge " (Hirschheim, 1985, p.56). Popper (1958, cited in Cotty, 1998) argues that positivist science is not a matter of making a discovery and then proving it right; it is making a guess and then not being able to prove the guess wrong. Logical positivists believe a clear distinction exists between fact and value, signalling a move from individual explanation (or laws) to theoretical networks of knowledge statements. Burrel and Morgan (1979, p.5) state that positivism in current usage may refer to one or more of the ontological, epistemological and methodological dimensions (but reaffirm their use in sociological terms as a characteristic of epistemology). For positivists, knowledge consists in the description of the invariant patterns that co-exist in space and succession over time (Bhaskar, 1991).

Anti-positivism came about due to the sterility of positivist enquiry, wherein a positivist approach "failed to appreciate the fundamental experience of life" (Hirschheim, 1985, p.64). Whilst many scholars advocated anti-positivism, Kant (1781) is recognised as having made the greatest contribution. For Kant, knowledge is achieved through a synthesis of concept (understanding) and experience (Hirschheim, 1985); he believed that it is illusory to describe the world without any reference to one's self (Heisenberg, 1962). "Objects are appearances that conform to our way of presenting" (Kant, p.24 cited Monod 2004, p.94), and "the object (as object of the senses) conforms to the character of our power of intuition", (p.21, cited Monod 2004, p.94).

> *Being appearances (phenomenon) cannot exist in themselves, but can exist only in us.*
> *What may be the case regarding objects in themselves and apart from all this receptivity*
> *of our sensibility remains to us entirely unknown. All we know is the way in which we*
> *perceive them. (Monod, 2004, p.94).*

Anti-positivists' sociology is to understand the subjective world of human experience (Burrell and Morgan, 1979). They further attest that some anti-positivist researchers have "sought to show how the supposedly hard, concrete, tangible and 'real' aspects of organisational life are dependent upon subjective constructions of individual beings" (p.261) proposing the study to be anti-positivist if it aims to "understand and explain the social world primarily from the point of view of the actors directly involved in the social process" (p.227). Schultz (1962, cited Lee & Baskerville, 2003) point out that anti-positivists' feel there to be a basic difference in the structure of the social world and the world of nature; and therefore the methods of the social sciences are different. That is not to imply that the findings cannot be deductive and proposed to fit a wider population.

The anti-positivists' domain includes phenomenology and constructivism. The epistemology of constructivism contends that all knowledge is contingent on human practices interacting with their world, and knowledge being developed and transmitted in a social context. The difference between the social and the natural world is that the natural world does not constitute itself as meaningful, the meanings are constituted by men.

The constructivist approach argues that there is no true or valid interpretation, but there are useful interpretations which stand higher than interpretations that serve no purpose. This approach is compatible with the nonimalist ontology specified by Burrell and Morgan (1979). For Schwandt (1994, p.125, cited in Crotty, 1998), constructivism "is deeply connected to the view that what we take to be objective knowledge and truth is the result of perspective". Constructivists claim meanings are constructed as they engage with the world being interpreted, bringing together objectivity and subjectivity. Constructivism is, in fact, the process of individual cognition, whereby experience and thought leave an impression of reality; it can have a social rather than an individual focus, looking not only at how individuals construct their reality, but looking at how groups of individuals communicate and negotiate their views and perspectives (Marshall, 2005).

Constructivism in IS research could rarely be found, Marshall (2005) proposed constructivism for IS research, terming it constructivism with a 'twist of pragmatism' – pragmatism as expounded by Rorty (1999), but did not use the approach. It appears constructivism would be a useful approach for IS research, as the organisation constructs a meaning of the IS, and the researcher can perhaps comprehend that construction and explain it. However, it is very questionable if this approach can be relevant to practice. Carlsson (2003) explains that the problem with constructivist IS evaluation "is its inability to grasp those structural and institutional features of society and social organisations which are in some respects independent of the agents' reasoning and desires but influence (affect) an IS initiative and the negotiation process. To develop theories of why an IS initiative (IS implementation) works for whom and in what circumstances requires a researcher to generate some means of making independent judgement about the institutional structure and power relations present in an IS institutive. This is something not possible in constructivist IS evaluation research" (p.17). For this reason constructivism has not been adopted.

Phenomenologists believe that things are as they are presented to us as human beings, we need to lay aside our previous meaning to appreciate them as they are, thus creating new meaning (Crotty, 1998).

Phenomenology looks for variations in human understandings and allows those variations to be present, the aim being to understand how the individuals conceive the world (Osteraker, 2001). There are instances of pure phenomenological research in IS, but the objective of phenomenology is not consistent with the objectives of this rserach.

Critical theorists like Lessnoff and Winch (1974, cited in Hirschheim, 1985), argue that the logical positivists' scientific method is inappropriate for the social sciences, proposing that the 'model of the person' is too simplistic. The critical theory is developed around the ideal that there can be an ideal society (Burrell & Morgan, 1979). Orlikowski and Baroudi (1991) contend that critical philosophy is the belief that social reality is historically constituted. This is the underlying principle of the Frankfurt school and the work of Habermas.

Critical realism is a 'modern' research approach that suggests research is about the unearthing of deeper levels of structure. Bhaskar (1991, p. 3-4), who is one of the major proponents of critical realism, is particularly scathing of positivism in social sciences; he identifies that "people are seen as isolatable from their normal social contexts" and questions "the whole language of operational definitions ... dependent and independent variables, and so forth is highly suspect." It assumes that "people can be reduced to a set of variables which are somehow equivalent across persons and across situations". He is also doubtful of the claims of anti-positivists and suggests it as being "a discrepancy between philosophical analysis and its intended object - a rift between epistemological principles and ontological presuppositions. And these are as evident in their Kantian prototype as in its contemporary avatars. For patently there is no way in which even if Kantian principles were all demonstrably valid, they could be used to justify any particular inductive reference" Bhaskar (1991, p.4).

Bhaskar explains the basis of critical realism is the belief that there exists an intransitive ontological reality and a transitive social epistemology which has intrinsic features that become known through 'metacritical' analysis which is critical and self-reflexive. Bkaskar (1992), proposes a careful or critical application of the scientific method to the social sciences and terms it critical naturalism. Bhaskar explains that all human sciences are extant in open systems and therefore, theory in human sciences cannot be predictive, but must be exclusively explanatory, and must be seen as constituted from a multiplicity of causes. Critical naturalism is based on a causal link between nature and social science; "social objects are the emergent powers and liabilities of natural ones, subject to continual conditioning and constraint by nature. In specific terms, the emergence of society is shown in the causal irreducibility of social forms in the genesis of human action (or being)".

The conceptual models of the positivism, anti-positivism, critical realism and constructivism are shown in Figure 23.

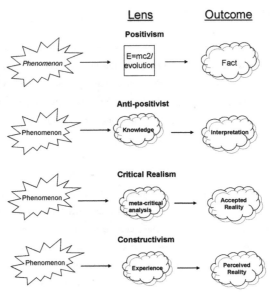

Figure 23.   Conceptualisation of epistemologies

In summary, conventional science based on 'rational positivist' thought has presumptions that a 'real world' exists; that data can be gathered by observing it; and that those data are factual, truthful and unambiguous. The subjectivists, on the other hand, assert that these assumptions are unwarranted; that 'facts' and 'truth' are a chimera; that 'objective' observation is impossible; and that the act of observation-and-interpretation is dependent on the perspective adopted by the observer.   They criticise social sciences, where the objects of study are influenced by extenuated factors that are extremely difficult to isolate (Boland & Lyytinen, 2004; Hirschheim & Klein,1994; Walsham, 2005). Fitzgerald and Howcroft (1998) propose that the positivist paradigm for IS research has been devoted to hypothetico-deductive testing, focusing on trivial hypotheses - "we are pursuing an incorrect cause with a maximum of precision."

Much debating occurs about the most appropriate research method for IS. If one of the research paradigms could be universally applicable and elevated to a position of supremacy it would have happened long ago

(Fitzgerald & Howcroft, 1998). The polarisation has led to entrenched camps that "arrogantly" see their research approach as true, but "paradigms should serve as a lens to illuminate research issues, not as blinkers to help closure." (Fitzgerald & Howcroft, 1998, p.27). Benbasasat and Zmud (1999) propose that interesting, but not necessarily relevant, articles for IS practitioners are those that address enduring organisational problems, challenges, and dilemmas, as well as articles that address timely business issues and those that synthesize a body of research or stimulate critical thinking.

Burrel and Morgan (1979) have proposed an isolation process to research approaches, where the approaches are mutually exclusive, but this does not appear to be the case in IS research. The IS community's' research methods in the US and Europe were analysed by Becker and Niehaves (2007); the results are shown in Table 4.

Table 4.   Methodological And Paradigmatic Diversity In IS Research

	US Journals	European Journals
Methods		
Quantitative	71%	40%
Qualitative	20%	49%
Mixed	9%	11%
Paradigms		
Positivist	89%	66%
Interpretivist (anti-posivist)	11%	34%

Interestingly, in Europe, the paradigm is predominantly positivist, but the method predominantly qualitative. This implies a positivist epistemology and an idiographic study. In the US there are more qualitative (idiographic) studies than anti-positivist approaches. Implying that positivist - idiographic study is taking place. Positivist studies can then, as Yin (2003b) proposes, be qualitative in nature. The debate about epistemologies then becomes somewhat vacuous (Fitzgerald,1998). Burrell and Morgan (1979) propose that "social scientists are faced with a basic ontological question: whether the 'reality' to be investigated is external to the individual – imposing itself on individual consciousness; whether 'reality' is of an 'objective' nature, or the production of one's mind." (p.1).

It is proposed here that the crux of the issue with IS philosophy is that researchers desire to find something generalisable, to help the discipline, not only through understanding, but practically, and this is likely to be, ontologically speaking, a realism. To this extent (Mumford, 2003) has asked for 'certainty' in IS research.

However, as (Kallinikos, 2004) observes, the complex nature of the interaction of IS and the social world means that IS must be evaluated against the background of a variety of organisational and human trade-offs that it unconsciously requires. For this reason the phenomena leads to an anti-positivist approach. In an attempt to overcome the dilemma (Lee, 1991) has asked that systems and organisations not be objects of the sense as proposed by Kant, but intelligible objects, objects of thinking and practical reason.

"The issue then becomes not whether one has uniformly adhered to prescribed canons of either logical-positivism or anti-positivism, but whether one has made sensible methods decisions given the purpose of the inquiry, the questions being investigated, and the resources available" (Patton 1990, p. 39). "In epistemological debates it is tempting to operate at the poles. But in the actual practice of empirical research, we believe that all of us – realists, interpretivists, critical theorists - are closer to the centre, with multiple overlaps" (Miles & Huberman, 1994).

> *Research, when it comes to a communication stage where papers are written for publication, is inherently positivist", "the interpretivist tragedy is to fail to recognise that research communication, in the traditional form, is inevitably positivist". (Fitzgerald & Howcroft, 1998, p.16).*

This research follows the lead of others including, Miles and Huberman, who seek an objective view from subjective information, terming the approach transcendental realism. This requires the researcher to plan rigorously when executing qualitative research, then contextualise the findings as "social phenomena exist not only in the mind but also in the objective world – and that some lawful and reasonable stable relationships are to be found among them" (Miles and Huberman 1994, p. 4). They seem to use the term transcendental realism as an arbitrary term, citing a lineage of theorists including Bhaskar (1978,1989) and Harre and Secord (1973) .

Miles and Huberman (1994) use the term transcendental realism suggesting it "calls both for casual explanation and for the evidence to show that each entity or an event is an instance of that explanation." Their perspectives seems to owe much to Popper (1980), who did not think science involved correct, right, proven or true theories. Rather, he contended there was a real world out there that we could translate from the really-real into an explanatory theory (Enigl, 2003). This investigation in the same vein, strives to identify relatively enduring social structures and processes operating in particular organisations and theorises that they may apply to other organisations.

Reality is socially constructed, multiple realities exist, and what constitutes 'scientific research' is both time and context dependent (Fitzgerald & Howcroft, 1998, p.13).

Crotty (1998) proposes that the assumptions that reality is socially constructed does not mean that it is not real: "Already present in the subject matter of the social sciences are the meanings that people create and that they attach to the world around them. In this sense, subjective meaning is an objective reality" (Lee & Baskerville, 2003, p. 230). ERP systems are not static in terms of physical components, data or human perception and therefore the IS forms part of the environment from which managers develop their shared meanings (Doolin, 1998). The ontology here matches that proposed by Seddon and Scheepers (2006) whereby "objective reality exists beyond human mind, though our perceptions about that reality are inextricably bound to the stream of experiences we have had throughout our lives ... we believe that the things that social-science researchers seek to generalize to other settings are *knowledge claims* from their research studies. Such knowledge claims are usually presented in the form of propositions, models or theories" (p.1146). Seddon & Scheepers (2006) suggest that "researchers who build theories and models to explain how the world works should clearly specify the boundaries to their knowledge claim" (p.1142), and, that researchers generally under generalise their findings.

It is important here to distinguish between society in general and organisations, as organisations are more regimented. That is not to disagree with Bhaskar (1991) that all of society, including an organisation, is an open system. However, organisations are bounded, although that boundary may be 'porous'; they are more strictly governed than society in general by hierarchies, structures, financial reporting procedures, depreciation rules and restrictions, understood competition and industry classification, identified management practices and IS methodologies. As Heap et al (1992, p155) explain, "... in even the most libertarian of free-market economies, individuals voluntarily surrender their freedom of action in order to form and join organisations".

The approach here could be described as soft positivism (Kirsch, 2004, cited in Seddon & Scheepers, 2006) which is somewhere between anti-positivism and positivism. Kirsch explains, "objective reality exists beyond the human mind, though our perception about that reality are inextricably bound to the stream of experiences we have had throughout our lives", and these "are likely to be different for different types of people (managers, teenagers, etc.), different cultures and, over time" (p.1146). Since man cannot transcend his language and cultural system, there cannot be any absolute viewpoint and the epistemology will be anti-positivist, where perceptions are sought (Hirschheim, 1985). For instance, if the interviews discussed later had taken place a year earlier or later, would the data have been different? What about a month earlier or later? Or a week? A minute? If the secretary hadn't interrupted would the discourse have been different? More importantly perhaps, can we be sure that it would be the same? If not there is no truth, but an opinion that exists while the phenomenon exists. The transience of the phenomenon is difficult if not impossible to conclude. This study is then, a perception of perceptions of a transient phenomenon, no more, and no less worthy for that.

3.3   Methodological Approach

Man must shape his tools lest they shape him – Arthur Miller

Two questions concerning the methodology need to be resolved, what form the method will take and how to justify the choice and use. According to Yin (2003b), the extent of the investigator's control and the focus on contemporary or historical events govern the research method . These three conditions and the methods that apply to them are shown in Table 5.

Table 5.   Relevant Situations For Different Research Strategies (Yin 2003b, p.5).

Strategy	Forms of Research Questions	Requires Control of Behavioural Events ?	Focuses on Contemporary Events?
Experiment	How, why?	Yes	Yes
Survey	Who, what, where, how many, how much?	No	Yes
Archival analysis	Who, what, where, how many, how much?	No	No
History	How, why	No	No
Case study	How, why	No	Yes

The research question renders all of the methods potentially appropriate. However, as the research is not controllable an experiment is not an option. The study being focused on contemporary events means that the method is limited to survey or case study.

The literature review has shown the absence of a normative theory surrounding the management and evaluation of ERP. As there is no concise identification of the factors relevant to the investigation, Cresswell's (1994) determination of a pre-scientific stage of research is indicated, one in which an hypothesis cannot be developed and tested. The only way to approach the pre-scientific stage is through induction or qualitative data (Paré, 2004). Nevertheless, consideration was given to a quantitative approach, but it was ultimately rejected, the primary reason being that the models assumed by survey methods do not correspond to the organisational context that has so many, potentially unknown, factors. Additionally, the number of variables identified from the literature is greater than the number of likely data points. The sample would need to take into account, as a minimum, the industry, size and type of organisation, position in the value system relative to its push-pull boundary, profitability, level of depreciation, purpose, age, and perceived success of the system, and whether the system is one of the applications that has been matured by the software authors. Arbitrary possible numbers of outcomes have been assigned to these variables, with total possible permutations of almost three million(see Appendix A for variables and permutations).

Chapter Three - Research Design

A further issue is that a survey could not tease out the nuances of the strategy process and each individual's perception of IS, as a survey's "ability to investigate the context is extremely limited" Yin (2003b, p. 13). Hasan (1998) intuits that it is an inherent difficulty in finding a rigorous, structured research methodology when the problem itself is context-dependent, complex and dynamic. For these reasons survey or quantitative approaches are not seen as being a practical choice of research method for this study.

Ethnography was also considered, where the phenomenon is observed and a descriptive study is undertaken. As Lutterell (2002) observes the best that can be achieved is to trace and document the data analysis processes. Whilst this has merit the research could have potentially lasted for a long time before any major findings were made.

The approach is, therefore, a case study. A case can be defined as an "integrated system" bounded by time and place (Stake 1995, cited in Paré 2004), and its research is useful when a phenomenon is broad and complex, where the existing body of knowledge is insufficient to permit the posing of causal questions, when a holistic, in-depth investigation is needed, or when a phenomenon cannot be studied outside the context in which it occurs (Yin 2003b). Stake (1994) stipulates that "case study is not a methodological choice, but a choice of object to be studied" (p. 236), while Lee (1989, p.34) assists the case study identification by maintaining the "MIS case study refers to the examination of a real-world MIS as it actually exists in its natural, real-world setting". The investigation of operational ERP envisaged here lends itself very well to this case study approach and explained by Yin (2003b, p.32) as, "The case study is the method of choice when the phenomenon under study is not readily distinguishable from its context. Such a phenomenon may be a project or program in an evaluation study. Sometimes the definition of the project or program may be problematic, as in determining when the activity started or ended – an example of a complex interaction between a phenomenon and its temporal context".

You would use the case study method because you deliberately wanted to cover contextual conditions – believing they might by highly pertinent to your phenomena of study (Yin, 2003, p.8).

Four fundamental methods characterise of case research: participant observation, direct (non-participant) observation, document analysis or by interviews (Yin, 2003b). Participant observation and direct observation were given significant consideration, the merits of these approaches lying in being able to obtain the values motives and practices over time of those being observed (Hussey & Hussey, 1997). Either of theses research methods would also enable a longitudinal study of the phenomena. However, the negative aspect typical of these two means of investigation would be of a single case study, and that the case may not yield good evidence.

The objective of the study being how organisations evaluate and manager ERP lent itself well to interviews where the insider's view is constructed using this interpersonal process. It enables the beliefs and motives of the subject to be better understood where these might have been unobserved with other approaches. Therefore, the interview approach was chosen.

Punch (2000) identifies two basic types of qualitative, interview based case research: explanative and descriptive. Descriptive cases aim to describe a phenomenon whilst explanative cases strive to understand the reasons and processes behind the phenomenon. This reserach seeks to analyse and explain, and is consistent with Weber's (1997) belief that understanding and explanation are two sequential components of social science inquiry. The methodology used is that proposed by Punch (2002), as a theory generating study that starts with a question, acquires data, and then establishes a theory.

Yin (2003b, p.38) also asserts that case study researchers "should generalise to theory". The most serious question this methodology must answer is, in the words of Schultz (1962) how can a researcher form objective concepts and form objective theory that is based on subjective meaning structures. To overcome this dilemma this research adopts Gregor's (2006) approach that focuses on the underlying theory rather than providing an epistemological perspective of the subject. She cites Popper (1980, p.59) providing the following definition of theories:

> *Scientific theories are universal statements. Like all linguistic representations they are systems of signs or symbols. Theories are nets cast to catch what we call 'the world'; to rationalize, to explain and master it. We endeavour to make the mesh finer and finer.*
> *(p.6)*

The approach to theory is influenced by the research purpose. Gregor (2006) suggests that IS theory has four primary goals: analysis and description, explanation, prediction and prescription. These are expanded into five types of theory that are conceptually very similar to the goals and are useful signposts for IS research as shown in Table 6.

Table 6.   A Taxonomy Of Theory Types In IS Research (Gregor, 2006)

Theory Type	Distinguishing attributes
I. Analysis	Says "what is" The theory does not extend beyond analysis and description. No causal relationships among phenomena are specified and no predictions are made.
II. Explanation	Says "what is", "how", "why", "when", "where". The theory provides explanations but does not aim to predict with any precision. There are no testable propositions.
III Prediction	Says "what is" and "what will be". The theory provides predictions and has testable propositions but does not have a well-developed justificatory causal explanations
IV. Explanation and prediction	Says "what is", "how", "why", "when", "where" and "what will be". Provides predictions and has both testable propositions and causal explanations.
V. Design and Action	Says "how to do something". The theory gives explicit prescriptions (e.g., methods, techniques, principles of form and functions) for constructing an artefact.

The research proposition is that ERP systems require ongoing evaluation and management. This study seeks to understand 'what is' in terms of what is happening, and is, therefore, an analysis study. There will also be elements of explanation to understand, where possible, "why" and "how". The method aims to create an explanatory case study using data collected through interviews. The process is explained in the following sections which follow the method identified by Paré (2004) for objective case studies.

3.3.1 Unit of Analysis

The specification of the unit of analysis is very important with explanatory case studies. Markus (1989) found the practical significance of the findings for the theory to rest on the study of the appropriate unit of analysis; and the clear definition of the unit of analysis helps to define the boundaries which in turn set limitations to theory applications. According to Miles and Huberman (1994) multiple case research, even more than single case, needs to be well defined prior to conducting the research. However, it is important that the boundaries are not so constricting as to reduce the case sensitivity. Par'e (2004) proposes that the unit of analysis should be governed by the following four criteria:

o   Each unit of analysis must be as specific as possible

o Each case should be a bounded system

o Each unit must be related to the initial research question(s)

o Literature must be used as input

Eisenhardt (1989) concluded that *a priori* specification of constructs helps to shape the research. The constructs derived from the literature review for each organisation is shown in Figure 24.

Figure 24.   Unit of analysis

The central aspect of the analysis is the evaluation of the ERP application and this is likely to be dependent upon the factors shown as discussed in chapter 2. The factors are largely those Yin (2003b) describes as contextual structures. The research, particularly the initial research of the pilot study, was guided by the various units of analysis. The domains were not seen as all encompassing and when the pilot study and subsequent cases identified other prevalent factors they were included in later stages of the research, and the data from previous cases coded and analysed for those factors.

3.3.1.1 Definition of the Research Question

"Defining the research question is the same as it is for hypothesis-testing research. Without a research focus it is easy to become overwhelmed with the data." (Eisenhardt, 1989, p.536). The main research questions is:

How should the ongoing value of ERP be managed and evaluated?

This gives rise to the following sub-questions:

o   What methods are employed to manage and evaluate ERP in the case examples?

o   How is the management and evaluation impacted by the strategic focus?

o   How have environmental characteristics impacted ERP management decisions and evaluation processes?

o   How do the broad objectives of IT effect management and evaluation methods?

o   How do ERP enhancements changes impact upon the frequency and method of evaluation?

o   What historical, political and industry influence impact upon management and evaluation?

3.3.2 Number and Selection of Cases

The term sample according to Yin (2003b) should not be applied to case studies, they should be thought of as individual experiments as they are not a sample in the statistical sense. Selecting case studies, therefore, is a matter of flexibility and selectivity (Yin, 2003b). Flexibility allows issues to be explored as they develop during data collection, while selectivity is concerned with deciding at the research design stage which features will be covered. The case study selection should replicate or extend the emergent theory (Eisenhardt, 1989). Qualitative samples tend to be purposeful rather than random. This is because the initial definition of the universe is limited: social processes have a logic and random sampling can be reduced to 'sawdust' and provide a biased 'hand' (Miles & Huberman, 1994).

It was uncertain how many explanatory cases should be undertaken as qualitative studies have no predetermined sample size (Punch, 2000, p. 56). Eisenhardt (1989) postulated that when case studies are being used to create theory between four and ten cases should be used as with less than four cases it is difficult to generate theory. Generally, case study research is finalised at the point of saturation (Paré, 2004).

Theoretical saturation is the point at which incremental learning is minimal because the researchers observing phenomena generate little or no new data (Glaser and Straus, 1967, cited Eisenhardt, 1989). However, the quantity of data can be daunting as case study research is open ended (Eisenhardt, 1989). In this instance the studies provided a good understanding of the phenomenon as they have provided many important constructs, but, as Eisenhardt points out pragmatic considerations will, and has here, limited the number of cases investigated. Choosing the cases also required a mixture of pragmatism and discretion, Miles & Huberman (1994) describe this approach as convenient and purposefully stratified.

A decision concerning the ERP applications to research was required. The ERP market is an oligopoly with three large protagonists: SAP, Oracle and Microsoft. Oracle and Microsoft have numerous ERP applications, although their main focus seems to be Oracle e-business suite and Dynamics AX respectively. It was decided the cases should ideally include all three companies in the research.

Bernroider & Koch (2001) outlined major differences in the selection criteria for ERP between small and large organisations. The literature review also identified that the evaluation and management of the ERP might be dependent upon an organisation's focus. This was seen as problematic with smaller organisations as they operate under more severe resource constraints, lack specialised managerial expertise, and have different, less aggressive objectives (Madapusi and D'Souza, 2005). For these reasons small organisations were eliminated from the study.

Other selection criteria were, that the research organisations have operational ERP and that the ERP has been operational for differing lengths of time, and that the organisations are from both the private and public sectors. The following organisations were selected: a global mining operation, a global aggregates company, a large Western Australian construction company, an Australia-wide service provider, and a large, publicly owned Western Australian utility. The organisations' revenue ranges from Au$50 million to more than Au$25 billion per annum. The ERP applications consist of Oracle e-business Suite (sometimes referred to simply as Oracle), SAP ERP and Microsoft Dynamics AX (alias Axapta). These applications have been operational for between two and 10 years. The original implementation costs vary considerably from Au$500,000 to Au$700m – Au$1bn. Between three and six interviews were conducted in each of the organisations, the following table providing an overview of the organisations researched, and the pseudonyms used.

Table 7.   Organisational Profiles And Interviews

Organisation	Industry/Type	Revenue Aus$m p.a.	Application	Approximate Cost of Imp. Au$m	Interviewees
Server	Service, Private	50	Dynamics AX	.5	6
Contractor	Construction, Private	800	Dynamics AX	35	3
Provider	Utility, Public	3000	SAP	40	5
Builder	Aggregates, Private	10000	SAP	800	3
Global	Mineral, Private	25000	Oracle e-business suite	500-700	5

The organisational profiles include company pseudonym, purpose, revenue per annum and cost of implementation, and the number of interviewees that were interviewed in each company. The following explains the companies in more detail.

o   The private company identified as Server services large retail organisations throughout Australia from six strategically located sites. The organisation replaced its existing ERP with a new ERP 24 months prior to the data collection.

o   The Contractor is a listed, rapidly growing organisation that provides personnel, plant and machinery to large scale construction and mining operations. In the last three years it has replaced the existing ERP with a new ERP for part of the business and is seeking an ERP for the rest of the organisation.

o   The Provider is a public utility provider that implemented an ERP system ten years prior to the data collection.

o   The Builder is an extremely aggressive global organisation that is growing by acquisition. It had originally implemented a global ERP over a 12 year period, it is now replacing the ERP globally with SAP. The aim is to achieve consistency of processes.

- o Global is a very large corporation that has standardised its worldwide ERP and processes. The consequence for Asia-Pacific is the replacement of the ERP, approximately 5 years ago, due to the introduction of global business processes.

A pilot case was undertaken in 2006 to test the validity of the conceptual model and the interview framework. Selecting the pilot case was seen as critical, Provider was chosen as the ERP system had been operational for approximately ten years, showed ongoing activity in terms of management and evaluation of customisations and additional modules, and appeared to have robust methodologies in place for the management of ERP.

3.3.3 Case Study Protocol

Reliability is considered an important issue in case research (Yin, 2003). The goal of reliability is to minimize the errors and biases in a study. The main way to achieve this is to create a protocol so that other researchers may replicate the steps (Burn, 1994). One prerequisite for other investigators to repeat a case study is the need to document the procedures followed in the earlier case Yin (2003b). This section aims to outline the procedures incorporated to manage the study in general allow and for replication of the case studies.

The organisations were selected due to the phenomenon being of merit to the research. In all but one case a site visit occurred prior to the case study process starting. The one site not visited was not represented in Australia, so numerous phone calls and emails were used to identify the validity of the case. Cases were accepted or rejected based on the criteria of access to key employees; particularly senior management, senior IS management, and finance personnel. The cases also needed to be relevant in terms of extent of ERP and organisational size. It was important not to be too prescriptive in terms of events and processes as this might impact the findings.

According to Yin (2003b), there are three types of interview: structured, unstructured and semi-structured. Structured interviews enable strong cross-case analysis, but can restrict findings: unstructured interviews restrict cross case analysis but allow new factors to emerge, which in turn, can cause constant redesigning of the processes; and semi-structured interviews offer a mixture of flexibility and cross case analysis, allowing open responses in core domains.

Semi-structured interviews were chosen as the best approach. Eight question domains were established from the research questions and the framework shown in section Unit of Analysis. They are as follows.

- o Original implementation, including controls of enhancements
- o Upgrades or re-implementations, including controls of enhancements
- o Strategy process
- o ERP evaluation process
- o Financial position
- o Environmental characteristics and forces
- o Influence of Software Authors and VARs
- o Perception of IS

Each question domain consists of a main question with the broad aim identified in the interview guidelines. The questions are both open and neutral (McMurray, Pace, & Scott, 2004). Each question had a series of probes that may be used to uncover information that was not forthcoming. In some instances the interview probes differ depending on responses.

According to McMurray et al (2004) there are different types of probes, elaboration probes, clarification probes, reflection probes, and repetition probes. The probes used here are mainly elaboration and repetition probes. Clarification and reflection probes were used in interviews in an impromptu manner, seen as appropriate to the discussion. As the data collection was conducted by one person, the researcher, it is proposed that the use of repetition and clarification probes was consistent. The data collection was conducted during 2006 and early 2007.

Prior to the interview, a letter was sent to the interviewee explaining the objectives of the interview, the length of time and the method. Burn (1994) refers to this procedure as a "cover story". The letter was amended slightly for each organisation to better explain the research.

The practice of active listening allowed the researcher to avoid making judgements or evaluations while participants shared their stories and experiences (McMurray et al., 2004). Each case comprised of three and six interviews so as to establish the 'multiple perceptions' that exist in organisations (Klein & Myers, 1999). The interviews were recorded and the recording transcribed. Where possible, documents and archival records were obtained for triangulation purposes. This was not possible in two of the cases and an explanation is covered in the limitations section of this chapter.

Patton (1990) formulates a clear and logical progression for analysis that identifies an audit trail which helps to validates the approach and removes some of the inevitable bias. In support of this recommendation the case study approach advocated by Yin (2003b,) has been used, see Figure 25. After each case, within-case analysis was performed (Eisenhardt, 1989). The researcher personally transcribed the interviews and noted what appeared to be key factors. A summary of findings for each case was produced. The case reports were then reviewed by the organisations' interviewees where practical.

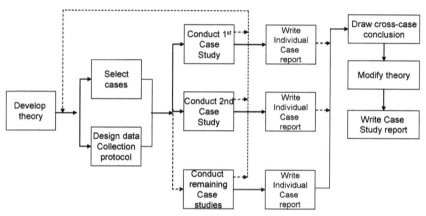

Figure 25.   Case Study Method (Yin 2003b, p.50)

It is acknowledged that the researcher is implicated in the phenomenon being studied, whether marginally through understanding and interpreting the participants' perspective or strongly by creating the reality being studied through the constructs used (Orlikowski & Baroudi, 1991).

3.3.3.1 Data Analysis

Tesch (1990) argues that there is not qualitative research but qualitative data. In this instance the data is spoken, and though language can be interpreted for how and what it communicates, it can be treated as data. Language may be studied in two basic ways: as structure by linguists in the interest of syntax and words; and for communication. This research focuses on the studying of regularities as communication in the data, an approach advocated for theory building by Tesch (1990).

The data analysis process is shown in Figure 26. To avoid possible research bias, the software application "Nvivo7 data indexing and theorizing tool" has been used. Nvivo 7 was utilised as its forerunner NUD.IST had been recommended by Weitzman and Miles (1995), for code-based theory building; they went so far as to say that "for many researchers it will be the best choice" (p. 256). The interviews were coded to the initial and emergent constructs. The initial constructs were inserted in the transcribed interviews as style headings, allowing for automatic creation of constructs as 'tree nodes' in Nvivo across the interviews. Two additional constructs 'position' and 'architecture' were inserted so that perspectives of people in similar roles and architectural similarities could be analysed across cases. Other coding (nodes) were developed to sift and analyse the data, so creating an understanding of each case. Each interview in a case was compared with the other interviews enabling a clearer picture of the case to emerge. New constructs were added and coded in Nvivo as 'free' nodes. A description of each case and the concepts formed is presented in Chapter 4.

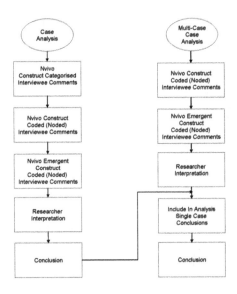

Figure 26.   Data analysis process

After each case had been analysed in isolation the cases were analysed together. Further conclusions were drawn and new constructs added as they became apparent. Nvivo 7 proved a useful tool for parsing the interview data and enabling the cross case comparison explained in chapter 5.

This process of within case and then cross case analysis was advocated by (Eisenhardt, 1989) as the cross case analysis 'sharpens' the theory building focus. Cross-case analysis is used to verify findings and ensure that findings have been identified in the data and have not been formed from the researcher's bias (Eisenhardt, 1989). This was primarily managed by creating a tree-node for each of the constructs then analysing the responses for the tree-nodes. The constructs were then analysed by attributes, particularly position. After the cross case analysis the emerging themes were checked against each case. Any emergent theory was then validated against the data and the constructs refined (Eisenhardt, 1989). The final step has been to compare the findings with the extant literature, to understand what is similar and what it contradicts (Eisenhardt, 1989). Discussion of the multi-case data analysis along with presentation of the theory that has emerged from the data is to be found Chapter 5.

> *The juxtaposition of seemingly similar cases by a researcher looking for differences can break simplistic frames. In the same way, a search for similarity in a seemingly different pair can lead to more sophisticated understanding. (Eisenhardt, 1989, p. 10).*

3.3.4 Limitations

> *Consciously or not, we listen and make sense of what we hear according to particular theoretical, ontological, personal, and cultural frameworks and in the context of unequal power relations. The worry always exists that the voices and perspectives of those we study will be lost or subsumed to our own views and interests (Luttrell, 2000, p. 499)*

Generalisability is concerned with extending the research outside of the population considered. Lee & Baskerville (2003) and Seddon & Scheepers (2006) suggest that generalising IS research is particularly important as the IS field is a vocation as well as a science. However, "Seen in traditional terms, the reliability and validity of qualitatively derived findings can be seriously in doubt" (Dawson, 1979, 1982; Ginsberg, 1990; Kirk & Miller, 1986;Kvale, 1989, Lecompte & Goetz, 1982, cited Miles and Huberman, 1994). Yin (2003b) sees the main limitation of case studies as a lack of methodological rigour and difficulty in generalization. The major issue for generalization of qualitative research is that it is sometimes envisaged in the same way as quantitative research where a sample is representative of a wider community (Lee & Baskerville, 2003; Maxwell, 1992; Mishler, 1990; Yin, 2003b) .

The ontological and epistemological approaches were discussed earlier in this chapter and are not elaborated here. The following discussion is primarily based on works by Mishler (1990), Maxwell (1992), Lee & Baskerville (2003), Yin (2003b) and Seddon and Scheepers (2006).

Chapter Three - Research Design

Mishler (1990, p.436) states that "the discovery ... of the contextually grounded, experience based, socially constructed nature of scientific knowledge ... should be cause for celebration rather than despair. It does not dispense with methods for systematic study but locates them in the world of practice rather than in abstract spaces of Venn diagrams or Latin Squares." The interpretations are subjective, so verification is not in question, but rather the importance of plausibility and ultimately applicability. Yin (2003b) refers to generalization from case study research as "analytic generalization", suggesting that "if two or more cases are shown to support the same theory, replication may be claimed. The empirical results may be considered yet more potent if two or more cases support the same theory but do not support an equally plausible, rival theory." (p. 32-33)

Mishler (1990, p.418) urges that "validity assessments are not assured by following procedures but by investigator's judgement", intimating that concerns of validity assessment are largely irrelevant in social sciences. However, he has also pointed out that validation is being applied to social science research in the same was as experimental research, with many studies being judged wrongly to lack academic rigour. However, validation should be a theoretical rather than a technical problem (Mishler,1990). For Mishler (p. 422), " ... knowledge is validated within a community of scientists when they come to share non-problematic and useful ways of thinking about and solving problems." He identifies the following 6 ways that exemplify quantitative data research:

1) Focus on a piece of "interpretive discourse"and
2) Take text as the basic datum
3) Reconceptualise as an instance of more abstract and general "type"
4) Provide a method of characterizing and coding textual units
5) Specify the structure of the relationship among them
6) Interpret the meaning of the structure within a theoretical framework

All of the recommendations by Mishler (1990) have been adopted in this study. The discourse has been transcribed to text and coded in Nvivo. The discourse has been carefully analysed and conceptualised this being presented in Chapter 4. The data has been reconceptualised using cross case analysis, relationships identified, and the theoretical framework created accordingly. The steps taken to achieve this are recorded in Chapter 5.

However, research also needs to be judged relative to the purpose and circumstance (Binberg and McGrath 1985, cited in Maxwell, 1992). These two components incorporate the validity of the concepts themselves as they are applied to the phenomena, and the validity of the postulated relationships among them (Maxwell, 1992). The theoretical validity can be broken down to descriptive validity, interpretive validity, theoretical validity, generalizability and evaluative validity (Maxwell, 1992). In the descriptive validity of this research, the factual accuracy of the account is assured because the interviews are transcribed, and much of the data is presented so interpretations can be verified. Interpretive validity is concerned with ensuring that the perspective of the participants' perspective is captured, so that the emic situation is captured. In this research the interviews have been read many times, and a great proportion of the interviewees' responses are shown, and thereby they are apparent to the reader.

Theoretical validity is concerned with the 'theoretical construction' by the researcher and the explanation of the phenomena. The theory construction is discussed in chapter 5, and it relies heavily on relevant theory. Evaluative validity is concerned with the value judgements made of the participants and their constructs, and of the inference made of the research. This is subjective and difficult to validate (Maxwell, 1992).

Yin (2003a) identifies four areas of validity: construct validity, internal validity, external validity and reliability: construct validity is to establish correct operational measures for the concepts; internal validity is about establishing sensible causal relationships; external validity is concerned with generalization; and reliability is concerned with the ability to repeat the study. This research strives to incorporate all of the controls identified by Yin, Mishler and Maxwell. The data analysis focuses on the transcribed texts and the meanings ascribed to them by the participants. The data reports were, in the main, validated by the organisations, the constructs have been rigorously applied and the theory developed in a reflective manner. Once internal validity and theoretical validity have been addressed generalizability becomes the major concern.

The process taken here is described by Lee and Baskerville (2003) as a description generalized to theory. This is similar to Yin's analytic generalizability where findings cannot only be generalized within cases but emphasized to a theory. However, that is not to say all assertions are true beyond reasonable doubt because they need to be tested, especially having regard to the setting's similarity (Seddon & Scheepers, 2006). If the research generalizes to a theory which can be defined as 'a coherent group of general propositions used as principles of explanation for a class of phenomena', the theory may help people make sense of similar events in different circumstances, even if different results are forthcoming (Maxwell, 1992). In interpretivism (anti-positivsim), theories pertain to the setting where they develop, but this does not necessarily prohibit them from being extended to other settings (Lee & Baskerville, 2003).

Triangulation occurs when different types of data or different methodologies are used to identify a juxtaposition of the phenomena and can be used to validate interpretive findings. "It involves looking at the research question from several view points rather as mappers will place instruments on hilltops to get overlapping data sets" (Olsen, 2004, p. 212). Relevant documentation was provided as were some archival records. However, while interviewees appeared to be very open in their discussion of events, concerns about confidentiality were real, and in some cases, the intellectual property of documents was of concern. For these reasons, triangulation, from different data points in its full sense was not possible.

Another potential restriction of the study was access to all key employees in an organisation. While it has not been possible to interview all of the key participants of an organisation it is believed that it has been possible in all instances to obtain a picture of the interpretations of the organisations' management employees and for the researcher to intuit an understanding of the phenomenon. McMurray et al (2004, p.245) contends that this can be the only objective of interpretative research.

The inevitable bias of the researcher concerning the research subject will undoubtedly have affected the interpretation of the data and the constructs. The study has been based on constructs derived from the literature, and these have increased during the study. However, the original perspective of the researcher will have biased the set of constructs. These second order constructs are derived from the researcher's interpretations; another researcher may have decided on a different set of constructs leading to a different study of the same organisations. As the biases have developed over more than two decades of experience in IS, it makes objective hermeneutics impossible. Accordingly, a "philosophical hermeneutic" (Denzin & Lincoln, 2000, p.194) approach was taken with the research recognising where possible the prejudgments, and in turn using the approach of "understanding the process of understanding" (p. 196). The aim is to describe, analyse and interpret relationships within a defined set of categories, "... it is always possible for there to be different equally valid accounts from different perspectives" (Maxwell, 1992, p.283). The best that can be done is to trace and document the data analysis processes, and the choices and decisions made, so that other researchers and interested parties can decide for themselves what has been lost or what has been gained (Luttrell, 2000).

The question of whether the theory can be deduced from the data analysis in this study may be open to debate. Suffice to say that the researcher was surprised by the findings and they were, as can be reasonably expected, derived from the data.

3.4 Conclusion

This chapter has outlined the rationale for the case analysis research methodology and the research design. The limitations of the approach have also been explained.

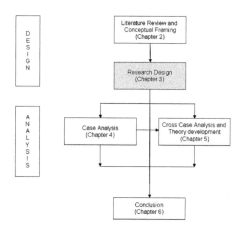

Figure 27.   Book design - chapter 3

The chapter forms the basis of the case analysis explained in chapter 4 and the construct analysis discussed in chapter 5. It also provides the platform for the theory development presented in chapter 5 and summarised in chapter 6.

Chapter 4 – Descriptive Case Analysis

A myth surrounding theory building from case studies is that the process is limited by investigators' preconceptions, in fact just the opposite is true. The constant juxtaposition of conflicting realities tends to 'unfreeze' thinking (Eisenhardt, 1989, p. 546).

This chapter anlyses the data obtained from the individual case studies. The technique is mainly descriptive and aims to illustrate what is happening in the organisations. The data is lightly related to theory and the case data is more thoroughly related to the theory in chapter 5. As advocated by Mishler (1990), many passages of the data are presented so that the reader can validate the interpretations. This makes the chapter lengthy and, to aid a shorter review, a summary of the processes and findings has been included at the end of each case study.

4.1 Pilot Case Provider

The project had an immoveable deadline and the project director at the time was also hell bent on making sure he didn't go over budget. However, by doing that, a number of issues needing to be addressed were left to after implementation. Other issues really, like some of the design issues, like customisation, or reviewing business processes, weren't really done thoroughly and we ended up having a fair chunk or our application being customised. That makes life even harder. (Financial Controller)

The pilot case was selected as it had a reputation of excellence for IS benefits' management, particularly with regard to the ERP application. A paper concerning the company has been published in an academic journal espousing the quality of its IT project benefits' management program. Therefore, the pilot case was seen as ideal for confirming or refuting the constructs of the model generated from the literature review of the study. The case has been very beneficial, the candid discussion by the senior managers concerning problems and oversights significantly added to thisresearch.

The organisation is a municipal provider with approximately $10 billion of investment in infrastructure in terms of installed plant capacity. Provider implemented an SAP ERP application in 1999, the cost of its application and implementation being approximately $40m.

The operations Strategy Manager, the IT Manager, the Financial Manager for IT services and two users were interviewed. Project documentation, process modelling analysis and a diagram of the applications were provided. The interview guide was followed in the conduct of the interviews.

4.1.1 Original Implementation and Its Antecedents

In 1996 a large scale IS was implemented to manage the majority of the activities of the corporation, it had been developed by three state providers, and was envisaged to manage much of the activity now managed by SAP. The application is still in use today but is limited to some customer orientated processes and functions; it has been referred to as 'Customer Service System' in the following description of the case.

The IT Manager identified the decision to purchase an ERP application as being based on "the year 2000 issues"; and because the organisation was moving to " a philosophy of buying rather than building". The mainframe applications were "reasonably ideal for the corporation but were "expensive to look after", so it was decided that the year 2000 presented a good opportunity to "come up the big step and go for a package". Chang, Gable, Smythe, & Timbrell (2000), when researching public sector ERP implementations, found that public organisations were moving away from in-house built applications and installing ERP. It seems Provider was following the example of organisations in the public sector.

The Customer service and SAP applications interface so that when a service request is created in the Customer Service system it creates a work orders in SAP. Status information is passed back by SAP, "There were some tensions between the two applications for a while, particularly in the plant maintenance, asset management type area." (IT Manager).

The IT Manager made the following comment:

> We have quite a number of applications; it ranges between who's counting
> between 3 and 5 hundred. We probably have 10 to 20 significant applications,
> ones that, if they stopped operating some within a few minutes and others within a
> few days, would cause the corporation some grief.

The number of applications is seen as interesting, as ERP systems are designed to replace legacy systems (Amoako-Gyampah, 2004). However, Themistocleous, Irani, & O'Keefe (2001) found that an ERP system supported only 30-50 percent of an organisation's IT requirements; consequently it had to be interfaced with other legacy systems. Markus et al (2000b) also found that, although ERP purports to support all functions, many companies find that legacy systems are required for specialised functions and require interfacing. Some legacy applications are indeed required due to functional deficiencies of the SAP application, but others, as explained in the following section, are being used due to internal politics. Davenport (1998) suggests that, if an organisation's systems are fragmented, then its business is fragmented and this appears to be the situation at Provider.

The response of IT Manager, when asked to explain the process for selecting the SAP application, was:

> We follow our normal procurement processes which is probably the most robust
> that you will find anywhere. Where we had a team of business analysts create a
> complex set of business criteria and evaluation and we went out to market and did
> the normal tendering process and had a number of applicants. Which covered the
> normal range of Enterprise type applications. They were all marked and ranked
> and accessed against a formal criteria and they had the normal processee people
> sitting in and watching everything that went on and it just came to the top of the
> pile. There were several consortiums that put in with SAP as the application
> anyway…….it came down to the functionality of the application plus the capability
> of the organisation to implement such a big bang approach over such a
> compressed timeframe. I think we gave ourselves under a year to implement and
> go live: configure, test do a few parallel runs and go live before Y2k.

Keen (1981) proposes that the acquisition of such a large system would usually require a cost benefit analysis where the cost of the system is established and the tangible or intangible benefits are identified. The researcher asked the IT Manager if costs were first identified then checked for the validity of the expenditure with regard to benefits. He replied:

> No, it came down to the good old traditional, 'this is how much we think it is going
> to cost where do we think we can get that back out of the business.' We created a
> specialised team of about 3 people we put in it, one who now heads-up support
> group. He and a couple of other guys came up with quite a sophisticated benefits
> realisation process and so that consisted of where the opportunities were how they
> would be realised, the process for realising them, which for the corporation was a
> little bit unusual and I guess that most organisations people claim benefits and a
> couple of years time they discretely forget about them because they rather keep
> hold of them [people] but they had quite a rigorous process of chasing them up and

getting people to sign off that at the beginning of the project you agreed to this 2
years out and here we are 2 years out so we want those savings.

When asked if the savings were actually achieved the researcher was told that they were and that this aspect was policed quite closely. The IT Manager continued, "a lot of people came around to have a look at that process because it was quite rigorous, well thought out and workable. A nice combination." The researcher presumed Provider's reputation for excellence in benefits management came from this positive interest of others.

The organisation claims a robust benefits management strategy, and it does indeed have very rigorous methods. However, unearthing of information and identification of issues revealed the process to be flawed. As an example, the Financial Controller provided the following perspective:

> *My perspective - it was less than ideal. The project had an immoveable deadline*
> *and the project director at the time was also hell bent on making sure he didn't go*
> *over budget. However, by doing that a number of issues that needed to be*
> *addressed were left to after implementation and other issues really, like some of*
> *the design issues, like customisation, or reviewing business processes weren't*
> *really done thoroughly and we ended up having a fair chunk or our application*
> *being customised. That makes life even harder.*

When the researcher inquired whether the organisation was still living with those decisions and issues today, the answer was:

> *Absolutely, it is to do with the way our organisation worked.*

The issues emerged over time and through some complex probing of the situation. The decision to maintain the customer service system outside of SAP was largely a political decision, but also necessary to demonstrate a return for the large financial investment in the application. The IT manager observed, "We have come up with this compromise where [Customer Service System] can log the faults and enquiries, and then it has a reasonably sophisticated interface to SAP to execute the work and get the responses back". Over time this compromise has cost the organisation large sums of money and was seen to continue to do so as the applications evolved.

The IT Manager, when asked about the implementation initiative and timeframes, remembered:

Yes, yes, it went in, my memory is a bit vague now, but it went a couple of months to spare. They did several trial runs to cutting over and there were a few compromises made along the way.

The researcher, probing to ascertain the compromises, recorded:

The functionality probably was not optimised in some of the modules and that was partly because you couldn't get good SAP consultants, if there is such a person. Who really understood the module and business functionality. It is all very well to get a plant maintenance configurer, but somebody who understand why you maintain assets and what the process is and therefore why configuring it one way or a process one way is better than another. You just couldn't find at that stage.

Some of the issues arising were also related as being internal:

Business people always revert back to what they know in preference to uncertainty so we villaged out ......it went in on time, we didn't transform any legacy data, which has caused the corporation a little bit of grief in some areas. Some places like finance people would grumble but finance historical data we can do without, but long-term asset data [is important] we had to come up with all sorts of creative solutions to make the mainframe data available but not in SAP.

The researcher, asking about data ownership, was informed:

I think it came down to time constraints complexity of transforming the existing data was going to be too time consuming so they decided not to go with it.......There was a little bit of politics in there, people who wanted change enthusiastically try and implement it without actually thinking what the implications might be, others want to keep it exactly how it used to be. So there was a lot of balance in there.

Dowlatshahi (2005) identifies that "the effectiveness of an ERP system design and implementation is affected by the company's ability to transfer the existing records and data into an ERP system" (p. 3758). The decision not to take over the data to ensure early project implementation has led seemingly to problems. It transpired that the operations people accumulated the 'most power' because day-to-day problems are the most visible. The planners, who prevent faults through analysing have less power and subsequently a less optimal solution. As the IT Manager explained, "It is something we have grappled with, especially in our warehousing, to elevate the visibility of long-term data analysis".

The word 'compromise' occurs three times in the IT Manager's interview: first, as the reason for maintaining the Customer Service System application; second, for explaining the lack of data conversion; and third, to moderate the decision on how to utilise the modules to meet business requirements. This type of compromise may occur if senior management does not impose control. When the Finance Manager was asked whether senior managers were involved in the implementation, he responded that there were "senior operatives". Numerous researchers have contended that senior management involvement is extremely important (Akkermans & Helden (2002), Legare (2002), McAulay (2003), Remenyi (2000), Rosemann (2001), Somers & Nelson (2001), Kroemmergaard & Rose(2002), Shang & Seddon (2002) and Baccarini, Salm, & Love (2004)). If more senior personnel had been included department conflicts might have been reduced.

Towards the beginning of the first interview the IT Manager informed the researcher that one of the reasons for choosing SAP was the knowledge of the consultants. Towards the end of the second interview he was asked whether the consultants' knowledge was as good as expected. His response was very enlightening:

> You know that they all operate the bake and switch system, where the guys who come for the presentation are the top guys, they are clued up, really know their stuff people, there in the room and immediately you know they know what they are talking about. Once they have got the job, they are doing what all of the others do, they are around all of the consulting firms in xxxxx, picking up anybody that knows anything about SAP because it is too expensive to fly everybody in.

This 'bake and switch' process, heavily used in the IT industry, occurs when the consultants involved in pre-sales have a wealth of expertise and when a project is won more junior consultants are utilised. In the evaluation stage, a large part of decisions can be based on the knowledge of these individuals, which, if they are immediately lost to the project compromises the evaluation. To overcome this possibility to some extent the contract can stipulate that the sales team should be part of the conceptual design. This solution has its limitations as it is not generally practical to stipulate names in service contracts because the contracting organisation cannot guarantee any individual's availability due to intervening impediments such as recreation leave, sick leave, or being no longer in contracted employment.

It was obvious the IT Manager had lost confidence in the approach adopted by the consultants, commenting:

> *A consultant can nod and agree but I have noticed with SAP guys that they are so*
> *fixed on what they did last time, that there nodding consists of thanking for paying*
> *me money and I am going to do it the way I thought anyway.*

As one of the key decisions for choosing the consulting firm's application was the quality and appropriateness of the consultants, the IT Manager was asked if, in retrospect, the decision was sound:

> *Of the product sets and vendors offered to us we believe we have selected the*
> *right product. When the selection was made at time business process was to be*
> *reengineered that was the outline. What the software suggested was the 'best*
> *practice etc. etc.' somehow that changed during implementation.*

When asked why the criteria had changed during implementation, the IT Manager responded, "Deadline, money and maybe some political pressure". He opined that there had not been a good change management process, saying, "I think those are the issues that pushed the project to end up delivering what, in my personal view, is a sub-optimised solution." He went on to explain:

> *In terms of evaluation process we should have done a lot more on our ability to*
> *change our business processes compared to the software. I think that we grossly*
> *underestimated the cultural change, also the capacity of this organisation to move*
> *the culture and change its long embedded work practices that wasn't really*
> *reviewed and looked at in detail.*

The Finance Manager explained that as this was a job-based organisation, planned maintenance being but a small proportion of the work, with the majority of necessary works being "unplanned or ad hoc". He continued:

> *SAP as software ... not quite matching that requirement ... We also have an in-*
> *house business rule that we have one work order for one task. That totally*
> *contravenes SAP's concept of a work order being for multiple tasks ... We weren't*
> *able to change that rule at the time of implementation as part of the budget and*
> *time constraints [so] we ended up having to customise our applications a lot in that*
> *area. In turn it also impacts on some of the capability of using SAP to analyse*
> *asset maintenance issues using the standard functionalities"*
>
> *We are cycling over 300,000 works orders on an ongoing basis. Normally an SAP*
> *implementation of say a manufacturing plant, a manufacturing organisation, might*

have 40,000 or 50,000 works orders as a maximum. Because we are cycling so many the granularity of the data and the analysis is really hard, trying to make sense out of it.

The IT Manager, when asked what he would change if he could re-address the implementation process, responded:

So there are a few things that we would change, it takes the organisation some time to accept that $100,000 spent at the beginning of a project is a $1m saved at the end.

A project lifecycle costing approach is clearly missing in the original implementation plan and the antecedents of this plan have directly and negatively impacted the organisation since. According to El Amrani, Rowe, & Geffroy-Maronnat (2006, p.85), one of the objectives of ERP is to get "users out of their functional silos and give them a cross functional view of the organisation" (p.85), and suggest that this can not happen "if the organisation remains stuck in a functional configuration supported by a patchwork of additional systems". Provider's organisation comprises a patch work of systems, and the interviewees were frank in their admission of a silo mentality. This mentality is even more evidence when the strategy process is explored.

4.1.2 Impact of Strategy Process on ERP

The strategy process was explained by the strategy manager:

There is a corporate information management strategy that's maintained and there is a cyclic process to review that and make it current. At least reflect the current intent of the business, it's based on the business knowing what it is doing, in terms of being a corporate strategy cascading down to individual process areas business units. Business unit have their own strategies which are aligned to the corporate strategy and then from there those are translated down to the branch plans etc. etc..

The type of strategy process used is defined by Johnson and Scholes (2002) as a 'formal' process, due to the formal planning process and a procedure for communicating the strategy.

The strategy process is interpreted by the business unit managers and then communicated to the IT department by each unit or department. The IT Manager explained that the process is more convoluted than that proposed by the Strategy Manager, averring:

> *There are at least 2 and probably quite a few planning processes that go on, the first one is our corporate planning process which cycles through every year and updates our long-term plan but updates our short-term plans – 1 and 2 year type plans. The corporate performance is a shorter timeframe, it has reasonable specific things that the corporation wants to do, that gets created and the process is improving as I speak, we used to find out about it more accidentally than by design, but it is being fed through now to our strategic information management process which interviews the business a slightly lower level of the organisation. Who theoretically are interpreting that corporate performance contract into their own individual outcomes and then interpreting what things they need IT- wise to achieve whatever it is.*

The stakeholder initiatives are then interpreted and result in individual departmental requests. This is typical of 'Management by Objectives' frameworks, which were seen as somewhat wanting in the 1990s, and have since been replaced largely by 'Management by Results' and 'Balanced Scorecards', in which the proposed initiatives are validated against the goals of the organisation with IT having a major strategic impact. When asked how the process was managed at the lower level, the IT Manager explained:

> *We dutifully note down what those needs are and I guess we interpret them back into the business speak into the information management strategy that theoretically guides which projects occur from year to year.*

The IT Manager was asked how IT had influenced the strategy process in terms of opportunities for technological developments, and he replied:

> *The corporate performance contract is created pretty much in isolation of IT input so some of things are scary and some of the things a bit of a surprise and they don't frequently take into account the opportunities that IT might provide.*

And when discussing how IT strategy came about, he said the Business Managers were interviewed, the outcome of which was quite poor, he added:

The strategic information management process interviews people and they have
forgotten about their performance contracts and talked about what they would like
to do, so you end up with two not quite aligned strategies.

Asked how the faulty interviewing process was being addressed, he explained:

Over the last couple of years we have tightened that up a bit, and now we have a
ranking process so a project, when it gets proposed it gets evaluated against a set
of criterion, one is in the performance contract: is it in the strategic information
management plan ... but it hasn't been traditionally but we are getting there.

This appeared to be somewhat less than a strategy and more projects were evaluated. The researcher asked
the IT Manager if there was a focus on distinct projects rather than the business goals:

We haven't really convinced people that we should be talking about what we call a
business story. Which is in 3 years time we will manage the organisation like this
and leaving it at that level and allowing business analysts to then tease out a path
and say in order to achieve that sought of objective we will need to set our
systems these ways. And therefore people have ownership of a particular project
and when an application falls out of that, they take ownership of that as well, and
guard it with passion. So trying to integrate applications becomes quite
challenging politically as well.

The strategy process appears to have been less than ideal with IS being managed mostly from the operational
level of the business. This faulty process has been recognised with remedial activity taking place in the form
of an appointed Strategy Manager who explained:

The difference in this role, is that prior to my engagement, the role of planning was
more about a program management function, which was, we have got a 100
projects and we have go so much money this year which ones are we going to
spend on and managing the ins and outs of the projects with a less of an emphasis
on, how are these projects aligned to the core objectives of the organisation.

Coming into the role my brief has been, "Don't worry too much about the dollars
and cents and the mechanics of managing programs, let's focus on making sure

we have a strategy from the business down all the way to the enabling IT level. We need to have visibility".

An operational approach to management of IS has been seen by application of the formerly prevalent IS theory to result in sub-optimal applications. Provider is now obviously trying to align better the IT strategy with the business. However, it has taken almost 10 years since the original implementation to address the issue and this has resulted in a proliferation of customisations and high expenditure.

4.1.3 Financial Procedures and Imperatives

As was seen in the strategy section above, the original project was estimated at AU$40m with the expenditure being planned in a 'business case'. A 'business case' was explained by the Finance Manager thus:

> *A positive business case is very much a financial return, a positive NPV, including a 5 year outlook after the project and take a $ point of view, including our maintenance costs and any licence implications.*

This approach appears to be a robust and tangible application of the prevalent approach in IS theory for automation of work.

When asked about the maintenance costs specifically the following response was made by the Finance Manager:

> *The estimate of the maintenance costs is fairly poorly done, because I don't think there is a lot of understanding of what it means. The disconnect between a project go live and maintenance is where TOC actually might hit you and I don't think we have a really good handle on this one.*

The researcher, queried the use of NPV, asking how the return was discounted, and whether inflation and cost of capital was included, heard:

> *Corporately we have a notional interest rate we discount and it is the same interest rate we use for all projects. Not just IT projects, there was no special interest rate. We adopt a corporate capital process.*

The Finance Manager further informed him that, in the previous year, the SAP application had cost $3m, and the current year having $5m budgeted for customisations and support. Salaries of all the personnel involved in the implementation were not included. These figures did not form part of the original NPV projection, "But that's what you get when you buy an Enterprise System," concluded the Finance Manager, who further explained:

> *If we account for our original investment plus our ongoing investment we have put into SAP, it is probably close to $100m. We won't be getting rid of a $100m investment quickly.*

The Finance Manager, asked if he believed that the maximum 5 year time period allowed in Australia for depreciation of IT was realistic for ERP which has a potential life-span much longer than 5 years, responded that he would personally not like ERP to be valued for longer, as the maintenance cost is written-off each year and money is "continually poured back in".

It transpired that enhancements are capitalised, being a possible reason why they are provided by an outsourced function, thereby the customisations are paid to a third party thus allowing those customisations to become assets. If the work was performed internally the cost would usually become an expense. Many companies find ways to capitalise such customisation, especially when a company has such large infrastructure as the one being researched, the IT costs disappear into depreciation of assets. This provides short-term advantage of reduced costs but has the potential of oncosts that outlast the benefits of the initiatives. Often little consideration is given to matching the capital costs with discrete application functions as is the case with the registration of conventional assets; policing of the 'assets' then becomes extremely difficult and is generally not performed. A subsequent discussion was had with the Strategy Manager concerning upgrades and the elimination of some customisations to reduce the cost of ownership going forward. He was asked if there was a potential problem with having to write off investments if customisations were eliminated:

> *Eemmm, ahhhh [long hesitation] Potentially. Although the major aspects of the system would pretty much be off the books by now.*

There are a 'few" enhancement projects that have internal recharging:

> ... *that comes and goes in organisations, you know we are going to recharge or*
> *we are not going to recharge. In an organisation like ours $50,000 will get you an*
> *analysis document, because it will take somebody 2 or 3 months to just figure out*
> *what the problem is, where the issues are coming from, and how to go forward.*
> *So, it is pretty expensive just spending $50,000 everywhere trying to get a grasp of*
> *what's going on.*

The financial imperative with the application is large. A change of application would have a major consequence for the organisation's financial performance.

The Finance Manager identified the following:.

> *There was a fairly rigorous benefits realisation project ... We still continue to have*
> *some benefit realisation review but we have not attempted to seek out TOC*
> *calculations. As the software matures in the organisation the TOC calculation*
> *becomes more complex.*

The original project was costed in detail but other activity has not been costed. Apparently, the original project is the 'tip of an iceberg' with the subsequent costs being the major expense, which were not rigorously policed.

4.1.4 Upgrades and Their Antecedents

There have been two upgrades with one of those being termed a 'major upgrade to 4.6C from 3.1H'. The IT Manager explained that there were also "various bits of upgrades", with the "Business Warehouse in 2001 being another upgrade to a newer version. ... We currently just went through upgrading Business Warehouse to 3.5" ... We have upgraded our operating system; and we changed our Unix so there is a number of upgrades that we have done."

The cost of the major upgrade to 4.6c, estimated to have cost approximately $3m dollars, was 7.5% of the original implementation cost. However, the upgrade was a "technical upgrade", one in which the functionality of the new release is not implemented with only the kernel being moved forward. Senior staff decided not to undertake a complete upgrade as there was insufficient time or money to move the customisation forward:

> *SAP is continually rehashing the application transparently, so you get a new*
> *version, the architects drive themself silly trying to put it in, but no functional*
> *changes to the user. Maybe a new look and feel but nothing tangible, so whatever*
> *you've got you're going to have forever. (IT Manager).*

The Fnance Manager explained that if the organisation does not upgrade the opportunity of using the technology for a quicker turnaround is lost; therefore an opportunity cost for not upgrading is incurred. Upgrades are discussed further under the Approach To Customisations section.

4.1.5 Re-implementations

> *The area that we have re-implemented is mainly in the finance area. There were*
> *two drivers, one, the organisation has had a change in its wholesale structure so*
> *we have to re-implement, another driver, was that we have changed some of our*
> *internal costing and internal recharging processes and, with the way SAP was*
> *implemented, we had to re-implement it (Finance Manager).*

When the Finance Manager was asked if the application had stifled the business he responded by answering, "Yes, mainly from customisations," adding he thought it was industry practice to try to match the business to the software rather than start the other way.

The IT Manager when asked would he re-implement the application, if he could, conjectured:

> *Yes, the biggest thing I learned was that there is a clear separation between a set*
> *module jockey and a good business analyst. If you follow the SAP methodology,*
> *which nobody seems to follow in the SAP environment, you would probably get a*
> *much better outcome.*

A re-implementation process is seen as a way of overcoming the negative antecedents of the original implementation. However, the cost and disruption make re-implementation prohibitive.

4.1.6 Perceptions of IS

The perception of SAP and IS in general is not consistent across the organisation. It varied as some parts of the organisation viewed the application as very appropriate to their work while others saw it as unimportant.

Managers also have different levels of application knowledge, the IT Manager explaining that "generally, the people who use it often find it good; infrequent users don't like it. "

When asked why he thought this was the case he explained:

> A lot has got to do with SAP the depth of menu structure within the GUI, it is not the easiest way to navigate. Some of the terminology and field descriptions aren't really as intuitive as one would like. The version of SAP we are running currently is 4.6C has a Window based GUI, but in reality it is still a halfway house between a real Windows based intuitive software and mainframe software. It is really just bridging the gap. So there are some useability issues and for people who are not used to it because they are infrequent they might only go in once a month or now and then to do a procurement function it is quite hard. So that is why there is a varying level of acceptance of the software.

Amoako-Gyampah (2004) also recognised that users of a system frequently have a better opinion of it than those who are infrequent users. The Strategy Manager divined a changing of perception, postulating that users were seeing the constraints of their own processes thereby being won over to adopt a "best practice approach rather than bespoke practice that they've had and developed over the years." Other interviewees did not articulate such an observation.

4.1.7 Influences and Consequences of Software Authors and Resellers

SAP asserts pressure on an organisation to upgrade by increasing the annual maintenance costs which stand at a 10% base charge plus a percentage based on the current version of the implemented application. The Finance Manager explained:

> One part is maintenance costs, SAP or any large-scale software escalates maintenance costs if you don't upgrade. SAP has a 5, 2, 1, what they call, 5% is normal maintenance, next year is 2% more, it is escalating, next year is another 1% more, after that it goes out of main stream maintenance. It becomes customer specific maintenance where it is negotiated.

The Finance Manager believed 15%-20% annual cost to be usual and proposed that authors such as "SAP, Computer Associates, IBM put a lot of the maintenance over to research and development." He was then asked if a limit existed as to what could be asked for annual maintenance. He did not believe that businesses would pay above 20%, but suggested that SAP would take more notice of very large organisations and not be influenced by smaller organisations.

When the Strategy Manager was asked about pressure from the author he saw it as a difficult decision to take new modules as this increases the ongoing cost of ownership. He saw that the power of determining initial and ongoing costs was largely with the Software Author.

There is perhaps also a disconnect between the Software Author's implementation aims and the expectation of the organisation. The IT manager explained the following.

> *When SAP was implemented they ran all of this training, I got nominated for*
> *training and my training course was how to create a cost code in SAP. I am there 2*
> *minutes with my hand up going excuse me why am I on this course, the response*
> *was 'well you have got such and such privileges in SAP and one of them includes*
> *how to create a cost code so you have to come on this course'. I'm going, 'I have*
> *no clue why I have to create a cost code and secondly when does this occur, when*
> *do I do it? I 'Don't worry about that go to screen such and such, type in a number*
> *press enter you have created a cost code you're certified'. So we have tried to*
> *change the culture through the organisation to more of a process orientated view.*

Amoako-Gyampah (2004) found that both users and managers did not generally believe that ERP training was adequate; Slater (1998, cited Amoako-Gyampah 2004) suggests that the completeness, length, detail, timing and even who to train, is an ongoing concern for companies implementing an ERP system. As Delone and McLean (2003) identified user satisfaction as a key determinant of IS success, the approach to training does not seem to maximise the chance of success.

4.1.8 Environmental Influences

The organisation does not see external factors as being important in managing the application, this is probably due to there being a vast number of customers and suppliers that reduces their individual power. Potential problems with the impact of Y2K on the internally developed bespoke applications, was cited as major reason to purchase an ERP application. There was also the perception that government service organisations were moving away from internally developed applications and starting to acquire applications from 3rd parties.

The author of an application appears to be a key consideration for Server, and the organisation only identified two acceptable suppliers of ERP.

4.1.9 Evaluation Procedures

This section discusses evaluation of the initial implementation, upgrades, re-implementations and, in the main, evaluation of customisations.

Evaluation is largely concerned with the small incremental projects continually proposed by departments. The IT budget is increased as each project is approved,

> *"There is a hurdle rate, but that is usually a smaller point. We categorise our projects into four, the hurdle rate only applying to the larger projects. When it is only say $50k or less, it is a fairly straight-forward run through." (Finance Manager).*

The strategist views the approach with a more strategic perspective, he claimed "It is NPV plus strategic alignment and strategic benefits that are less than quantified. They are based on anticipated benefits but not necessarily hard benefits tied into an operating budget."   The researcher initiated further probes, inquiring if it could be inferred that it is not practical to identify benefits:

> *You may claim a link between a $5m SAP implementation and the fact that you met a major contract for $50m and as a result the guy didn't bid $50m he bid $48m, is that a direct attributed benefit to the SAP process.*

And, asking if it were possible to relate benefits to numerous initiatives:

> *Generally the benefits go to the business and the costs to IT!*

The following explanation by the IT Manager demonstrates how the approach to evaluation is changing to a strategic perspective:

> *I guess the easiest way to put it, is from a capital point of view it is a nice surprise if the project has a positive return and if it had a strong case it might get some ranking above another project. But in general most of our projects would either be infrastructure, maintaining the status quo or described as a strategic project. I think*

the corporation needs to mature a bit, the reason they are generally labelled as a strategic project is because it is a little bit hard to identify what the business outcome is and so on. They do have an immediate objective and immediate benefits to whoever ask for it, but when you get into the benefits realisation role where you are saying there should be a noticeable benefit to the organisation at that level and therefore should be tracked like that a lot of our projects haven't quite got there. So our process for identifying a good project over a not so good project is more down to strategic indicators like is it in our corporate performance contract which is set by executive. This is in our information management strategy rather than a rate of return.

The approach is to maintain the infrastructure and identify key strategic projects and others that have a high anticipated NPV. The discussion concerning strategy highlighted considerable concern with the strategy process, this bringing into question the authenticity of the strategic projects. Keen and Digrius (2003) propose a method of scoring these different type projects which enables comparative initiatives using tangible and intangible techniques. The IT Manager was asked how projects were ranked or analysed: and how, for instance, would an infrastructure project be ranked against a strategic project. He explained that a scoring mechanism is used:

It has to be over 90 to be guaranteed, because over 90 it means that the corporation won't be able to operate an IT system if this doesn't happen. So usually hardware and licensing are the 100s. We have got a couple of applications that are using Oracle forms, which is not a supported product anymore so those generally get a high numbers because we are concerned about maintaining the thing. They are really stuck in a time warp you can't enhance them because there is noting you can do. Then you have the 60 – 80 which are strategic projects, one that the corporation have said you shalt do and we rank them accordingly. Then we have the 30 – 50s which are the ones that are there because they have got the good pay back.

Having the high payback projects ranked the lowest and ongoing business the highest represents an interesting approach and is possibly due to the enormous consequences of failure to deliver the product and a mentality of risk control. The IT Manager was asked whether 30-50 type projects with positive return had a time lag due to their low priority:

Yes, a good example was the SAP Business Warehouse that was identified as a
critical need in 1996 and we implemented probably 2002/2003 because people
were fed up with it being pushed out another year…. We have the traditional bow
wave there is only so much money to go around and everything that is below the
line for one year has to get what we called smoothed out to the next years and if
you are a little guy you will get smoothed a long way out.

This obviously opposes the positive NPV espoused earlier. When asked about cost of ownership calculations, the IT Manager admitted there was no measure. The Finance Manager was also asked this question and he identified some of the budget increase as being for staff to support the application or enhancement, adding, "However, having said that, some parts are real, some parts are very hard to actually realise - for argument sake, when a project using equivalent 0.1 of a FT employee(full time) wants to increase the number of hours, to support the application is difficult as in reality it is really hard to mobilise a fraction of an FT if the adjustment of hours is internal." This problem is exacerbated by different types of projects as indicated below:

It is alright if we buy consultants or outsourced hours, they have a much more
flexible manpower management process than internal. And so that in essence
what we have to deal with is step changes, so a number of projects accumulates
up and then we build up until we recruit one person. The challenge there is the skill
set, there will be a number of projects that only give us fractions of an FT in
support. Let's say that 5 projects contribute to 1 FT, 5 projects can be very different
in their technology skill set. To try to amalgamate that and put it back into a
support group that ties to support all the applications, the overhead of actually
learning is more than the staff allocation. And that is not catered for at all.

This strategic approach, requiring the strategy to be interpreted by each business unit and department, results in project proposals which by necessity means the proposals are individually evaluated. This has created a complex mix of evaluation processes and difficulties for supporting the many initiatives. Irani, Themistocleous and Love (2003) noted that evaluation becomes very complex both in terms of content and time-frames with an extended systems environment that includes legacy application and it is, therefore, perhaps not surprising that Provider has such complex procedure and faces the difficulties described.

4.1.10 Approach to Customisations

It became apparent during data collection that the aspect of ongoing customisations is critical to aligning the system to meet business needs. The following discussion outlines the approach to customisations.

> *The process that was put in place when the project was implemented was that for each SAP there are 3 modules, there is a process manager who is in charge of the business so in our customer service division for arguments sake they look after the planned maintenance version, finance division have a business process manager who looks after the cycle area etc. They are the ones that drive changes and make requests, so if they want to change a field description or move the screen layout, or have a small enhancement because some minor process change they have to decide what needs to be done in the business, then negotiate with ISD and my position, a group of business analysts that all came out from the project work in this group they will work with the business process manager trying to define the specification. Then some of the configuration is done by ourselves but some are done by outsource provider.*

Probing further, the researcher asked whether a cost benefit analysis of the customisations was undertaken:

> *Unfortunately no. At the maintenance level that was never considered, only when a job becomes too big, the benchmark of being too big is governed by our capital process. At one stage it was $25,000 so anything close or above that mark we would question if that should have been done under maintenance. Rather it should have been done under a capital project.*

The Finance Manager had identified earlier that the threshold was currently $50,000. The IT Manager was asked about cost of ownership of these "small" customisations that cost less than $50,000:

> *I think this is where the more we do under maintenance the harder it is to upgrade. This is not necessarily pointing the finger at individuals but because maintenance issues are always dealt with fairly quickly because of time, documentation is not completed and it is not necessarily integrated into the previous version so some of those things make maintenance harder. Therefore, we now have to rely on personal knowledge of some of the business analysts, as well as documents of knowledge.*

According to the IT Manager some unsanctioned customisations happen on an ad-hoc basis, "If you are working away and somebody rings up and says can you fix such and such, and you have only got to spend half four, you will go and make the change." He contended that a process of sanctioning small, urgent jobs increased costs and disrupted support. What happens is that the business asks, "How many people do you need to support it, and you go 10, and they go wow that's a lot of people but this is because they are all doing these little 10 minute and ½ hour jobs everywhere rather than saying, 'no that's actually a proper project'. The IT Manager agreed it was a "business continuity risk" and they were trying to improve knowledge management and embrace the ITAL (see literature review) framework.

Larger projects have a planning process to identify requirements and create a project proposal. "Only if it comes through with a positive business case will it go on the flow line." The researcher was told on inquiry what constituted a positive business case:

> A positive business case is very much a financial return, a positive NPV. Including a 5 year outlook after the project and take a $ point of view, including our maintenance costs and any licence implications. But the estimate of the maintenance costs is fairly poorly done, because I don't think there is a lot of understanding of what it means. The disconnect between a project go live and maintenance is where TOC actually might hit you and I don't think we have a really good handle on this one.

If a project proposal is not seen as strategic and the benefits are only in monetary terms it may not be implemented for a long time. The Strategy Manager made the following comments concerning customisations:

> There seems to be a willingness from the business to potentially review some of the customisation, probably now recognising that non vanilla implementations present a whole set of challenges moving forward

The existing controls are still allowing for many customisations – those below $50,000, and any strategic or maintenance projects will almost certainly be implemented. The IT Manager explained that many requested customisations could not be implemented because the applicants "do not understand the function" or "we have modified the module away from standard." He continued, "Rather than going back to generic and starting again we do the quick option of implementing a bit of what we call a front-end. Then the front-end morphs into a more user friendly front-end, which usually means that it doesn't have any of the fields that SAP has."

When asked about controlling the release of software, the IT Manager responded with:

> "We are still struggling with our development test and production environment as it's very expensive to maintain a full blown, fully compatible environment. You get the thing in development, it works great, in test it seemed to be Ok, and you put it in production and everything comes to a stop."

As this problem in not atypical and usually indicative of an IT department that is reacting rather than proactively managing releases, the IT Manager was asked how the situation might differ from the situation when the organisation built its own applications. He replied that the "rigour" had changed, explaining:

> People think that it was paper chasing but everything was thoroughly tested, people knew what they were doing and it worked first time. There was always somebody who oversaw the entire process, there was a way things were done, that was sort of lost and even SAP has that internally but when you put the application in the consultants are in and under a deadline and under estimate it because they want to get the job so they cut all of those corners.

The Strategy Manager, when asked about the size and release of customisation units, stated his belief that the organisation was responding to a lot of "noise", and that where SAP became concerned the "horse had bolted" with it being almost impossible to regain control.

The IT Manager, during his interview, made two telling comments:

> I won't mention the project name, it is an enhancement to SAP, and because they don't like SAP, and it's an implementation of a function that SAP has but somebody would like it in a web environment, so we are going to essentially duplicate the functionality for $290,000. So that somebody doesn't have to use SAP.

> I think [Provider] has continued and behaved as if it was a custom application when indeed it should have changed that behaviour (IT Manager).

At the beginning of his first interview the IT Manager stated that one of the reasons for buying SAP was its "philosophy of buying rather than building", the organisation is now in danger of buying and building, a very costly process. The Strategy Manager when asked how the process might be changed, rejoined:

> I think there is an opportunity identifying itself in the next 18 months, we need to have a major version upgrade. In the past, and this is only going on what I have been told, it has been very much a technically driven upgrade based on reasons of maintaining support etc. Now with this particular version, which is a major upgrade with the application moving to a completely new architecture..... there is an opportunity to eliminate some of the business barriers [re-engineer processes] that were there within the business to prior to adopting SAP .

> We need to understand how things work first and then superimpose the application on the top. Just don't implement an application in the hope everything will fall into place. People will always revert back to what they understand and manoeuvre the application.

The researcher observed there appears to be a culture of customising applications and that this needs to be stopped if IS to take a strategic and lead role in the organisation.

4.1.11 Restrictions and Limitations Imposed by ERP

Bannister et al (2001) identified what he terms as disbenefits of applications, where applications have a negative impact on benefits. Although not a major construct, the potential of the application to restrict the organisation is interesting. It was apparent from the interviews that the number of work orders was difficult to manage with SAP and the continuous customisation are indicative of a mismatch of the application and the business. Also, the number of legacy applications, with the need to interface and maintain them causes the organisation ongoing cost and management which is not usually envisaged with an ERP application.

The Strategy Manager echoed that 'if you are a relatively newer start-up organisation where you can literally align your process from day one to the ERP, then I think there is the opportunity to really leverage it'. However, he saw the current application restricting the organisation moving forward, contending the "retro-fitting to organisations is really probably under-estimated" and limiting as SAP is not a tool for the business but a way to manage a business. Interestingly, when asked how SAP viewed this contention, he proposed, " they probably see it as an opportunity to load the price". SAP then, to some extent, represses the organisation resulting in customisations and/or re implementations to effect change.

4.1.12 Expected Lifespan of the ERP

All interviewees were asked how long they thought the application would last and what they believed would be the reason for changing the application. The Finance Controller believed the organisation would use SAP as long as SAP was a major vendor. He cited a product from Computer Associates known as Masterpiece as being utilised for many years until the vendor ceased supporting it. He also believed that SAP was lagging behind other applications in terms of technology, but was catching up, and that this would not be a reason to change the application.

The Strategy Manager's view was that the system would be changed either for business reasons or due to lack of sufficient investment to maintain the current application. He made the following comment.

> WWWWooooeerrr. As it stands at the moment I can't see in my vision a day when it
> won't be in place and I would probably use certainly a 5 to 10 year timeframe from
> today. I say that because I believe that if anything there is another 5 years of SAP,
> we might then do a strategic evaluation to see if it still fits or if there is anything
> more suitable in the market place. Assuming there was there probably is a 2 to 3
> year decision process and implementation process to move to a new platform, so
> that is why I said 5 – 10 years may be.
>
> I think once you make the leap it is not a short-term decision. I think fundamentally
> I don't see too many people backing out of an implementation of SAP onto
> something else unless it is driven by business downsizing or not able to maintain
> the investment that is required.

The IT Manager did not see any horizon for SAP replacement, asserting that SAP invests between 10% and 20% of revenue in the application and it would remain at the head of the competition.

4.1.13 Approach to Business Process Analysis

The proliferation of customisations and the difficulty of customising a function already modified for other purposes have created a post-live focus on the analysis of business processes. The objective is for staff to think in terms of a continuous process and then identify gaps or restrictions in the process according to the IT Manager:

We wanted to work out some simple method that the business could understand where to priorities their energy in terms of where SAP enhancements went, and you can look at the whole of SAP and be overwhelmed with a 101 things that you could do but where would be the value and where would be the business buy into it. We came up with a really simple methodology that the business really latched onto and it consisted of using tools that SAP provide and don't know that they have. A thing called, I think it is called The Solution Builder.

Two years after the application had been implemented a process of 'run through' was undertaken with all employees responsible for particular processes. Issues with the processes were identified and logged and these were colour coded. The IT Manager explained that red indicated that the process 'had a lot of opportunity, the interpretation being it is stuffed and we need to fix it'; orange indicated that it could be 'lived with but might be better'; and green showed 'we can put up with it'. After spending AU\$100m the best to be hoped for is that 'it could be put up with'!

The IT Manager made the following comment:

If only we had known about these tools before we went live. We didn't actually learn about them from SAP and the application of the tool isn't actually designed for this. It was actually designed for a marketing person to sell SAP and all of the SAP consultants that we had on site had no idea how to do it like this. This process recently helped to prioritise investments as the dilemma had been how to fit the'10s of million dollars of asks into a smaller budget with a level of agreement.

Interestingly, the IT Manager did not see the results of this evaluation as an opportunity to re-engineer the business processes. The Strategy Manager indicated his noticing of a "willingness" for the organisation to move away from customisations to re-engineering processes so that the new functionality could be utilised. He maintained that historically there had be a reluctance for people to change their process, and they would rather alter "out of the box process based on the fact that I have been doing this process so many years in the same way." When asked what was winning them over he acknowledged:

I think they are now seeing the constraints of their own processes versus the tools they have got out of the box to use, and there almost being won over a bit to adopt best practice approach rather than bespoke practice that they've now had and developed over the years.

Whilst he has mooted a change, there has been no reverse engineering of the customisations to date. The IT Manager deemed the lack of initial focus on the business process being due to the time allocated to the project. The re-engineering of business process was planned as part of the original implementation, but had been managed by the operational managers responsible for the process. A BPR doctrine advocated by Sethi and King (1998), is that any re-engineering should be managed by a manager who operates above the function being reviewed. Apparently, during the original implementation as well as with the recent business process review, the process has been analysed by employees close to the process, which is unlikely to result in a step change.

4.1.14 Findings and Interpretations

It appears that the ERP implementation has suffered from a flawed strategy process, this is in spite of what appears to be a robust method of business strategy development. IS is not an integral part of the strategy process and the two do not appear to be adequately aligned after the strategy process is completed. Johnson and Scholes (2002, p.566) describe a strategy process having an unrealised intended outcome, as having an emergent strategy "that comes about through everyday routines and activities".

The strategy process is shown diagrammatically in Figure 28. The strategy is communicated to departmental heads, their initiatives in support of the strategy result in project request for IS changes. The amalgamation of the project requests is then used to create an IT plan. However, this is less than an IS strategy per se. The appointment of a Strategy Manager by Provider is an obvious recognition that the organisation's strategy process is flawed.

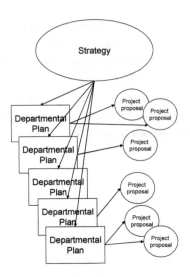

Figure 28.   Provider Strategy Process

The powerful groups in the organisation have optimised processes while other less powerful groups, such as the planners, are not serviced as well. The operational manager's responsibility for identifying process changes ensures it is less likely that business processes will be changed than customisations made. One of the major complaints about BPR is that people are not sufficiently involved in the process (El Sawy, 2001); however, one of the major reasons for this state of affairs is that the changes require an enforced new way of looking at the process.

The culture of developing systems is still apparent in the organisation and is manifesting itself in continuing customisations. The threshold of $50,000 before an evaluation is required for a proposed customisation allows for a vast number of minor customisations to be made. This impacts the support environments where the current state of the test system is unknown, dilutes the effectiveness of the support team, increases the support overhead and impacts the ability to upgrade. When tangible evaluations are undertaken, the positive NPV projects have the lowest ranking meaning that IS is not being managed with a focus on the return on capital. This is a questionable strategy in what is a capital intensive business.

The management and evaluation process is shown diagrammatically in Figure 29. Many development activities, shown on the left of the diagram, are undertaken without any evaluation. These are ad hoc '30 minute' customisations performed by either by support staff or customisation projects costing less than $50,0000; which are automatically approved after a short risk analysis.

The high pay back projects are given one of the lowest priorities and either do not get sanctioned or wait a long time to be sanctioned. The strategic projects are those identified by departmental managers to be directly related to the organisation's strategy; however, all the interviewees doubted the robustness of the strategy approach. The status quo projects of hardware upgrades and licences are automatically sanctioned, but a great deal of money is being spent to maintain the status quo. The 'front end' add-ons demonstrate that the system is being modified by additions because of the difficulty to develop some functions further. The belief that evaluation and management of customisations is less rigorously executed than for applications developed in-house demonstrates the lack of control of the total cost of ownership of this highly customised application.

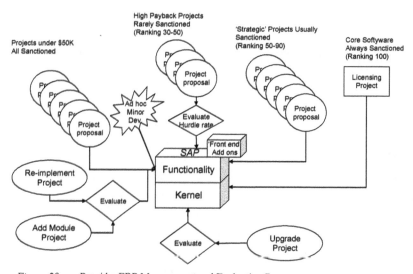

Figure 29.   Provider ERP Management and Evaluation Process

The wish to reverse-engineer the system to be as close to vanilla as possible seems to be a reasonable strategy to reduce the cost of ownership. However, no one involved in the process has the seniority to issue an edict for the change.

The problems observed in the Provider's organisation can be summarised as follows.

- o   senior management involvement is lacking;
- o   original implementation deadline impacted extent of business reengineering;
- o   antecedents of the original implementation are having a long-term impact;
- o   application is seen to have been too extensively customised;
- o   evaluation processes can be circumvented;
- o   powerful groups are optimised and others sub-optimised;
- o   IT is not considered as an enabler in the strategy process;
- o   IT projects and corporate objectives appear to diverge: and
- o   extensive customisations restrict upgrades.

4.1.15 Conclusion

According to all interviewees the initial implementation was poor. The focus of 'on time; on budget', prompted by the Y2K phenomenon, did not allow for sufficient consideration of the necessary changes to business practices or to the application. The culture of developing software to meet the organisation's needs has continued after ERP implementation, leading to a heavily modified, difficult to upgrade application. This has led to a loss of opportunity in utilising the functionality of later releases.

Two further constructs from those identified in the literature review were included in the subsequent case studies. A business process view was critical at Provider's organisation; therefore the approach to business process analysis was added as a unit of analysis for subsequent cases. This case made it obvious that the process of managing an ERP is much more fluid than originally envisaged. Customisation requests are being continuously generated so the approach to customisations was added to the eight original constructs. The pilot case was very beneficial, identifying the new constructs and reinforcing a number of the constructs already identified. The latter were: implementation and upgrade antecedents, effectiveness of strategic management, finance procedures, perception and culture, and the influence of the application's author.

4.2   Case Study Server

Server has five sites across Australia with approximately 180 employees. It services and maintains assets at retail outlets for a major consumable product. The outlets are primarily owned by very large global corporations. The service is, generally, provided by contractual agreement and includes both preventative and general maintenance. Server operates a 24-hour help desk and has service engineers available throughout Australia, 24 hours a day, 365 days a year.

The ERP application is the Dynamics(AX) application from Microsoft. It was implemented at a cost of approximately Au$600,000. Six interviews were conducted with the management cohort, consisting of the CEO, IT Manager, IS Support and Development Manager, Finance Director and two key users. The organisation provided a reasonable amount of secondary data in terms of project reports and associated documents. Server is the smallest organisation researched.

4.2.1 Original Implementation and Its Antecedents

Prior to the implementation of Dynamics(AX) the organisation had two applications: one for the front office functions of service management; and the other for the back office function of accounting. The systems were not interfaced and there was much re-entering of information from one system to the other.

The IT Manager explained that the back office application had been used for 18 years and that the organisation had "taken it along with" them by applying customisations. The front office application had been in place for four years. A major reason for change was the double handling, "So when we were doing our work, we had to enter our service information into the *Front Office System* and then relay that information again into our accounting system so we could charge out our invoicing. So it was double handling" (IT Manager).

The Finance Manager saw the deficiencies of the old system as

> *less accountability and was more labour intensive. You had many more physical*
> *actions to get to an end result, under the new system, the way the system has*
> *been designed and the way it's working for us is that as soon as a service call*
> *comes in all parties have relevant functions and they've only got to perform one or*
> *two functions to get what they want.*

The application was acquired with long-term debt. The organisation, which has grown rapidly recently via acquisition of a larger organisation, uses factoring to manage cash-flow. The application was implemented at a very precarious time for the organisation in terms of debt ratios and cash-flow. The CEO confirmed that the application had been purchased at a difficult time for the organisation but recognised the need to "provide information to predict where the organisation needs to go in the future". He saw the previous systems as "totally antiquated" and unable to service the organisation in the future.

The CEO when asked how he communicated the business directives, replied:

> *Some directives for what I needed to see from the position of the field staff and how it was going to affect our guys externally, but predominantly, most of the operational issues were done by the administration staff as to what they believed was the best package. My main drivers were flexibility and growth potential. That is not to say the people from the administration internally weren't looking for the same things, but they were my drivers. I wasn't looking to invest the money for a short-term solution, I was looking for a long-term solution.*

The IT Manager when asked how the budget for the application was identified, explained that she conducted a review of products in the market place and then established a budget to provide a reasonable selection of products in a price range the company could justify. She further explained that there were cost increases of approximately 33% during implementation. The project information shows that the cause of the increase was created by the value added reseller who originally bid for the project with a lower cost application. The reseller was short listed but failed to secure the tender. They immediately re-bid with the Dynamics (AX) application, using discounts agreed with Microsoft, bidding the same cost as they used with the original failed application. The service costs were never revised and the Dynamics (AX) application was far more sophisticated resulting in additional services. While the initial estimates were the same, the contract was agreed on a time and materials basis. The subsequent cost escalation created a great deal of consternation for Server. When the IT Manager was asked if the implementation went as planned she responded:

> *No, ha ha ha! But I expected problems no matter what, but not to the extent that it happened. And I believe that us, as a company, we try to be as forgiving as you can in these sort of situations because you know it's not going to run smoothly, and you expect problems and you try and work with everyone to help things go along but sometimes the frustration with it was just a bit too much. Especially when you had to repeat things.*

The IT Manager stressed the difficulties saying that the six months of familiarisation was for longer than she anticipated. This disruption period is what Markus and Tanis (2000) refer to as the shakedown stage. The CEO said the organisation was so concerned that the management was "worried if we had actually bought the right sort of software".

After approximately six months Server moved into the "onward and upward" stage. A user of the application explained that "without the system that we have taken on over the last two years I wouldn't be able to perform as many functions." The debt recovery function had been entirely automated providing more time and allowing for the emphasis to switch to development activities. The application was seen to have reduced the debtor payment cycle from about 87 to 56 days.

The Finance Manager explained that one of the benefits was that he could obtain "snapshots of history" for review and easily extract information to Excel when reporting and analysing. The CEO identified provision of information to improve the organisation's ability to win projects and lever the information to increase the value of projects as key drivers. The tangible benefits noted by the IT Manager were reduction in personnel, and cost avoidance from less personnel being necessary as the company grew. When asked if the benefits had been realised through staff reduction the IT Manager's response was, "We actually did get rid of a couple to start off with, but now looking back at that I wish we hadn't, because if we'd kept the people that we had we would have grown perhaps a bit faster. We jumped the gun really".

A number of functions requiring customisation were allocated to a second phase of implementation. This is common practice with complex ERP, as explained by Wilcocks et al., (1997) who propose that IS implementations should ideally be made in many phases that provide investment returns throughout the project rather than one large implementation. This phasing also reduces the complexity of the implementation. Due to the difficulties with the initial implementation Server decided to address the functions themselves through an in-house capability rather than use the reseller.

The IT Manager, asked about the information gains, answered that the process had been slower than hoped for because of difficulty with customers providing the required information and staff capturing it. Additionally, to report information in the application was more difficult than anticipated.

4.2.2 Impact of Strategy Process on ERP

The CEO explained that the major influence on strategy was from "discussions with our main contractors; they give us an idea of where they would like us to go, but the reality is what you would really like to do is to try to provide them with a reason to spend money." The customers with their anticipated requirements, drive the strategy, which is passed on through meetings and informal discussion. The Development Manager was asked how he became informed of strategy, answering, "They tell me, lately there has been talk of mergers and we might merge an organisation into our own".

Server is primarily owned by a family. The IT Manager is related to the CEO so many discussions are held on an informal basis. This type of informal strategy process is not untypical of a medium sized privately owned organisation. Johnson and Scholes (2002, p.578) define a strategy of this type as logical instrumentalism, where strategy evolves from "partial commitments rather than global formulation of total strategy".

4.2.3 Financial Procedures and Imperatives

The implementation was a significant cost to the organisation, particularly as it was already highly geared. The financial position of the organisation was seen to have an ongoing impact on the application, described as being very unlikely to be replaced in the short to medium term; and that any upgrade would need to provide significant benefits to the organisation to be justified. Due to the cost of upgrades it was decided on a cessation of the annual maintenance agreement. The impact of upgrades are discussed further in the next section.

4.2.4 Upgrades and Their Antecedents

The Dynamics (AX) ERP application when purchased did not contain a 'core' service module. However, Microsoft operate a process whereby a reseller can develop a module, have it certified and sold by Microsoft as part of the application. Server acquired a 3rd party service module in this way through Microsoft, and heavily modified it to meet what they believed were their specific requirements. The next version of Dynamics(AX) included a service module that was different to the one that had been acquired; therefore to upgrade Server would have to develop another service module to meet the organisation's requirements. This obviously caused consternation as the investment in the current module would be largely lost.

During the sales process Server was informed of the cost of maintenance, but claimed the cost of applying the upgrades provided under the agreement had not been discussed. The Development Manager when discussing the cost of applying a service pack (a service pack is something less than a release and is generally to overcome issues in the application and fine tune rather than to release functional enhancements), observed:

*Our reseller came out and offered us a service pack, service pack 4. We were told
that it would cost between $30,000 and $40,000 to apply it. For a service pack.
Can you imagine how upset we were with that! This is our service provider, we can
implement it for you but we will charge you $30,000. We ask "don't we have a
maintenance agreement". That is not part of the maintenance agreement, the
maintenance agreement provides you with the service pack but to implement it we
need to charge you. Well this isn't working then.*

The customisations to improve the application by applying the service pack cost approximately $210,000,
this cost being almost 15% of the customisation costs. The maintenance agreement is approximately 25% of
the current list price to which must be added support desk charges that vary according to the value added
reseller engaged. If one service pack were implemented a year the cost would be $65,000 plus support and
other service costs. For a major upgrade the cost would be much higher. It is probable that the cost of
applying upgrades, and/or the time required, would slowly reduce as the procedure was consolidated. This
may not seem a large amount of money, but it is a significant cost to the organisation, and high when
compared with the initial investment. The CEO summed up his disappointment:

*I have an issue with the way that is approached, if you pay for the software through
the maintenance system you would expect the system to be updated on a regular
basis. To download information is a push of the button exercise to a degree, ... I
am disappointed that above the cost of the maintenance there is a cost for
installing the upgrade, as you go along, which I find perplexing.*

The IT Manager acknowledged a review of the process since they realised the cost imperatives, "We
thought, hang on let's just step back a bit, because since we've done all of these modifications in some of the
versions we're actually not part of their standard system in the service side of things. So we thought, no
we'll wait until we're ready to move." A small internal team was established to maintain and support the
application: accordingly. The maintenance and support was cancelled.

This decision seems reasonable with regard to functionality as the application supports the current business.
However, the maintenance agreement also provides the organisation with an avenue for future proofing in
terms of technology. This was seen as the major advantage of acquiring an application from Microsoft by
the CEO, who said would be maintained by Microsoft and therefore be a long-term asset. Since the original
implementation a new version of the software has been released which includes the new technologies,

Chapter Four – Descriptive Case Analysis

Microsoft Share Point and RFID recognition. Both of these would be very useful to the Server, simplifying both their PDA rollout and automated product identification of their installed equipment.

The following line of questioning is perhaps not ideal for a researcher, but the exercise was aimed at eliciting a response from the Development Manager about how the application was managed over time. Asked whether the modified system will be upgraded in the foreseeable future, he replied:

No, it just doesn't work for us.

A further probe sought to know what the situation might be if the author withdrew all support for the organisation's version. He replied:

We are quite happy with the product we have got, we have the ability to modify it and we don't need 3rd party support. The company can continue for the next 10 or 20 years using the same program, which is fully up-to-date with today's technology.

Another probe suggested to the Development Manager that the system might be out of date in 10 or 20 years so he opined:

I honestly believe the product will exist in its form or a similar form in 10 or 20 years time. You can customise it just so much. It depends what you mean by out of date, it might not have the most up-to-date wiz bang things that don't relate to us anyway...

Pressed, he was challenged about his certainty of the system's longevity considering what technology from 20 years ago might be used today:

No it doesn't work that way [looking back 20 years]. I honestly believe that this product is built to last more than a 5-year lifespan. You can't make an assumption unless you know what you need to update. I honestly believe Axapta [Dynamics AX] can be modified to keep up-to-date.

The Development Manager was allowed that his explanation related to functional level but he was further probed about the possible future technological changes, specifically significant Kernel change. He explained:

If the Kernel changes dramatically we will have to upgrade. But we shouldn't have
to pay $50,000 a year in maintenance for something that might not happen in 5
years. So in 5 years let's just pay out the $250,000 for the new product and
upgrade.

Ultimately, this is either a reaction to an unexpected cost leading the organisation to 'step back', (IT Manager), or it is a reasoned and considered approach to evaluate the potential of financial releases prior to committing to the annual cost of maintenance. It certainly alleviates the pressure to upgrade simply because the maintenance agreement represents a sunk cost. If all customers took this approach, ERP vendors would quickly be in financial difficulty. Markus et al (2000b, p.255) found that " extreme difficulties in the shakedown phase appeared to have strong negative influences on companies' willingness to continue with the ERP experience ... Even when the ERP system was retained there was great unwillingness to upgrade to 'enhanced' versions of the software. In essence, these companies implemented 'legacy' ERP systems." It may be that Server already has a legacy application.

4.2.5 Re-implementations

None of the modules have been re-implemented. The CEO explained his realisation that the advice he had been given concerning the setup of the system was not necessarily the only solution thus:

We found that we got advice from an IT individual or software person and that is
his opinion saying that you can or can not do a process ... we find that we ask
more questions of more people and sometimes get a choice of a number of options
and find one that is better than we thought it was to start with.

Whilst there has not been a re-implementation, the organisation does not necessarily consider the system to be optimised yet.

4.2.6 Perception of IS

The interviewees had a positive attitude to IS. The IT Manager said, "With computer systems a lot of it is a learning process, because everything's moving so fast, changing so fast, it's hard to keep grasp of". She also explained that the ERP application had not changed her perception of IS which was very positive. The CEO further added that organisations fundamentally relied on IS.

4.2.7 Influences and Consequences of Software Authors and Resellers

The application being provided by a large organisation such as the Microsoft Corporation, and the implication for long-term support, was seen by both the CEO and the IT Manager, as a major factor in the acquisition decision. The Development Manager did not see it as a factor and explained, "We are persuaded by cost. The system was in our price range and seemed to provide the benefits we required".

The support given by the value added reseller was seen as less than ideal by the IT Manager and, as the following explains, some of the blame was allocated to Microsoft:

> *I think support people try their very hardest to help, they are supposed to be supported by the people that produce the product, but I've always found there's a lack of communication between people that actually produce the product and giving it to the support people who are supposed to help other.*

This disconnect between the software author and software reseller has caused the company to cancel the maintenance and support agreements. This has reduced the revenue stream for these organisations and may, in time, result in Server implementing another application. This should be of particular concern to the author as the initial acquisition decision was largely based on the product being provided by Microsoft.

4.2.8 Environmental Influences

The external environment, other than the author and reseller discussed earlier, impacts the management and evaluation of the application through customer expectations and satisfaction. As the major driver for the implementation was the value of information to the organisation's customers who are operating as an oligopoly. The CEO averred:

> *We could see that the [industry] was suffering from the amount of resources they had available to them because they have not been making profit for the last couple of years. They have only just started to make profit, and had reduced personnel in maintenance area, at some point you are going to have to spend money again which they are currently doing to catch up because they have tried to get as skinny as they can while things have been lean and now they need to go back. But, they don't have any people now, so the point is they can't justify buying a [product] so we have to let them know why. We can justify the expenditure in terms of cost of ownership and support.*

The ERP system provides the information to enable customers to justify expenditure to upgrade and maintain plant and machinery. This obviously increases revenue for the Server and makes the Server more valuable to the customer. The IT Manager saw the industry as highly specialised with only four competitors. The complexity of the industry has meant that the ERP solution is also complex. The IT manager pointed out, "You can't just get a general clerk off the street and expect them to do this, it takes quite a bit of training to get them up and running" . Presumably this is increasing the customer's switching cost as well as entry barriers.

4.2.9 Evaluation Procedures

The financial benefits of the application were not calculated. The CEO made the following comment to justify the expenditure, "We knew we were in an upswing market, the information that was demanded from us due to our customers retrenching some of their staff provide a sales opportunity". He believed that the system was only being used to "a 10th of its capacity" and that the senior staff was "waiting for technology to catch-up in other areas". He was also certain that the benefits had not been sold adequately internally, in turn preventing the recording of valuable information. He explained that "When the customers are provided the information they are apparently very impressed, but it has not materially impacted the bottom line yet". He went on to comment:

> But we are just about at that point in this financial year, where we will actually see the benefits of the investment we have made ... .But more importantly our customers can also see that a private smaller organisation has managed to compete with a multi-national in providing data for the decision makers in the larger organisation to work out which way they should be spending their dollars... .Our revenue has increased, but it's not a direct issue on any one thing, but it is there based on an underlying capability.

The Finance Manager pointed out that the system also aims to improve efficiencies, by reducing cycle times and avoiding the additional cost of personnel as the company grows, saying:

> We are about to embark on some electronic information now that will afford us to reduce our paper work trail, dramatically in the 1st quarter of this year. Given that it all works together that will be integrated in our services department where all of the information of parts and time that are installed on site will be updated

electronically and fed straight into the system. This will allow the system to
automatically invoice out.

The Development Manager saw the most important aspect of the application to be ease of customisation, in spite of the 33% cost increase for implementation, contending:

> *There wasn't a specific system that suited all of our needs of off the shelf. We had*
> *to get a system that could be modified quickly enough to meet our needs. It was*
> *demonstrated in the presale process that Dynamics(AX) could be easily modified in*
> *24 hours. We initially accepted that those modifications were easy to do. ...*
> *because forms were built very quickly we thought it would be easy in the event it is*
> *much more technically difficult but we got there in the end."*

When the IT Manager was asked if the envisaged benefits had been achieved, she responded,

> *The modification of the system actually stacked up quite well. There has not been*
> *one task that we cannot perform internally to solve an employees request.*
> *Management and other staff are continually bombarding me with requests and*
> *there has not been one task we have not been able to perform. We have had to*
> *receive some assistance for complicated programming but we are getting there.*

When asked about the rigour and process used to identify customisation requirements and to sanction programming activity, she repeated, "There is no real sign off of costs as it is just time. Presumably, the cost of customisation personnel are seen as committed costs, and customisation is a matter of resource utilisation. The Development Manager when asked how the priorities for customisation were established acknowledged, "I set the priority; it depends who is screaming the loudest and where it comes from"!

This informal cost or benefits procedure perhaps parallels the informal strategy process.

4.2.10 Approach to Customisations

The Development Manager stated, "I can make modifications to the system as I am talking to users and when they refresh the system they have the modification, even before they put down the phone." He added further about his responsibility:

> *[my] ... job is to make sure everyone is happy with relation to the system, and I will*
> *do whatever it takes to make that happen. If I can show them what they want to*

see with 5 to 10 minutes work then my job is done in that case. As demand occur
they really are stacked up in priority in which ones gets done first.

A user when asked how requirements were identified, explained:

That's easy, whenever I come across an obstacle ... I use 'Play' [test system] and
try to create whatever I need to do from that and if I can't I go to our IT specialist,
he is very clever, I tell him exactly what I want, I sit down with him, he shows me
what he is doing as he goes along, we generate the report or function that I want
to the spec. I need.

This informal approach to customisation of the application appears to be lacking in procedures and controls. To change a multi-users' system at the bequest of a single user, without consideration of the impact on other users and upon a process is very questionable. However, all of the users at Server seem happy with the situation, even though the question remains as to how long this will be the case given the cost of upgrading the application is continually increasing.

4.2.11 Restrictions and Limitations Imposed by ERP

The IT Manager thought it would take four months to fully utilise the new application, but it took approximately seven months. During this period the constraints of the application severely hampered the organisation, particularly through lowered staff efficiency and the inability to create customer invoices. The invoicing problem had a serious impact on cash flow, the CEO contending it nearly put the organisation "out of business".

In examining the project documents it transpired that invoicing problem was one of systems failure but an organisational issue. Prior to the system being implemented the sales invoicing had been performed by the accounts department; but after the implementation the service support staff performed invoicing. As there were two systems previously, information from field service and support staff was verified and sanitised by accounts personnel prior to sales invoices being created. With the new system all work had to be accurately coded to new time codes and part numbers, thus moving the coding discipline forward in the organisation and creating an overhead for staff.

The CEO's identification hinted as much with his riposte at the time:

> *What I have seen with software is, there has to be a trade off from what happens on site and getting them to feed the information directly into the system without getting other individuals between them and the reporting process. If you can get that person to report that information and it goes all the way that's fine. In the past we have had a situation where we have had to palletise the information to sanitise it to a point where that's what the system will accept.*

The IT Manager commented:

> *I had people ringing me up crying because they couldn't do their work, they were so frustrated, it was a nightmare! But, the system is not a user-friendly system. if I bring new people into the company, I've got to train them, they're just bamboozled, absolutely bamboozled. In the accounting side of it, piece of cake, but as far as doing our install and our service side of things and doing the tracking for the [industry] they are just absolutely bamboozled.*

The researcher pointed out the previous mention of the industry and information needs being complex, and so was a possible factor, to which the IT Manager responded, "I think it's a bit of both. Oh the complex business is more of it than anything, but I think also it's not as user-friendly as we had hoped because when we're looking at it and you're entering in your information it's not flowing as we had thought." Amoako-Gyampah (2004) revealed that managers, more than end-users, perceived that ERP would be easy to use and easy to learn. These organisational bottlenecks and the resultant problems is similar to what was proposed by Markus and Tannis (2000) .

4.2.12 Expected Lifespan of the ERP

The Development Manager thought the application would last "not less than 5 to 10 years", and that the reason for change would be requirements the application could not provide. One of the users thought that the technology "was one of the best around and he could not envisage ever changing it as I would find it hard to believe what more a system could do."

The IT Manager was of the opinion the system was bound to be changed, but thought the potential life span was between fifteen and twenty years. Interestingly she argued the change might come about due to Microsoft keeping at the forefront of technology, this requiring a new system, saying, "They will not continue to keep on supporting our system, they'll want us to go with their new one."

The CEO suggested that it was a matter of "crystal ball gazing when the system would be changed". He identified that flexibility more than anything else was important; and "if I am paying people to palletise this information to get the software to work I will change it".

4.2.13 Approach to Business Process Analysis

None of the interviewees saw the need to modify the business processes to fit the system as the intent was, when acquiring the system, to customise the functionality to meet the company's needs. The Development Manager when asked if there were processes in the organisation that were less than strategic and could be altered, he asserted there were such processes operating but had no desire that they be changed.

4.2.14 Findings and Interpretations

Controls and documentation of customisations are lacking. However, the organisation is focusing on its strategy of satisfying customers by providing information. This appears to be an instrumentalist view of strategy, which is described by Johnson and Scholes (2002, p.579) as managers who "see their job as managing adaptively, continually changing strategy to keep in line with the environment, whilst maintaining efficiency and keeping stakeholders happy". Server has only four competitors, accessing and is situated in a dynamic and competitive environment. This causes many changes in the information required.

There might be an issue with the communication of strategy, as it was identified that the benefits of the application were not being communicated internally, which appeared to manifest itself in the service staff not providing the required level of detail and frustration on the part of the field users who have to increasingly enter more data. This is a dilemma because the organisation is not comfortable with maintaining the granularity of information needed to service customers. This is possibly indicative of the informal strategy approach (Johnson and Scholes, 2002) which is incremental and not formally communicated to the organisation. Server staff see service and maintenance information as an overhead, but better communication of the organisation's strategy might change the staff's opinion.

The management process shown diagrammatically in Figure 30 shows the CEO as having informal discussions concerning objectives with department heads, which combined with discussions with customers enables a strategy to emerge. The interpretations of that strategy will result in customisation requests being made to the development department, for initiation as soon as practical without an evaluation of benefits. The cost of the customisation is absorbed through the payroll.

Whether the customisations are made for strategic purposes or to satisfy a user's demand is unknown to the development department and appears to be of little consequence. Upgrades have been put on hold for the foreseeable future so the Development Manager monitors future releases to ascertain which are beneficial to the organisation. However, it is realised that the RFID and SharePoint technology embedded in a later release would give the organisation tremendous advantage for both deploying their PDA devices and reading the serial information from installed base parts.

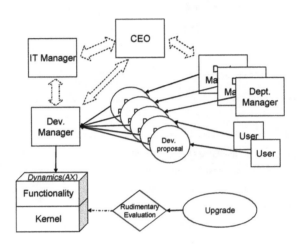

Figure 30.   Server Strategic Management Process

The continuous customisations are likely to make the system increasingly rigid. One of the major drivers for the purchase of the application was the belief that Microsoft would keep the system up-to-date; however, customising the system and ceasing the maintenance agreement has compromised that key purchase decision.

4.2.15 Conclusion

The informal strategic approach noted is understandable, given the operating environment and the type of company. It seems to be important for Server to improve the communication of strategy and to try to align ERP procedures to that strategy. The need to customise the application is open to some debate, particularly when much of the information is standing data concerning product versions. However, accepting the need to develop the application, there should reasonably be more rigorous methods of establishing the need to customise. To negotiate individual user customisation needs by telephone may be efficient, but limits the consideration of the best approach, particularly as the CEO has stated that consultants' opinions are open to debate.

This case study caused a change in the researcher's perspective concerning the relationship between the author and the maintenance agreement for no consideration had been given to the agreement being deliberately aborted. Maintenance is sometimes seen as a source of frustration for organisations as new software versions are paid for but not implemented due to cost, disruption and difficulty in applying customisations. It seems from this case that if the application was purchased for a finite period, the strategy to cease the maintenance would be sound. However, for a strategy that calls for the system to last as long as possible and be maintained for a similar period, the decision is dubious. The financial situation and the antecedents stemming from poor implementation have seriously impacted the management of the ERP application, particularly in regard to cancelling the maintenance agreement and the building of an in-house capability.

4.3   Case Study Contractor

The Contractor case study is of a rapidly growing contracting and service provider. The revenue for financial year ending June 2007 was $906m, which had increased from Au$800m the previous year and Au$650m the year before that. The interviews consisted of the finance director, the CIO and key users in the order shown here. The company provides, broadly speaking, contracting service to the construction and mining industries through a number of subsidiary organisations. The Contractor is not highly profitable with earnings before interest and tax of between 5% and 6%. It sees itself as an aggressive organisation. The Contractor is a distributed organisation, with 45 sites in Australia and a presence in three other countries. It needs detailed information concerning leased assets, projects and contract services to operate efficiently.

The case study was selected as the research vehicle because Contractor had implemented Dynamics AX. After the data collection was completed, the organisation divested itself of the divisions which installed Dynamics (AX). Whether this was the reason or not for the purchase of the software is difficult to identify for certain. It is apparent that the information requirements of the division that implemented Dynamics AX was different to the rest of the organisation, and it was poorly supported by the existing application. For the division to be sold is at least a coincidence, although, it appears from the financial information that, if the division had not been sold, the company would not have been profitable in 2007. The company is listed on the Australian stock exchange.

4.3.1 Original Implementation and Its Antecedents

The system replaced by Dynamics AX in one division is to be entirely replaced in the near future. It is a Unix application that has been operational for over 15 years. The application has had three significant releases with many interim releases. A number of problems were identified with the system: the project costing functionality was not adequate for the organisation's growing requirements; it could not provide "human resource information or contract safety information"; and the provision of management information was also problematic. The applications were seen as "very poor". In addition to the main system there are 18 other stand alone applications.

The CIO explained that the application "had been heavily modified, which was a mistake, we shouldn't have done that, so the vision is to return back to either an ERP or best of breed using industry best practices, purely from a support point of view." There had been 30 programmers employed full time to customise the application. The CIO said, "We're not a programming house, and we should not have been a programming house".

The latest version of the application had Windows functionality; however, to move to that version "was at least as difficult as implementing a new application in the organisation" due to the extensive customisations needed to be applied and lack of skills to apply them. "So the vision was turn back to either an ERP or best of breed applications," the CIO said, continuing, "We can't continue to lock ourselves into one vendor, if we ever have an argument with that vendor, we're stuffed. So we've turned back to vanilla."

Interestingly the finance manager said " we've got a support contract in place for the current version, now, the skill base to support the existing version is almost non existent, OK, so we could have a disaster coming up with our existing system in that it will no longer be supported, and therefore that's also significantly contributed towards a decision to look at a replacement system." It seems that dismissing the staff who knew the application was a risky move that could have dire consequence.

The reason for purchasing Dynamics (AX) was explained by the Finance Manager:

> XXXX business has a labour hire, fabrication, and plant hire business with very small jobs, quick turnaround. Cheops could not cope with those type of jobs, Cheops was designed for long term construction mainly in the building industry, whereas we are doing quick turnaround jobbing in maintenance and the Cheops system simply wasn't working for us. So what we wanted to do was to find a system, a short term system that would cope for the next 2 or 3 years, where we could get a little more accurate information, so we were automatically pushed into an area of a business that needed an urgent fix.

The Dynamics (AX) implementation has gone well. Issues with reconciliation of the project with the general ledger resulted in disputes over managers' end-of-year performance bonus.

The project had a relatively short 'Shakedown' phase, this possibly being a consequence of the relatively small scope of the implementation. However, there does not appear to be any major antecedents of the implementation impacting the ongoing management of the application.

4.3.2 Impact of Strategy Process on ERP

The CIO is not a member of the Board, but meets with the CEO and CFO at "least once a month". Board level meetings discuss strategy but there is no formal process in place to disseminate the discussions about strategy. When an organisation is operating in a complex environment as diverse and changing as that the one Contractor operates in, it is possible that managers will recognise that "specialists lower down in the organisation know more about the environment in which the organisation operates" (Johnson & Scholes, 2002, p.592). The Contractor has employed external consultant Ernst and Young and Gartner, to work with the operational managers to provide reports to the Board. In two instances external consultants had also been used to assist with the selection of the organisation's application.

The CIO, after a few months in the position, wrote a five year strategic plan for the CEO and the CFO explaining the direction he wanted to take the organisation. "It was a five year IT strategic vision, outlining how to change every aspect of IT, from service to telecommunications infrastructure, to redundancies, to business continuity, to systems," he said. When asked about the focus of the document, the CIO stated, "If you don't have a good mixture of technology we're going to use and how it's going to fix the business, it just will not succeed." This was apparently the first IT strategic plan the organisation had produced, the CIO concluding, "IT is now moving from a service division to an enabling division; enabling the business units, goals and objectives." He then gave this explanation:

> in America now CIOs can run the organisation and he leads the business change,
> with IT enabling them and that's exactly what we're trying to do.

Rather than commenting on the document, the CFO sent it for review by Ernst and Young and Deloitte who largely endorsed the strategy which had four main components: network provision, tele-communications, applications, and hardware. The CIO added to his earlier comments saying that he regularly put an expenditure request on the CFO desk for signature. Asked if any of his requests were ever rejected, he retorted that in the early days requests were questioned but now they are generally signed. This process of managers providing expenditure requests and seeking approval is sometimes known as the 'Bower-Burgelman' (Johnson & Scholes, 2002, p.580), where managers put forward proposals and resources are allocated. However, the process is only as good as the approval process, see (Keen & Digrius, 2003), and in this case there appears to be a lack of rigour in the sanctioning of expenditure.

4.3.3 Financial Procedures and Imperatives

The organisation is growing rapidly, it has spent sparingly on IS, but made major investments in telecommunications, hardware and networking. The organisation had a net profit of $44 million from $966m of gross revenue with a net profit after tax of $33m. This was achieved in the main by disposing of the divisions that had installed Dynamics (AX) for $66m. The organisation's capital is approximately $350m so the company has made a reasonable return of 12% on capital which is, obviously, achieved by a high asset turn of almost three. The organisation is geared to approximately 65%, which is not high in general terms, but the low profitability means that a downturn in activity would severely jeopardise the company's operation if debt were any higher. The organisation claims an order book of $2 billion dollars.

In the researcher's opinion, the organisation is severely sub-optimised with information; the rapid growth is occurring at a cost to profitability. It is not always easy to establish financial performance in a project organisation because rules surrounding earned value can impact a growing organisation's apparent profitability. This type of organisation generally needs timely information concerning project profitability and asset utilisation. But it does not have the level of information required, for instance, it takes two to three weeks after month end to obtain the previous month's results. The situation was described as 'quite poor', as this type of organisation requires much scheduling of services and plant.

The Dynamics (AX) implementation was approached on a low cost basis, the application costing approximately $500,000. The expected cost of the new system is approximately $25m., which is low for a billion dollar organisation. The CIO explained:

> We are looking at SAP and Oracle...... if we like what we see there we'll proceed.
> If we don't like what we see, if it's too costly, or if it's unrealistic for us well then
> we'll drop back a step and we say right we've got all these people in place, we will
> use best of breed.

Subsequent conversations to keep in touch with the organisation and complete the data collection revealed the CFO had changed, and the organisation was investigating best of breed applications by functional area. One reason for this was the cost of the application making it apparent that the financial performance of the company is having an impact on IS evaluation. Conversely the IS strategy and IS management seems also to be having an impact on the financial performance of the organisation!

4.3.4 Upgrades and Their Antecedents

The CIO explained that if upgrades are maintained a system should last an organisation a decade or so. The proposed change, from the existing application to a new application, had been decided because of the high cost of upgrading the customisations into the new version of the existing application. Dynamics (AX) had not been upgraded at the time of data collection but was planned to be in the coming twelve months.

4.3.5 Re-implementations

There had been no re-implementations of specific aspects of the applications.

4.3.6 Perception of IS

The CIO believed IS has made "a significant contribution" to the organisation, but explained, " The systems we have require a lot of administrative support because of fragmentation, it's all over the place, and we need to pull information out of a lot of different areas, so we need a lot of administrators accounts to support the system." Whilst IS is highly valued there are obviously issues with performance and the provision of information.

4.3.7 Influences and Consequences of Software Authors and Resellers

The CIO has created a strategy for hardware, telecommunications, networking and systems. The first three elements are largely in place. The approach taken is interesting and has implications as to why the selection of the major ERP has been so prolonged. The following is an extract from the interview with the CIO:

> The first guy at [Telecom] we got just didn't understand It ... and then we
> eventually got a young executive over there, and I took him out one weekend and
> said look this is where I want to be, you know virtualisation, everything
> collaboration and data, and everyone coming back from any location, from
> anywhere in the world we want it coming back here .So we got him on board ... so
> we got [Telecom] ... to put a fair amount of money in upfront ... .

The investment by the partners is typical of the partnership approach adopted by the Contractor. One partner has "put in" $1m and the others have given large discounts. The company now has a very good telecommunications and infrastructure with a Novell network said to be very robust, as well as IBM hardware. The group of 'partners' from Novell, IBM and the Telecom organisation hold monthly management meetings. The CIO reported,

> We've gone from an infrastructure with 516k modems to an infrastructure that's the
> same as the top 4 banks .... Our CEO's happy because our initial outlay hasn't
> been that much, and our sites are happy because they have instant access to most
> systems now, to most information".

The intention is to move the remaining organisation over to Citrix during the next 12 months. The cost benefit thus far is questionable, the degree of difficulty of deploying a Citrix thin client is not high, and without centralisation little improvement can be expected. Much time has been spent cajoling and working with providers and convincing them of the merits of investing in the strategy, but the benefits to the organisation appear slight as the information provided is still inadequate.

The CIO expanded on the part of the organisation's philosophy:

> *We don't enter into any relationship with a reseller who just wants to sell us things ; they will only come on board if they partner with us to some degree. We don't directly deal with any resellers either, what we do, again coming from a retail background I know ... where the reseller normally figures we've gone straight over the reseller gone straight to the vendors"*

The Finance Director told how the executive staff had pressured SAP into becoming directly involved with the tender even though it was a much lower value system than they would usually become involved. Both Oracle and SAP and been paid a reduced rate to provide a functional proposal. He explained the *modus operandi:*

> *Oracle weren't keen on it, because normally they don't do that stuff until they get into design stage, it's not the way we work, OK , you want to partner with us, then you've got to tell us how you can come and help us, then we'll tell you how we can help you. So the only way for us to make a great evaluation in our opinion was for us to throw the doors open and say look there's 2 of you , we possibly will partner with 1 of you , both of you come in , we'll pay you, spend 6 to 8 weeks here, looking at our company, looking at our processes and learning about [Contractor] and to be honest I think it will be a philosophy that these guys will be using a lot more of because both companies have come back and said it was a fantastic process for them. (CIO).*

It seems that Contractor was trying to exert pressure on the Authors and has been quite successful in doing so. The partnership concept appears to be sound but there also appears to be a lack of focus on the information needs of the business.

4.3.8 Environmental Influences

The CIO believing generally that one of the strongest influences on aspects of Australian business came from America:

Then when America realises it's not going to work ,like they did with outsourcing in about 2001, we seem to think , we can make it work, we're better, the problem with us in Australia is we don't have the communication infrastructure like America. ...[Contractor] "is trying to buck the trend."

He observed that IBM USA is very much into partnering whilst IBM Australia want to partner but, as yet, have not found a suitable organisation, although the company was very happy to form a partnership with Contractor. The Finance Manager observed that, when bidding for work if two 'bids' from organisations were similar, the customer was likely to choose the supplier with an application with which it is easier to integrate, saying:

If [mining co] are looking to tender and it's between us and [Competitor] and our systems make it easier to interact with on a daily basis, and the price is about the same, who would you pick? That's where competitive advantage comes in.

When a key user involved in the selection process was asked if he thought that the customers, suppliers or competitors would have any influence on the ERP selected, he replied:

None, oh look, all of our main clients are on SAP, linking SAP to Oracle's not a problem, mention Oracle, you've still got to do all the connectors, whether it's SAP to SAP, or SAP to Oracle, so there's no real advantage to either one.

The CIO concluded, " It's definitely an internal decision as to what direction we take" adding, when asked if the competitive environment of an industry was diluted by competitors having the same software:

There's always something that's more unique within one organisation than another organisation that makes them successful ..is it going to be the IT system, or is it going to be the drive of the CEO, the CFO? At the end of the day it comes down to drive of the CEO, CFO which makes the businesses differ. When it comes down to the IT infrastructure, you will find that the IT infrastructure will be very closely aligned between organisations, not entirely but will be very closely aligned.

At the time of the interviews some articles in the press concerned implementation failures with SAP. The CIO mentioned,

> *I recall the National bank had SAP and it went terribly wrong, there was some very*
> *bad press about SAP ... we won't let that publicity influence our internal decision.*
> *During the review process we had a number of press releases that came out, and*
> *we obviously asked questions from our general review process and tender process*
> *to those suppliers asking them for a bit more detail . We certainly won't allow that*
> *press to influence our decisions.*

It is interesting that information concerning failure did not influence the purchase decision, the only explanation obtained for this was that all implementations can go wrong, and that it is probably not product related.

The environmental influencers are a large reseller and the breadth of the product set. Customer information needs are an important factor but due to connectivity of applications but they do not determine the application.

4.3.9 Evaluation Procedures

An organisational review by the general manager's group led by Ernst and Young took place in January 2004. The team identified a number of business areas needing to be addressed, these have become the current focus. The Finance Manager reported this to include, "Financial reporting and also our internal procedures and controls, risk management, that type of thing."
The focus was seen as a high level strategy specifying annual revenue growth.

When asked if there was a formal report was being used for business objectives, the Finance Manager responded, "I really don't know. I believe there would have been some sort of report that came out of it, but I've only been given the section that related to finance type issues and payment issues", adding the report had identified the systems as being very poor for the type of organisation. He then commented:

> *Oh look, everyone knew there were shortfalls in the systems, but how significant*
> *they were and what sort of impacts they had really was highlighted after we did a*
> *very detailed review.*

One of the major issues with company and systems was seen to be the tendering process. The Finance Manager noted that a competitor had entered into receivership due to poor tendering processes, explaining that with such small margins, the tendering process is fundamental. Feedback information concerning profitability and margin erosion of previous contracts and projects is required. He regretted that information of sufficient granularity was not available and what is available is taking many weeks to produce. He further observed:

> We started looking at our information requirements at our reporting requirements and that's how we sort of moved on to looking at the types of reports people wanted to see, how was it being done now, it was still being done in spreadsheets. Can it be done better? Which systems was the information coming from, its coming from a lot of systems, a lot of manual systems I might add, and it was just a natural progression.

The CIO explained the process of acquiring a systems as follows.

> We have a vision on how we want our systems to benefit our users, our divisions, our group, our stakeholders, and our clients. Most people would only have a.. how is this going to benefit our business. So we're going 2 steps past that, looking at stakeholders, and looking at our clients. That's where you become more competitive.

> The main driver for the system is to support the growth plans of the organisation. What we've done is, we've gone through a tendering process , and invited a number of consultants, IT companies to give us a price for a replacement system , we then came down to a shortlist with SAP and Oracle , EY once again helped us with the tender process , we had our shortlist of SAP and Oracle, these products are very well known in the industry, and we're now doing our final review. They should meet all our requirements; from safety, management, HR, payroll, to financial management, project management, the whole lot.

The researcher asked the Finance Manager if other less expensive systems had been considered, "We did get a price for Pronto and a couple of other products , but once again they didn't give us the overall solution, the HR, payroll, plant maintenance, people, plant are key in our organisation. Those other products didn't support our requirements in those areas."

The CIO explained the following with regard to cost benefit analysis for acquiring the ERP application.

> You can't sit there with an ERP and say this is the return of investment we're going to get, it just doesn't work, you need to say, your business case has got to be

based around efficiencies. How efficient can we make our lives on site? What is the cost savings, because time savings on site will lead to cost savings here. That's the reality, you're not going to get cost savings by just putting in an ERP, you'll only get cost savings by saying, by putting in this ERP this process that used to take a day will now take half an hour. (CIO)

A formal evaluation of the benefits had not taken place. The justification was based on senior members of staff spending less time producing reports in Excel and more time running the organisation, facilitating growth. The CIO's explanation follows:

A lot of the IT terms like Return of capital they're valid, and you need to use them, but at times you can sit there and say I'm going to get an ROI in 2 years or an ROC of 22% it doesn't work.

The appointment of EY was seen as a very important part of the selection process as they "had done it before" and would be able to identify "anything that was overlooked". However, without formalised objectives and goals EY would presumably find the selection difficult.

The researcher persisted by asking the Finance Manager how the organisation would know if the systems supported its needs and provided benefits:

I think that what you'll find is that we'll have a better turnaround with our reporting for the month, from time to time our senior management will ask our general managers, how we're going throughout the month, our current systems we simply can't tell them, you know if we're only 2 weeks into the month we cannot tell our CFO how it's going or how it's tracking. We tend to know what the results are 2 weeks following the end of the month.

The decision to acquire Dynamics AX was taken because a project costing system, relatively easy to implement and supported by an organisation for the "foreseeable future", was required. Dynamics AX was a particularly good fit. As the plan was to implement a replacement system in two or three years, the costs were very tightly controlled.

Contractor does not have a standard capital expenditure request, the process being that if the people in operations want a significant piece of equipment they have to write a report, justification, cost etc for the

CFO. He will then evaluate it, and then, depending on the extent of its proposed budget, it will go up to the CEO and the Board. The CIO's explained that if IT expenditure had not been identified in the IT strategy document it would not be sanctioned. Efficiency gains were to be the yardstick, but the report did not include tangible benefits.

The procedures and control seem to be commensurate with strategy formulation in so far as there is no formal dissemination of strategy, and there are no standardised procedures for evaluation. The use of consultancy organisations seems to enable strategic decisions to be made but detail between strategy and revenue growth seems to need further clarification.

4.3.10 Approach to Customisations

Customisations to Dynamics (AX) are being limited to what is "absolutely necessary", and the implementation was as vanilla as practical, in recognition of the previous application having been overly modified.

> I would suggest that my predecessor was a business systems person, she was very focussed on the business, and she would have said well can we do it, yes we can, let's do it. And that's why we've got to this point today, no review on cost ... it was, someone from the business has asked for it so I'll put it in. That's why in certain areas of Cheops, there's 3 or 4 ways to do things. Because they just develop bolt-ons because someone wanted them. (CIO)

For an SAP or Oracle implementation to be successful the application would need to be flexible. The CIO had presumed that Contractor would develop the application in-house when he said:

> We've gone to visit a number of organisations during our review process, these are organisations of significant size, who've taken on both Oracle and SAP, what they've done is they've actually developed, within the IT department significant skill base in the products and what's happened is, they can then drive change in those products to suit the business.

He further intimated that the ideal is not to customise the application and change process flows, but it was obvious that the application would inevitably be customised to meet business requirements.

4.3.11 Restrictions and Limitations Imposed by ERP

The existing application has restricted the organisation for many years in numerous areas, particularly in terms of reporting, information for business decision making, and information to enable the monitoring of project profitability.

The Finance Manager predicted there would be only two major ERP products in the market place and that these would become increasingly similar. He suggested that this would restrict organisations and prevent IS from being a differentiator. The CIO also believed this, and commented that organisations are "going to be more and more closely aligned in regards to IT infrastructure."

4.3.12 Expected Lifespan of the ERP

The CIO challenged that 10 years in the IT industry was like 100 years in another industry, averring the Contractor was thinking "of a 25 year period, 25 years down the line... the only way you would disband it is if the system is not doing the job, it's not producing the outputs that our clients requires, and there is a system that could provide us with competitive advantage"

The Finance Manager also saw the acquisition as a 25 year investment; he could not envisage the system changing, explaining:

> ... because all you'd be doing is upgrading the version that you're on. So if you choose a product like Oracle or SAP, and provided you keep up with the upgrades and pay your licensing fees and continue to upgrade it, there won't be a need to change. It could easily last 25 years.

Apart from business premises, it's possible that ERP applications are the assets expected to last the longest. This is quite surprising from a technology perspective, as a quarter of a century is an extremely long period to expect technology to last.

4.3.13 Findings and Interpretations

The data from this case have been carefully scrutinised in an attempt to understand the rationale for, and method of, IS strategy formulation. An initial outcome is there seems to be a lack of focus on information which could be due to gaps in the information obtained from Contractor because of confidentiality considerations. However, a major focus is on the annual revenue being $1b, all of the interviewees mentioning this focus on more than one occasion. As a goal it is commendable, but to be healthily profitable would also seem to be prudent.

The Contractor uses the strategy process shown in Figure 31, whereby the CEO and CFO create strategy and at times turn for assistance to outside consultancy organisations. Organisational deficiencies have been defined to a high level in a strategic report by the management group supported by consultants Ernst and Young and Deloittes. At the time of the data collection the document was four years old but was still the cornerstone of initiatives. None of the individuals interviewed knew what was in the report other than the contents of the sections allocated to them. The CIO had produced a strategy document in the first year of his occupying the position. He had been in the job for 4 ½ years at the time of data collection. He generates expenditure requests against the document which are almost always sanctioned by the CFO.

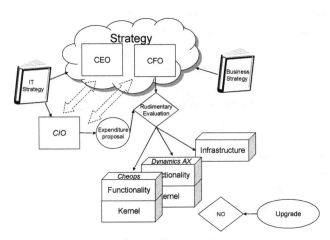

Figure 31.   Contractor Management and Evaluation Process

The strategy documents appear to be old and possibly needing review. The organisation now has networks to compete with the largest bank but does not seem to have identified information requirements for the networks. The systems are still distributed, with each of the sites having a version of the core application. The introduction of Citrix (a technology that relays screen changes from a server to thin clients) will not improve the information component vacuum. It appears that the Contractor is sub-optimised with information and has a lack of controls around the ERP application.

The risk associated with an 18 year old application, having no in-house expertise and a supplier knowing the customer will not require their service in the future, is very high in an organisation that has almost $1bn of revenue from numerous and disparate projects and contracts.

4.3.14 Conclusion

The only component of the discussion concerning information involved human resources and on-site safety details. The conclusion reached is that the organisation is not sufficiently focused upon understanding its information needs and is consequentially selecting an ERP without known objectives.

4.4   Case Study Global

The case was selected because the organisation is a major global corporation and, in its Asia Pacific region, has replaced an ERP application that has only been operational for a few years. It has implemented the Oracle ERP e-business Suite (Oracle) both in Asia-Pacific and worldwide. The case was considered very relevant to this research which was seeking to understand the business drivers and evaluation surrounding the decision to install and maintain a global ERP application. The CIO, finance manager and users were interviewed in the order shown here.

Global has 300 sites in 44 countries, with operations in mining, refining and manufacturing. The organisation is the world leader in its product set and has enjoyed tremendous success over the last 10 years. Revenue in 2006 was in excess of US$30 billion, an increase of US$5 billion from 2005.   A cost reduction program in recent years has saved US$1 billion. The return on capital employed has reached a high of 16.2% (using end of year rather than mid-year capital values) which has risen from 6.5% in 3 years.

The case is of interest for the strategic motivation to use a single application, and the organisation's recognition that to achieve the desired benefits local optimisation may have to be compromised. The interviews focused on key members of the management team in the Asia Pacific region, including the person responsible for corporate applications and infrastructure referred to here as CIO.

4.4.1 Original Implementation and Its Antecedents

The decision to have a single ERP was motivated by a restructure with a global emphasis. As the Finance Manager explained, "We want to align globally; we want to report globally on what our costs are and what our profits are, and compare our businesses. That is where the real benefits come." The ERP implementation is part of a global strategy that aims to compare organisational and regional performance, and identify best practice.

The Oracle application is being implemented globally and is housed in four strategic global 'regions'. The application has been utilised in Australia for three years and is still being implemented in some parts of the world.   The Australian organisation had previously implemented Peoplesoft ERP. The decision not to adopt Peoplesoft for the organisation's operations worldwide was made because its supply functionality was considered to be inadequate for global business requirements.

The CIO when asked whether ERP was working well for the business he responded:

No, in most areas we would say the system is not ideal at all, and in some instances has taken us backward. The business would certainly say that. Which is where the measurement of value becomes an interesting proposition. I guess, this packages has been put in on a global business case which basically says over all [Global] which operates in multiple regions and multiple countries and across a dozen different types of businesses and we will be a better company and it will be more effectively managed if everywhere is using the same HR system, if everywhere is using the same procurement system, the same financials, the same order to cash solution. Because the management visibility and ability to compare across business is hugely beneficial. So in terms of strategic management of the business it is a much better place to be.

In terms of a guy sitting at [site] refinery who wants to order an item for his stores he will probably say it has gone backwards. That it was easier before, because before that he had a system that had been tailored to his Australian requirement by our IT group. We had a long tradition of providing very tailored solutions for our business people that did exactly what they wanted them to do. And if they decided they wanted to do it differently 6 months down the track and, they told us, if they had the money we made it do it for them.

A strategic decision was made to install the system for commonality and standardised information rather than being optimised for users or individual organisations. The CIO explained: "It is targeted at keeping us aligned with the other regions so that any changes we need to make has to go for an approval process back to the US." The approval process has significantly reduced the local developments from the previous application.

4.4.2 Impact of Strategy Process on ERP

Apparently the CEO sees the organisation as a single enterprise and wants to answer "numerous global questions" (CIO). The latter explained that the organisation has seven refineries and without the system the organisation "couldn't compare costs" of procurement. Prior to the global ERP initiative, "the information was held in 15 systems in Europe, 3 in North America, and 3 in South America". A strategic driver for a single ERP is the increasing number of global contracts with large organisations.

The strategy process can be defined as 'formal' with initiatives being communicated throughout the organisation by reviews and notices. The CIO said of the system that "it was very well publicised what

Global wanted to achieve." But due to this centralised strategy there is increasingly less business autonomy at organisation and regional levels.

The ERP application is then a cornerstone of the globalisation strategy, being used to control, compare and co-ordinate the disparate organisations, and enabling strategic global alliances to be established.

4.4.3 Financial Procedures and Imperatives

The Finance Manager explained that the organisation was in an extremely strong financial position, with high revenue growth over the last decade. The growth in revenue was largely attributed to a strong worldwide economy. The cost of the investment in the Oracle application was not known but estimated to be between $700m and $1b worldwide. There is, perhaps not unsurprisingly, "no possibility of abandoning the system" in the foreseeable future.

The strong financial situation enables upgrade decisions to be made without costs being a major factor. However, upgrades are viewed as very expensive, the Finance Manager explaining the key consideration to be the global strategy and commonality of information across the organisations. All of the upgrades are co-ordinated globally with each region managing its part of the global initiative. Costs of upgrades are borne locally, and, if necessary, a module or function would be re-implemented; but as they are "as vanilla as practical" this was seen to be unlikely.

In summary the healthy financial situation means that cost is not a major consideration for the management and evaluation of ERP.

4.4.4 Upgrades and Their Antecedents

The organisation has upgraded twice in 3 years, each upgrade costing the Australian organisation approximately Au$2m. The cost is seen by the CIO as high as upgrading benefits the Australian component of the business only marginally. The CIO suggested:

> *Ideally in Australia we would run a business case to say do we upgrade or don't we upgrade, you could basically do a cost benefit on it, to see if it was worth doing. But at the end of the day the drivers are different, we were dragged along to have to do it, we had no choice.*

The cost is absorbed locally, and as each business is responsible for its performance, the Finance Manager saw any upgrade as an overhead to the business. As the CIO explained: "You have got to align globally, you loose control of the agenda to a certain extent".

The researcher queried whether the possibility existed for a region to decide not to upgrade? It's possible, asserted the CIO, but such an event would have impacted on support at a "global level", and as the organisation is "off-shoring support to India, we would have undermined their ability to support us alongside the other businesses". He also explained there were some necessities to upgrade, as "the payroll requires upgrades and patches to produce group certificates in the right format". The system also requires "continuous patching" to resolve problems, "So you get on a train of upgrades".

The benefits of upgrading were seen as minor, a user explaining: "That is the price you pay for best practice"! The process of upgrading was seen as problematic by the CIO who argued: "It is necessary to ensure customisations work with the next version, and even with the few modifications we have made, upgrading is very difficult". He also warned: "For someone who is an IT professional, who has enjoyed a career of creating slick software, Oracle is not great."

Restrictions placed on customisation allow upgrades to be performed, but they are still difficult to achieve, expensive, and provide minimal benefit.

4.4.5 Re-implementations

Re-implementing the system was not seen as something that was likely as the system is very close to vanilla and when the organisation deployed the modules they "made pretty reasonable modifications and customisations. " It is also the intent wherever possible to change the business process rather than the application.

4.4.6 Perception of IS

It was identified by the CIO that IS is "not core business as it is for a bank, it is an enabler, except for process control where it is key to some processes". The ERP implementation was seen to have largely had a negative impact on users. A key user explained that "in terms of a guy sitting at a refinery who wants to order an item for his stores he will probably say it has gone backwards. "However, apparently the more senior staff are now viewing IT more favourably. "Over all I am satisfied it hasn't hurt us, because it was a huge upheaval for the company to get there." CIO. The CIO explained the following.

We aspire to be not noticed. If the system can be used without people feeling negative about it that would be the best we could hope for we didn't have any great hopes when we put it in, because we knew it was going to hurt in a lot of places.

It is obvious that the useability of the ERP is not as good as it was previously and in turn the perception of IS has reduced at an operational level. It is interesting that senior management perception of the contribution of IS has increased. Sedera, Gable, & Chan (2004) and Lim, Pan and Tan (20004) found differences in operational and strategic perspectives of ERP. It seems that it might be difficult to optimise for both global standardisation and local useability.

4.4.7 Influences and Consequence of Software Authors and Resellers

Oracle asserts indirect pressure to upgrade the system by not supporting systems that are not at the current release. The CIO explained that "we could go to them and say this doesn't work and they say are you patched up to there, and if you say no, they say come back when you are patched up to that point. So if you don't keep level with the patching or with the upgrades you become unsupportable."

Oracle were seen as instrumental in the decision to select the software. The CIO explained that "the Oracle organisation worked very hard to make sure that it secured the business. They were very flexible, the Oracle system did not have a maintenance module and they agreed to write one to meet our requirements.". The finance manager also said that "it really is a pretty much strategic relationship we have. The deal was cut at a very high level and gives us a lot of leverage with Oracle ".

The researcher probed to understand the process that was being utilised to develop the maintenance module. The module is being created to the organisation's requirements and will then be marketed as a " best practice" module. It was seen by the CIO that this was how most of the ERP modules are created, they are written for an organisations requirements and then sold as part of the package in future releases. Global tries to convince Oracle to include required customisations in the core application to reduce upgrade overhead and they have been quite successful at this. It was seen by the CIO that it is very questionable if these developments amount to best practice as they are not designed to be generic, and little time is spent seeing how they meet the broader community needs.

4.4.8 Environmental Influences

The environment impacts the organisation in terms of key customers demand and the need for global relationships. A key user explained that most of Global's customers have the SAP ERP application, but it was not seen necessary for Global to have the same application as customers. It was explained that the industry was supported by only three applications and that two of those were now provided by the Oracle corporation.

4.4.9 Evaluation Procedures

The CIO explained that a common application, "if you are a global company, is almost a prerequisite." He explained that the evaluation process allowing for the application "was a global strategic decision based on ability to cover the ground. The only real contenders were SAP, Oracle and to a lesser extent Peoplesoft." Peoplesoft did not "have the coverage in terms of manufacturing, order management and maintenance", and SAP were seen as too rigid - "You either do it the SAP way or not at all."

The Oracle application was selected at the highest level, the Finance Manager asserting: "There were negotiations on the software licensing costs; we got a significant percentage reduction on the base cost, due to the global deal." Each regional implementation initiative was managed and costed separately, with separate contracts, but there was no evaluation at the regional level, with the CIO observing: "I was a bit facetious perhaps saying we didn't evaluate it, but in Australian terms we didn't."

Apparently the benefits at the regional level were not that important, the Finance Manager observing: "How worthwhile it is for me going back over the benefits of putting in HR and finance when it was a push basically? I am not sure it is worth the time and effort." He explained that analysis was more important for discretionary projects, saying:

> If we have project A and B and we need to decide where we put our time and effort it is very important. Your cost and benefits upfront is very important and by coming back at the end you fine tune your understanding, you can't improve that project, but you might find ways to improve future projects.

As it is expected to be sometime before an installation such as Oracle occurs again, any learning was thought to be irrelevant. The Finance Manager explained:

> It is a capital expense but it was pushed down. They put together a high level Cap Request, to cover the whole program globally and got that signed off by the board. It was driven by our CEO, he is the one who said we need to do this, this is what we need to do to be the best company, which is our vision. You can't be the best

company in the world if you have 20 different business in four regions in 40 odd
countries all doing things in their own way.

When the researcher asked the CIO whether the capital expenditure was almost $1b, he was told, "Probably not, but before we started deploying they knew what it was. So the original cap. request has not been extended. It is not a project that has blown out beyond anyone's dream." The CIO was asked why the project cost more than originally envisaged, asserting, "The scope has changed, we are doing some stuff that we didn't think we were going to do and we have not done some stuff we thought we would. "

From a user perspective the view of the system is quite poor, the CIO suggesting that "some will say it is terrible, it is much worse than the previous application, and others will say it is not so bad. They are getting used to it. They're taking a while." An operational manger explained:

> *It is very hard to get quantified benefits out of these things. Some business will just*
> *refuse to do it in money terms as, as soon as they say they have saved $200k then*
> *management will come looking for it and ask why isn't your budget less.*

Managers are being wary of defining benefits, and, as the CIO intimated, "You really need to nail it down before the project begins. ... You generally try and look at the operating budget over a year. But you might look at business process and how do you quantify it, it can be done but it takes a lot of work."

4.4.10 Approach to Customisations

Customisations to the application are rigidly controlled by a central team which evaluates the need for the change to it. The CIO explained there being a "constant pull" from users to customise the system, but that this "undermines the vision" of the global company. If the region is convinced of the requirement, it tries to convince the global IT organisation to include the customisation in all regions; if global IT are convinced they in turn try to have Oracle include the customisation in the core application. Achievement of a modification will take a two to three year cycle.

An IT manager observed that if the users are prepared to "wait two or three years you know it is something they require"! However, a counter view raised was that if three years could elapse then the customisation is not really necessary.

Change is going to be much more costly from now on, before you could change
bits and pieces but now you've got to change how a whole ERP works not just one
module (IT Manager).

The rigid control of customisations imposed during implementations has been continued. Very few
customisations are now being sanctioned; the business having to make do largely with the standard
application and the customisations made before implementation.

4.4.11 Restrictions and Limitations Imposed by ERP

A key user avers that using the application "has created quite a lot of frustration". And the CIO contends the
company is profitable enough to employ more staff if the overhead of the application requires it, but, "Most
areas would say the system is not ideal at all, and in some instances has taken us backward. The business
would certainly say that. This is where the measurement of value becomes an interesting proposition." The
CIO noted:

We had a session yesterday, down at our xxxxx refinery with our management
there. Part of their presentation was what was working and what wasn't working
with IT and what could be better. And I was very relieved that he didn't mention the
Oracle application.

The system is as cumbersome for users but not to the extent that it restricts business operations. However,
the application has had benefits at a global level as the organisation is now able to interface globally with
customers and provide best practice information across the group. The researcher concluded that it seems
impossible to optimise the application both locally and globally simultaneously.

4.4.12 Expected Lifespan of the ERP

None of the interviewees thought the system would be changed in the foreseeable future. The CIO said that
he could not see the company ever doing something similar again, and if the system were changed it would
be provided by an outside hosting organisation. He believed that, as the IT industry matures, hosting
operations will be managed by SAP and Oracle. The move to hosting houses by major ERP vendors was
proposed by Fulford (2003).

4.4.13 Approach to Business Process Analysis

Formerly process analysis was based on the application and as such the users simply "have to do what the system says". The organisation has changed processes to work with the application and users have created what are referred to as 'workarounds'.

4.4.14 Findings and Interpretations

The proposal that "IT is not core as it is in a bank" is interesting considering the organisation has spent approximately $1billion on an application. As $1bn constitutes only 3% of revenue, it is around the average annual spending on IT. The expectation of benefits of this level of application expenditure in the Australian region is extremely low. An observation by the CIO was very telling:

> *A lot of people here would say we should have put in SAP. A lot of people would still question the whole strategy around Oracle. Oracle is a problematic package, Oracle is not slick software by any means; it is basically a cobbled together batch system with a pretty front-end that allows you to enter data that kicks off a lot of background processes.*

This statement was not a compelling argument in support of spending $1 billion.

The strategy process is depicted in Figure 32. The organisation make request to the global IT department for inclusion of customisations in the application. If they are agreed, which may take three years of consultations, the customisations are added to all regional applications. Sanctioned customisations are sent to Oracle requesting they be included in the standard application. The upgrades are implemented rapidly to ensure ongoing support by Oracle.

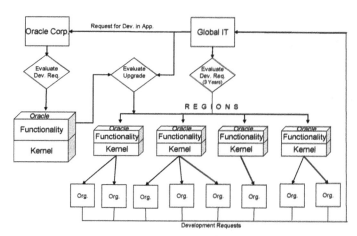

Figure 32.   Global Management and Evaluation Process

4.4.15 Conclusion

The major conclusion is that customisations to support local and non-strategic processes are not seen as necessary. Using a vanilla application may be cumbersome but if the decision is an edict and well communicated then users have to accept it. The company's success, albeit in a buoyant market, demonstrates that standardisation can be very beneficial.

4.5 Case Study Builder

The case study of the Builder organisation is a remarkable story of ERP management and change. Builder is a very aggressive organisation, growing rapidly by acquisition, so that in ten years it has created a presence in 20 countries. The worldwide revenue of the company is almost US$20 billion, with over $3 billion of net profit.

The European region has undergone a complete re-implementation of an SAP ERP application. The replaced application had only been live four years and had cost approximately Au$200m. The re-implementation was driven by the organisation being taken over. It is very interesting to this research to understand the reasons to re-implement a successfully implemented system at a re-implementation cost of approximately $250m. Interviews with the European region were undertaken with IT management and financial personnel. The worldwide coordinator for IT (referred to hereinafter as Coordinator) was also interviewed and provided tremendous insight into a complex business environment. The Coordinator talked at the beginning of the interview unprompted for 12 minutes concerning the background of standardising business processes worldwide.

4.5.1 Original Implementation and Its Antecedents

Builder had originally implemented J.D. Edwards in its regional organisations but found that the large number of customisations and the different processes in the organisations around the world meant that the organisation could not upgrade for Y2K purposes. The organisation formed a group of senior managers to identify core processes and the content of the processes for ongoing implementation in all of the organisations around the world. The case has three ERP implementations: the initial world-wide implementation of J.D. Edwards at Builder, the original implementation of SAP in Europe by the group acquired by Builder, and the recent re-implementation in Europe of SAP to meet the Builder's worldwide standard process.

4.5.1.1 Original European Implementation

The original SAP implementation in Europe was made live in 2002. The purpose of the implementation was to create commonality and reduce the number of applications across the group of twenty-four organisations. The Finance Manager explained there were "twenty-four individual operating companies and each one had their own administration centre." The objective was a shared service centre, a particular benefit being one set of customer information rather than 24. The implementation was deemed to be very successful, with both local optimisation and the required centralised information.

4.5.1.2 Re-implementation

During the 1990s Builder had tried to implement common systems and processes around the world but had been unsuccessful, the Coordinator explaining there had been "common technology, a common ERP, which was J.D. Edwards, but it was configured differently and interfaced with different local systems ... the way we managed the businesses was really different."

To overcome the issue the company split the IT "personnel into two main domains; one very technology orientated domain, and another organisation that we called Business Process Centre, being very much involved in the concept of the [Builder] Way. It is now called the [Builder] Way group." The group identified the core processes to be used worldwide, the aim being to create commonality, best practice and ease future acquisitions of organisations. The processes were originally implemented in J.D.Edwards, but it was decided that the product did not offer sufficient capabilities for the global processes, so Builder proceeded to find an application better matching the processes.

The Builder created a task force to review potential applications. They reviewed a "great many" applications but the decision to choose SAP "was not difficult". The Co-ordinator explained that "it would allow the integration of business processes and the level of fit with the Builder Way processes being the key factors." The SAP roll-out included the re-implementation in Europe.

4.5.2 Impact of Strategy Process on ERP

The re-implementation in Europe has less local optimisation than the former application, and is thought by users to be more cumbersome than the previous implementation. However, users in finance and HR prefer the new system as they can more easily produce reports across the group. The Finance Manager in the UK identified that performance is monitored at a country level, but the strategy process "is very much driven from the centre, globally. ... Strategy formulation is top down, the CEO is a strong individual, there is an Executive Committee of the regional presidents plus representatives of co-ordinator functions." The organisation has three distinct product sets having different markets or ways to market. As the UK IT Manager explained:

> We have a department that is responsible for global strategy, we consolidate global needs, global requirements, evolution of process, evolution of countries and regions which creates the initial discussion for analysing the portfolio for the local strategy group.

When asked if there was tension between the global organisation and the local business the finance manager admitted there was, but he " wouldn't say it was that acute, global focuses on consistency, by benchmarking and that causes friction as locals always consider they know their business KPIs best." Interestingly he suggested that the global system added to the tension as it is where the emphases are most obvious.

It became apparent that the Builder operates in a very fragmented, global market with many small players, but Builder was the second largest organisation of its type at the time of data collection with 4% market share, the largest having 5% (Builder's organisation is now probably the largest following a very large acquisition). The products are commodity priced and Builder is looking to reduce the indirect cost of finance and HR through centralisation while introducing best practice in support of global customers.

As a final comment the UK IT Manager revealed, "Builder will continue to make acquisitions; there will be a strong emphasis of getting these processes in so that we can apply them to new acquisitions. As this makes the acquisition process much easier, we obviously like to lever knowledge of cash, process and customers". Johnson and Scholes (2002) identify the reason for acquisition, amongst others, as being able to exploit an organisation's core competencies in new global arenas, and due to a very ambitious Senior Manager. Both of these reasons may be influencing decisions at Builder.

4.5.3 Financial Procedures and Imperatives

The key financial performance indicator is cash generation. The Finance Manager explained that cash generation is managed by having a "very short reporting timescale, for instance sales, prices and volumes that is daily or at least weekly." The researcher asked whether the focus on cash generation made the planning horizon short and perhaps stifled investment. The Finance Manager gave the following response:

> If anything, the organisation is looking longer term than it was before; there is a
> little bit of reserve of our [product] where we try to keep coverage of 10 or 20 years.
> We have a strong balance sheet and we are not using it to hold back the business.
> There is a blueprint process where the business tries to look 5 years ahead, where
> they identify what they want to do and invest in during the next 5 years. The cap.
> ex. process is such that the maintenance of the business and cash generation are
> covered with so much of one and so much of the other.

Whilst cash generation is the focus there seems to be very solid financial controls, the Finance Manager explaining: "Business people are held responsible for variations from previous month, last year, on budget.

Information on its own won't change the organisation but people being responsible for their result and the focus on the numbers will improve the business."

The IT manager explained that the company would change the application if it did not provide the processes required; but, this seemed unlikely as it was chosen because it could fulfil the necessary processes. However, if the CEO wanted to re-implement or make large changes to the application it would be done. The ERP application has been implemented to provide financial returns for the business and as such is not handicapped by lack of expenditure if the expenditure is deemed necessary.

4.5.4 Upgrades and Their Antecedents

One of the main factors for acquiring SAP was the high cost of upgrading the heavily modified J.D. Edwards application worldwide. The Coordinator argued it would have cost in excess of $10m to upgrade the procurement process in J.D. Edwards alone:

> *One of the factors when we contacted Mr. xxxxxx (CEO), how can we have the business applications ready for year 2000 with these disparate systems. This helped him see the value of the business case and standard applications for our businesses, as we could not manage IT upgrades.*

Builder plans to upgrade SAP two and possibly three times a year which seems excessive and possibly more than the releases available. However, the strategy is to implement process changes when upgrading rather than customise interim releases. The Coordinator explained, "There should be a version strategy to be related to how we manage the portfolio evolution."

This approach contrasted to the approach of previous SAP implementation in the UK which was 'technically' upgraded once in 4 years. The IT Manager advised: "There was one technical upgrade to apply patches and things like that - quite a big one; it took 3 or 4 months and everything needed to be retested. "The reason for the upgrade was identified by the UK IT Manager:

> *The timing of it was such that the different projects and implementations had stopped, we had got behind on our upgrade path. So it was always a matter of looking at the projects and when they came to an end, and so when can we slot this in to the schedule, It was put off for a period of time and then a window was found to do it.*

There appears to be the significant difference between the approach to the original application and the re-implemented one. Heavily modified applications are very difficult to upgrade and tend not to be upgraded whilst lightly modified implementations with well defined processes can be upgraded easily. As the IT Manager explained, "Certainly many of the restrictions on development are so that upgrades will be easier."

4.5.5 Re-Implementations

The re-implementation in the UK has obviously been driven by the acquisition of the European operation. The application will be incrementally re-implemented with enhanced processes, the UK IT manager suggesting re-implementing and optimising processes is likely to happen:

> *If we have to respond to global market changes or requirements or one country comes up with a great idea then we can take that advantage we have gained or that idea we have got we can implement it in one country but very quickly put it in the other countries because that are all working on the same systems and processes.*

4.5.6 Perception of IS

The UK Finance Manager thought that at the user level the system had not been well received, "the front-end users would say we have gone backward with the implementation of SAP", and the organisation has not done enough "to sell the benefits". He went on to argue that, both from a back office perspective and his, the perception of the capability of IS had increased, as

> *Now we can mine the information. One of the major benefits is balance sheet control, and we have a good picture of balance sheet risks, where in the past we relied on an audit or a bi-annual check.*

An interesting slant on the perception of the business was narrated by the IT Manager when he contrasted the original implementation of SAP with the re-implementation:

> *You try to convince the business community that it is project for the business and on behalf of the business. But they still think of it as IT. The first project was a bit scary for the business as it brought about a big change, as it changed platforms – they had been using Vaxes for a long time, it was a big change but seen as an IT project.*

The Builder Way is not seen as IT at all, it is just seen as a complete change. OK we are getting new systems but it is seen as a Builder company initiative. And a continuation of the acquisition possibly. But people understand it is about countries wanting to work in the same way and is therefore an initiative form the Builder Way and not about IT.

The implication is that the perception of an application can be directly impacted by the way it is presented and perhaps who is presenting it.

4.5.7 Influences and Consequence of Software Authors and Resellers

The increase in the cost of SAP's maintenance agreement when the organisation got behind a recent release was a factor in the decision to upgrade the original application in the UK company. As the upgrading was to be much more pro-active now the author has less influence. The Coordinator explained that the evolution of SAP was seen as so important to Builder that a company has been established to "capitalise on the relation with SAP", and "analyse change in technology and make reports on how the ERP market will evolve."

4.5.8 Environmental Influences

Customers and suppliers are seen as key factors in the decision to implement a standard ERP application, but not seen as important in the actual choice of application. The coordinator identified global contracts with key customers as key driver, and a regional manager averring that one interface with customers was advantageous because we are "able to use EDI for invoicing as we can do it across the customer organisation, and we can target our invoicing cycles to suit their administrative cycles."

The procurement process has also improved, the IT Manager explaining the company now "are able to make global deals" for raw materials. Another reason he gave for the implementation is to improve the organisation's competitive position in the fragmented market place, passing on:

At the moment our systems and processes are seen by Builder as being an advantage over our competitors. To such an extent that in our joint venture organisations we are refusing to implement the systems as our partners will have access to them.

In conclusions the environment impacts the management and evaluation of ERP, through competitors, customers and suppliers.

4.5.9 Evaluation Procedures

The decision to implement a standard solution was for both business improvement and cost savings. The Worldwide Coordinator explained that "the first business case stated how much it is costing to maintain and upgrade the service and versions of the applications; and how much it would cost if we had it as standard. So it was very much cost centred ". The company had what it believes is very good process in the South American Business, the coordinator explaining:, "there were some business cases of savings that would be produced by utilising these processes"

The decision to move away from J.D.Edwards to SAP was because the product "was becoming obsolete and there was consolidation of the ES industry worldwide". The cost was considered as not "too bad" when viewed in the context of business improvement rather than IT expenditure. The Coordinator explained further, "SAP is not cheap. It is a very expensive technology. But it would allow us to integrate business processes and the level of fit with the Builder Way processes were the key factors."

The worldwide budget for the total implementation is at a very high-level, but becomes much more fine grained for each region or country. The Coordinator continued, "When we know the number of people and the size we can budget. We have a firm estimate." When asked if he could identify the value of benefits realised, he recounted:

> Well, not without inventing. I can offer to give you some of the benefits we have achieved. I can give you one example, procurement, this is typical, having standardisation of the business that we use for managing [Product] plants and having software that is common in Europe and Mexico we have information on consumption of material. Having the information of consumption of material worldwide we can make very good purchasing decision worldwide and where we want to buy materials.

Interestingly, the reason for the original implementation of SAP in Europe was because of stock market expectations, the IT Manager suggesting:

> There was a major financial evaluation but at the same time the non financial factors weighed very strongly. One of the major reasons was that XXX, the organisation at that time, was one of the few companies quoted on the stock exchange that didn't have an ERP system.

The IT Manager explained that the organisation didn't undertake a "rigorous justification " but did get Price Waterhouse Coopers to investigate. The decision to implement SAP was influenced by the application being used in one of the organisation's companies in Germany. When asked if other applications were considered the IT manager made these comments:

> *We paid lip service to looking at other applications but because Germany already used SAP, we had favourable licensing costs, and it was always going to be SAP ... the CEO had a clear vision of how he wanted the UK company to change. ... part of the program was to put in one single point for administration, called shared services centre.*

The centralisation process was not without problems as "a lot of the issues originate at the front-end, so the emphasis shifts from a collection exercise to a query management exercise." This is due to the relationship with the customer being managed in the remote business and the collection at a centralised function".

The implementation that replaced the original SAP system had a cost benefit study completed, revealing the cost over-ran by approximately 20%. A large portion of the costs, including implementation, was capitalised and is still being depreciated, "but aggressively."
The benefits were to be based on the shared data centre and increased customer satisfaction. The monetary value of benefits were not a significant enough consideration for follow up. Other benefits to the organisation were explained by the Finance Manager:

> *The benefits were about head count reduction, mainly in back office processes. Once we had established the shared service centre we lost focus on that and the focus has shifted to information collection and the benefits of having standardised systems. Having one view of the customer, one view of suppliers, work in capital improvement ... there was a perceived work in capital benefit, in terms of better management of payment to suppliers, in terms of how we manage work in capital around reporting of quarters and year-end.*

Another major benefit was benchmarking, the organisation had "already seen where cost comparison of manufacturing improves practices." The system will "allow us to reduce costs and later to focus on the customer when cost savings have been delivered." The researcher suggested that the emphasis on cost might imply a tangible evaluation process to which the IT Manager responded:

> *Yes it would, I suppose what I am finding difficult is the evaluation of the system ...*
> *we are now using a shared service centre in Hungary to reduce costs. There must*
> *be a cash benefit but those decisions are taking globally rather than by the UK.*

Asked if costs were taken locally or centrally, the Finance Manager replied, "Some costs that are directly attributed to the UK are absorbed locally, but the SAP configuration and implementation costs are being met centrally". The researcher ascertained that the centralised cost would be allocated across the group. The IT manager explained the local costs are for specific local customisations which are allowed under the guidelines explained in the Customisation Section. The IT Manager, explaining that a local IT budget is controlled by the business centre which "brought the business case", said:

> *All the equipment costs, all the PCs, are in a central pot, which is budgeted for. If*
> *there are projects that are put in the budget for next year obviously they have to be*
> *made known this year a business case created and evaluated. Apart from*
> *infrastructure, networking, servers and equipment, they are IT costs that are*
> *budgeted for and taken within the IT budget. There is some small amount of stuff*
> *in there for projects. But business projects come out of the business and a*
> *business case has to be signed off and budgeted for.*

4.5.10 Approach to Customisations

The major problem with the initial implementation of J.D.Edwards was the number of customisations, the Coordinator explaining, "In just one of the processes we had over 900 variances in the process for the different countries." The lack of conformity of these variances, prompted the organisation to standardise the overall processes, and ultimately to change the evaluation surrounding customisations.

Customisations are now very tightly controlled and unless they are very small they must be sanctioned by a global process owner. Only two types of customisations are now sanctioned: country specific legal and market requirements. The IT Manager advised:

> *First of all there is definition of the process, and OK it includes the system, but it*
> *could be the way that purchase orders are created, approved and released and*
> *[Builder] have a definition of that as well as the people who are involved in it. It is*
> *the same in sales, so there is a definition that is pretty tight. If you think you need a*
> *modification, you have to ask yourself if it conforms to the [Builder] process. If it*
> *does, then what we are trying to do fits the standard process then the expectation*
> *is that the standard system can be configured to meet that. Because the definition*

is meant to be able to be met by the standard system. But if it is changing the process, we identify if it is a legal requirement or a local market driven requirement as to the way we do business, the requirements are then evaluated by the project and, if there is change requested, there is a hierarchy tree in the project to evaluate if the modification should be made. Small changes may take place, but larger changes, of only a few days are evaluated by a committee. It could go to the steering committee, it could also go to the person who is responsible for that part of business, for example [Product] has a worldwide owner. They would identify why that modification had to be made for [Product]. So it goes from the project and to business management depending on the size of the modification.

When the IT Manager was asked if cost of customisation was a factor in the decision he ruminated, "Cost is a factor, but in the project world it is about keeping the processes standard between countries and inline with the Builder model. That is the major driver." When asked how many requests are approved his response was, "The legal ones obviously get through, other requests get through where we are allowed to add extra fields to the system; but we are not allowed to change how the basic front-end screens look and operate. The option is to put fields on other tabs". He then added:

They say we can't change the main transactions because it will invalidate our support or warranty, but you can put it on this additional data tab. That is allowable but you can't change it on the front screen! Percentage that get through? On volume it is probably 30%-40%, on value, given that we are not making the [system] mods for £1m, it is a lot lower. It is very much about what is needed, things that are nice to have will not happen.

Some technical requirements not included in SAP in specific areas of the business have caused Builder to interface with another application. Interestingly, the IT Manager informed, "SAP has promised to incorporate that functionality in the future," which variation will presumably be 'best practice'.

The IT Manager when asked how the control of customisations differed in the original application, he disclosed, "We made more changes to meet user requirements and to make it more user friendly. There were more nice to haves in that model". When pressed the IT manager conceded there would have been more than twice as many customisations in the original implementation.

The Coordinator explains hs perspective on the reason for the strict controls around customisations in the following:

We really have a business process governance. We go to a new country, such as
the UK. We find different functionality in different parts of the business. We need to
be very positive and very strong of how we manage the business processes.
Otherwise we will become disparate as we were in the 90s. There are elements
that are required and necessary to change functionality, they are where the
process of manufacture is imperative, legal regulations, something that is required
by the government, and thirdly what we call market critical elements. We need to
be very firm on the governance of business processes and we need business
process standards. And the group needs to be firm enough not to reproduce ten
different procurement systems.

The controls on customisations continued after the implementation.

4.5.11 Restrictions and Limitations Imposed by ERP

The users in the UK organisation did not believe the re-implementation was an improvement because the
previous system "worked perfectly well" and the new one "requires working around". The IT Manager there
said that "it would be difficult to see the benefits of the current implementation, but from a global position as
we are looking for global processes, I see that as a very strong benefit." He continued, saying that compared
to the old system the new system was difficult for users; and, "In sales they have to use several screens
which they don't like. It is a similar problem in other areas."

The Coordinator was queried about his belief that a single set of processes worldwide would hinder the
business in certain areas, expanding:

In our case it is proven that the group can change, we are depending on
managers. If there is a reason to change we will change our processes. On the
contrary this is power as it were.

The following is quite an amazing situation explained by the Finance Manager.

In the UK we have a couple of businesses, one that is very unique to the UK,
retention of the business is accepted as it is good for the UK business. But we
haven't got a system for it and we are continuing with very antiquated systems so
the business is now seen as a back water - to the extent where we question
whether to keep the business or not.

He added that it was "unfortunate" that the business was so profitable otherwise Builder would have sold it already! Davenport (1998, p.2) proposed that ERP pushes a company toward integration even when a certain degree of business unit segregation may be in its best interests.

4.5.12 Approach to Business Process Analysis

The Strategy Manager explained the process of standardisation:.

> Along with external consultants, in 1999, we wrote a story to the CEO from what
> we called the executive committee, his response is very simple it says we start
> analysing the finance, administration, and operations etc. And you contact the
> presidents and all the people in charge of operations in the different parts of the
> world.

> Always we have 6 or 7 presidents or senior executives from all over the world, plus
> legal and external consultants. The CEO and his directors report. I led the
> discussion. We made analysis, we analysed the processes and the applications we
> had. We presented our recommendations and the way we should proceed with the
> implementation. It was a very good discussion. The outcome - they decide these
> are the main processes that we should standardise.

The Coordinator was asked if the discussions were difficult with Presidents representing their own interests. He made an interesting response concerning the restructuring:

> No, no. I think not, Richard. I would call them the basic processes. I would say
> that people realised, because of IT, we have to have common business process
> and the Builder Way.

> I didn't mention a very key piece of information. One of the purposes of the
> committee was not only to change the way we manage processes and the way we
> manage IT, we required a very important change in the way we manage the
> company and we manage profit, we need governance. The governance the way
> we manage the organisation. The collective power. The first important change of
> the executive committee was that all IT personnel all over the world reported just to
> one head. So the person who design and build the applications in Venezuela,
> Mexico, Europe all report to one person and at a corporate level. This was very

key. This meant that the IT personnel were not trying to serve the country president or there customer but the guy who leads the executive committee and the IT function at corporate. This was a very important change.

He further intimated how the process evolved:

When we made the recommendation to the executive committee we asked them to provide us with groups of the procurement managers, the HR managers, etc, so we have excellence in the business processes. Then we have business process consultants and we build the process view and map the process, etc. We also have the IT solutions role. IT solutions meaning to provide to the group a study and facts about the IT applications that is supporting the organisations all over the world. So the group did not only provide recommendations concerning the processes but also regarding the IT support tool that the processes should have. We had very different commercial applications, one in South American Country, one in Spain and one in the US. The group recommended that we need to use one of these as the basis for creating the standard.

The Finance Manager explained that a common platform is important for business process evolution:

We are trying to achieve a common platform and common way of working, when it is all in and settled down, if we have to respond to global market changes or requirements or one country comes up with a great idea then we can take that advantage we have gained or that idea we have got we can implement it in one country but very quickly put it in the other countries because that are all working on the same systems and processes.

The IT Manager explained in the sequence of implementation, the new SAP the processes changed first and then the application followed:

With Builder Way the reorganisation was done upfront and the existing systems creaked and we had to tweak them a little bit to work with the new business structure. We knew that Builder Way was going to come along and join the structure and systems. It was all part of the same initiative.

This focus on process has changed the view of the organisation from an IT initiative to a business initiative. The Coordinator explained that the processes will continue to evolve with a group to educate companies through the processes. Strategic benefits are likely to accrue only to organisations that treat ERP implementation as a business process rather than an IT project; and orchestrate a culture change to capitalise on the potential benefits that integration provides (Davenport 1998, 2000; Markus and Tanis, 2000; Somers and Nelson, 2001; Bendoly and Kaefer, 2004 cited Abdinnour-Helm and Lengnick-Hall, 2005)

4.5.13 Expected Lifespan and of The ERP

The Coordinator did not know how long the system would last but:

> *It will be a lot of years, we really can manage the requirements and support for a long time and manage the evolution of the process and the way we do business. I have no idea how technology will change. I think not less than 10 or 15 years, something like that.*

The Finance Manager thought the application would last at least 10 years with an aspect most likely to change being regarding the SAP application. The IT Manager identified the expenditure of vast sums on the implementation as a reason for not changing readily. He saw that a driver for change might be that competitors achieved an advantage through a different application. Then he added:

> *If SAP wanted to charge an extortion amount for support, or there was a major market opportunity that SAP couldn't support then they might change it. Unless there was something substantially better, better could be functionality, not need so many people to operate it, I can't think of too many reasons to change it..I think this implementation is here for the next 10 – 15 perhaps 20 years.*

4.5.14 Findings and Interpretations

The management and evaluation processes of the organisation are depicted in Figure 33. The global process and IT groups oversee the country implementations and ensure that the processes are standardised throughout the world. Customisation requests are received under the three categories and, when sanctioned, are added to all systems. Project managers can sanction local, very minor customisations, but they cannot alter the core transaction content, and must add new fields to additional tabs on forms rather than the main tabs.

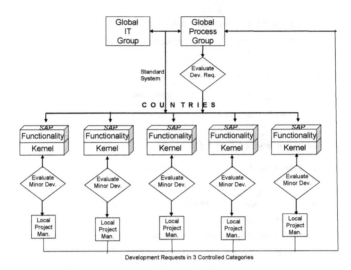

Figure 33.   Builder Management and Evaluation Process

The consistency of the process is assured by the very stringent controls on customisations. While 30% of proposals may be sanctioned, many proposed customisations will not fit into the legal, market or manufacturing requirements categories and will therefore not be requested. The standardisation of the process worldwide is being well received by the businesses. Even the users, who now find the system less efficient than previously, are content to use it as they recognise the benefits to the company.

The separation of the IT and process team is an interesting concept. It means that the process team looks at optimising the organisation going forward; and the IT team provides support for process team initiatives.

4.5.15 Conclusion

The approach to managing the ERP appears mature and all interviewees agreed that it is delivering substantial business benefits. The strategy of the organisation is fundamentally linked with ERP management with the ERP considered to be a major component for aligning regional businesses. The standardised approach was borne out of the frustration of trying to manage disparate applications worldwide. The lack of disruption to the UK of a re-implementation with many less customisations is testament that customisations can be effectively restricted. The IT Manager made this final enlightening comment:

Builder isn't a company that is afraid to make big decisions, and their success is based on that they are not afraid to take on many things at once. What we are doing now has a huge scope; once it has been done I am sure there will be other things that they want to do.

4.6 Conclusion

This chapter has described the five case studies and drawn conclusions concerning the management and evaluation of ERP in each of the organisations. This analysis forms the first stage of the case analysis process. It has utilised and increased the constructs identified in chapter 2 as well as the research methodology explained in chapter 3.

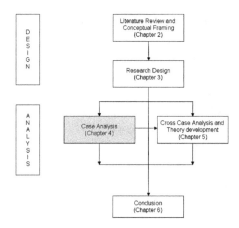

Figure 34.   Book design - chapter 4

The explanation in this chapter is used in the construct analysis and theory development presented in chapter 5. The chapter is summarised in chapter 6.

Chapter 5 - Cross Case Analysis and Theory Development

"The dialectical process is ... as follows: a concept is posited as a starting point. It is offered as a potential description of reality. It is found at once that, from the standpoint of logic, this concept must bring its own negation with it: to the concept, its negative is added automatically, and a 'struggle' ensues between the two. The struggle is resolved by an ascent to the higher plane from which it can be comprehended and reconciled: this ascent ... generates a new concept out of the ruins of the last. This new concept generates its own negation, and so the process continues, until, by successive applications of the dialectic, the whole of reality has been laid bare." Scruton(cited, Giddens, 1984, p.42)

This chapter anlyses the case studies against each of the constructs and proposes interpretations and findings for them. It builds on the last chapter's description of the cases and generates explanative meaning. The aim being to identify, as far as possible, within the theory "what is", "how", "why", "when", and "where" in line with the theory process identified by Gregor (2006). The chapter concludes by amalgamating the findings of the constructs, and from this crystallising key factors into a framework.

This is the final stage of the theory generating study that started with a question, acquired data, and establishes a theory (Punch 2002). The theoretical proposal provides explanations, but as Gregor (2006) explains, it does not aim to predict with any precision, and there are no testable propositions.

5.1 Original Implementation and Its Antecedents

This section of the book does not aim to understand in detail the factors that influenced the original implementation but to understand how the antecedents of the implementation impact the ongoing management of the application. This section first discusses the acquisition drivers in terms of the events that led to the decision to acquire the application. It then, briefly, looks at approaches to implementations and their drivers, and finally the antecedents of the implementations are discussed.

5.1.1 Acquisition Drivers

Server, Contractor and Builder acquired ERP applications because their existing applications had been heavily modified and, as a consequence, were difficult to upgrade. All three organisations had the option to upgrade the original applications but the cost and burden of doing so meant that a new system became a viable option.

Builder had used the J.D Edwards application in all of their worldwide locations but had implemented different processes, customisations and configurations in each one. The need for standardisation meant that the J.D. Edwards application had to be re-implemented throughout the world, prompting the decision to identify an application that best matched the current business requirements. Server was not able to upgrade the original application due to the large number of customisations. The application ultimately, according to the CEO, became 'antiquated', and had to be replaced. Initially, Contractor also heavily customised their application, but after changing the CIO, curtailed customisations and retrenched employees with application expertise. The application no longer supplies sufficiently detailed information to manage the organisation, and, partly due to the lack of expertise, the organisation is to install a new ERP.

Global used the Peoplesoft ERP in some of its sites, including the Australian region, but chose to implement a common ERP globally and replaced Peoplesoft with Oracle e-business suite. Oracle had also been used in some locations but, interestingly, was not the most prevalent application. The selection of the Oracle application was heavily influenced by the Software Author's willingness to work with Global to create a required maintenance module and its promise of being receptive to proposals to change the application to meet Global's business requirements. It is probable that a smaller organisation would not have been able to secure such guarantees.

Provider wanted to move away from bespoke software and used the implications of Y2K as the impetus for the implementation of SAP. SAP ERP was chosen as it was seen to have the most appropriate functions as well as strong consultancy support.

Provider identified that during the original implementation there was a lack of focus on cross modules processes; the IT manager describing the consultants as 'module jockeys'. El Amrani et al (2006, p.100), identified the importance of cross module processes, when, after undertaking both qualitative and quantitative research of ERP implementations, concluded that, "research indicates the importance of cross-functionality as an effect of ERP implementations", and only when it is understood will it "allow managers to more efficiently integrate business process and functions". Kuldeep & Van Hillegersberg (2000) found that consultants may not have enough knowledge to configure packages to organisations' needs. The module approach reinforces traditional hierarchical organisational structures and Davenport (1998, p.22) suggests that, if an organisation's systems are fragmented, then its business is fragmented. Which is the case with Provider as it has more than 300 legacy applications.

It seems that organisations need to make decisions concerning cross functional business processes pre-live. However, being able to make considered pre-live decisions is very difficult as an organisation may not have sufficient knowledge of the ERP. Pozzebon and Pinsonneult (2004) identify three levels of transfer of technical knowledge in ERP implementations. The lowest level has the consultant responsible for project results; the mid- level requires cooperation between consultants and client; and at the highest level, the client takes responsibility for the project. However, Pozzebon and Pinsonneult (2004) also identify training to be largely inadequate and propose that managers, even at a junior level, need to have systematic training on IT concepts and management. The training programs in the case studies were unanimously criticised. For the case examples it became clear that much more comprehensive training and education was required, it being insufficient to rely on the training by consultants which consists of parameterisation of modules. The lack of knowledge of organisation when implementing the applications is cause for concern and is addressed further in other sections of this chapter.

5.1.2 Implementation Topology

Markus et al (2000b) propose that large scale projects require a high level of organisational authority and broad organisational participation, citing ERP "studies have revealed that strategic and managerial benefits such as global consistency, efficient resource control, or improved decision making are planned or realized mostly by the central offices of international businesses" (Mitchell, 1999; Newing, 2000; Stahl, 2003 cited Shang, 2005, p. 2135). The two largest organisations Global and Builder are operating in an international markets, figure 35 shows diagrammatically that international organisations can have a global, international, transnational or multinational focus.

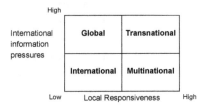

Figure 35.   Classification of international business operations (Clemmons & Simon, 2001, p
209)

The organisation types in the figure have the following characteristics:
- o   Global firms have a strong focus on seeking global efficiencies through consistent operations
and centralised world resource management.
- o   Multinationals have a strong national basis and concedes substantial autonomy to subsidiaries.
- o   Internationals have products derived from central customisations with local discretion for
customisation.
- o   Transnationals are seeking global efficiency and flexibility while promoting communication and
organisational learning among business units.

This implies that not all organisations have the same implementation focus. Different international
oraganisational structures are ideally reflected in different international IT operations and management
(Shang, 2005). Head office and local offices need to be aware of their affect on total business operations,
and the trade-offs necessary between global controls and local responses (Clemmons and Simon, 2001).
According to Ives & Jarvenpaa, (1991): centrally co-ordinated business structures should have globally
centralised IT and focus on cost advantage; multinational organisations should have IT that primarily
supports country requirements; transnationals should focus on worldwide integration of information and core
processes; whilst international organisations should have a federal approach to IT.   In the same vein,
Markus et al (2000b) identified five different types of multi-site organisational configurations requiring
different ERP topologies. They propose that geographically dispersed organisations could possibly have
unique, technical and managerial choices and challenges.   Davenport (1998) agrees, explaining that some
companies operate in regional markets so profoundly diverse that a different version of ERP needs to be
implemented in each region. He contends that the federal model is perhaps the most difficult requiring
decisions on what should be common and what should vary.

The topologies found at Global and Builder are different, but the difference is restricted to the dissemination
of the application servers. Global and Builder are both operating large scope, centralised global IT strategies
with the aim of standardising information, and have created central centres to control these global projects.
The implication of supporting theory is that the models implemented by Builder and Global will not
necessarily apply to other less centralised organisations. It is also concluded that the Builder and Global
centralised approach matches the proposal by Davenport (2004) that the fewer instances of ERP applications
in multi-national organisations, the better chance there is of integration. For the reasons explained above it is

difficult to generalise on the ERP topology needed to best operate an international organisation. However, it can be argued that organisations with centralised control and rigid management are more suited to ERP than those wishing for regional autonomy.

At Builder and Global senior management are dictating SBU processes so they are able to compare business performance. Boonstrap (2004) found that stakeholders might acquire ERP so that senior managers can regain lost power; this appears to be the case with Builder and Global. However, Lim et al (2004) warn that if users perceive an ERP implementation as a way for management to regain control of processes, and a weapon for disempowerment, this can result in what is referred to as 'effort-performance dissonance'. The unease of the users at Global is possibly a result of the unconsultative implementation and, the probably correct perception, that the central organisation wishes to regain control.

5.1.3 Implementation Antecedents

All of the companies experienced an initial period after the implementation of poor organisational performance. Markus et al (2000b) labelled this the "shakedown stage" and point out that a performance dip after initial implementation of an ERP system is very common.

All, except the Provider, ultimately viewed the implementations as a success. Interestingly, Provider did view the implementation as successful for a number of years. Newell et al (2007) when investigating process optimisation with ERP found organisations come to view ERP differently over time, and coined the phrase 'best for when'. Provider's implementation was viewed as a success as the system was implemented on time and to budget, and the proposed cost reductions sought were deemed to have been achieved. However, the 'rush to make the system live' meant that historical data concerning asset maintenance was not transferred and this oversight seriously hampered the ongoing maintenance of assets. The customisations made to the application have meant that Provider has not been able to functionally upgrade. Internal politics and a short implementation cycle have led to the Provider having more than 300 legacy applications, giving rise to a wish to 'start again' and reverse engineer the customisations. It seems that the decisions made early in an application's life have long term consequence and therefore, require much consideration of the potential impact.

Server has similar issues and, whilst it may currently have high user satisfaction, it has found that due to inconsistency of underlying information, and complexity of the application, the organisation is unable to provide the required management information. It has already ceased upgrades and will ultimately have to undergo a very expensive upgrade, or replace a heavily modified application when it becomes "antiquated".

In all instances the implementation procedures and ethos have continued throughout the applications' life. The organisations which commenced developing the applications continued to do so with what appears to be gusto. This is the case at Provider where customisation continues even though this practice has prevented functional upgrades for almost ten years. Provider now wishes to reverse engineer the application but continues to spend approximately $5m a year customising the application. This seems contradictory, but is perhaps what Johnson, Scholes and Whittington (2008) term path dependency, where organisations have difficulty changing or relinquishing base strategies.

Global and Builder are also consistent in their approach, with what is a second round of ERP implementations, having put in place firm controls to resist customisations during implementation, they have continued with these controls throughout the systems' life. Builder adopted this approach after experiencing the difficulties of managing a diverse, heavily customised ERP. The decision to strictly control customisation at Builder appears to be well received by management and operations personnel. At Global there has been much more disquiet.

The early customisation of ERP or other large scale IS is evidently a factor in the ultimate abandoning of an application. All the organisations ideally wish to have vanilla, upgradeable, applications but believe that a certain amount of customisation is necessary. The level of customisation varies, but obviously some organisations control customisations much more stringently than others, and with the exception of Server, subsequent implementations have tighter controls than earlier ones.

Brown and Vessey (2003) identified that the late majority implementing ERP can save time and costs by applying templates, and that organisations can benchmark success so avoiding some of the pitfalls of early adopters. The ERP implementations studied here, other than perhaps that of the Provider, can be described as late adopters; nevertheless, the organisations seem to be wrestling still with activities as if they were early adopters. It seems that the organisations, as well as the Software Authors, have not learnt from others' mistakes. However, Global and Builder demonstrate evidence of self-learning, deciding to implement new applications and alter their approach.

Tan and Pan (2002) produced a model of ERP success, shown in Figure 36, it is based on the IS success factors deduced by Delone and Mclean (1992).

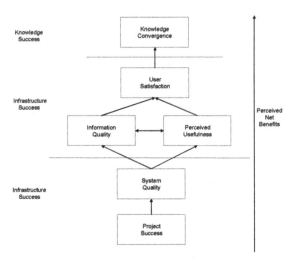

Figure 36.   Proposed ERP System Success Model (Tan & Pan, 2002, p.931).

Noteworthy are the distinct boxes for information quality and perceived usefulness. This research implies that information quality is achieved at the expense of perceived system usefulness. As it is apparent from this research that it is very difficult to have standardised, largely vanilla application with a high level of user satisfaction, and also that it is difficult to have ongoing customisation to improve user satisfaction along with standardised multi-site information.

5.1.4 Interpretation and Findings

This research indicates that the potential of the application is decided very early in the process, possibly as early as the strategic emphasis placed on the acquisition. The proposal here is that this is a major factor because the antecedents of the implementation are long lived and may well prevail throughout the life of the application. The fact that Provider, nearly 10 years after a poor implementation, is still trying to recover the situation, emphasises these long lived consequences. To overcome this an organisations needs to, as proposed by Willcocks and Sykes (2003), build in-house capabilities in the areas of IT leadership; including business systems thinking, relationship building, architecture planning, technology fixer, informed buyer, contract facilitation, contract monitoring and supplier development. This must be done as early as possible and pre-live. If this has not occurred pre-live, organisations need to focus on these competences and re-evaluate the ERP vis-à-vis business requirements and cost of ownership. Particularly regard to the length of time that they believe the application will last.

Chapter 5 - Cross Case Analysis and Theory Development

For the case examples the following are the primary interpretations and findings concerning the original implementation impacting ongoing management of ERP:

- o The functional processes implemented when the systems are first made live are long lived and therefore, critical
- o Customisations need to be controlled and should probably only be sanctioned where absolutely necessary
- o Centrally controlled international organisations are much more likely to have success from an ERP implementation than decentralised organisations
- o The organisations are not learning from others' implementation mistakes and are not following critical success factor guidelines

	Provider SAP	Server Dynamics (AX)	Contractor Dynamics (AX)	Global Oracle	Builder SAP
Original Implementation and Its Antecedents	- Main driver Y2K and desire to move away from bespoke software. - Chose the application by comparing functionality and processes. - Identified application cost and established a team to find the required savings: benefits were achieved. - Implementation poor due to extent of customisations and lack of focus on processes	- Main driver over modified out-of-date legacy application. - Cost of application identified from potential applications. -Benefits identified as personnel cost reduction and cost avoidance when growing. - Considerable post-live problems that lasted 7 months. - Viewed as a success. - Customisation of application seen as necessary.	- Main driver extensively modified legacy application. - Implementation justified against the information needs of each division. The division being sold subsequently may indicate an underlying reason. -Implementation considered a success - Business-wide implementation of application in near 'vanilla' form.	- Main driver global standardisation, replacing robust, recently acquired ERP in Australia. - System chosen from a short list of three vendors, the Author considered the most flexible. - Intention was for the application to be as vanilla as possible. - Local opinion is the system is not ideal constituting a backward move. The global perspective is very positive.	- Main driver standardised global processes, prior application being modified to sub-unit requirements. - System chosen for match with processes. - Organisation did not identify an overall cost but costs each implementation. - Thought of very favourably by users and management.

Table 8. Case findings on original Implementation and Its Antecedents

5.2 Impact of Strategy Process on ERP

I can say with some confidence that the companies deriving the greatest benefits from their systems are those that, from the start, viewed them primarily in strategic and organisational terms (Davenport 1998, p. 11)

ERP studies consistently argue that ERP projects should be business rather than technology driven and that an ERP requires alignment with a firm's source of competitive advantage if it is to yield positive strategic outcomes (Abdinnour-Helm & Lengnick-Hall, 2005). Parr and Shanks (2000 cited El Amrani et al, 2006) point out that, as the scope of the ERP modules implemented takes in most of the company's functions and departments, the ERP projects should automatically assume strategic importance.

The strategies in the three organisations Builder, Global and Provider are formally planned and disseminated: Builder recognised a market opportunity for best practice in the area of production and product delivery; Global, due to an increasingly global focus of its customers, required enterprise-wide sales and contractual information; and the Provider has a business strategy process which is communicated to business units, that in turn spurns IS projects' that are to be amalgamated into an 'IS strategy' by the IT department.

Server has a more informal strategy process which, nonetheless, identified that an ERP application could provide strategic advantage through increased customer satisfaction. The CEO had recognised a deficiency in the information capabilities of customers and chose to implement the system to provide customers with important installed product information with the aim of increasing sales. The Contractor has a formal strategy process that does not seem to be well disseminated in the organisation. The Contractor is proposing to focus on internal information needs, a large component being accurate tender information. It is also suspected that an ERP application was purchased so a division could be divested. All of the ERP initiatives studied can, therefore, be termed strategic.

Figure 37 shows a traditional SISP alignment model. IT, business environment and internal capabilities are examined in a similar manner to a SWOT analysis (Porter, 1980). From these a business strategy and an IT strategy are developed. The model then identifies that the applications become implemented and the process resumes with the new applications. This method presumes the traditional iterative approach to strategy.

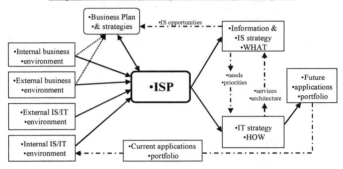

Figure 37. Planning process for a strategic information system (Burn, Marshall, & Barnett, 1999, p.82)

According to Hackney et al (2000) this type of SISP model is based on the following assumptions:

1. A business strategy exists
2. IS Strategy can be aligned with IT strategy
3. An IS strategy and business strategy are different
4. IT is a source of competitive advantage
5. Strategic information systems exist
6. Strategic applications of IT are planned formally
7. SISP encourages organisational integration
8. SISP works

Hackney et al (2000) further suggest that research proves that this is not likely to be the case. This formal process which is performed at intervals, is also not seen to be the process in the organisations researched. Abdinnour-Helm & Lengnick-Hall (2005) aver that the strategy discussion has moved on from an intent "to compete on the basis of cost leadership, differentiation, or innovation", and has expanded to "diversification, organisational-level strategic activities, expected financial concerns, core competence development, dynamics capabilities, and the nature of competition in an industry". The case study organisations function in dynamic, competitive and generally technology enabled industries and appear to operate much more according to the Abdinnour-Helm & Lengnick-Hall (2005) proposal.

Madapusi and D'Souza (2005) propose the following 5 components of ERP and strategic alignment.

Chapter 5 - Cross Case Analysis and Theory Development

1. Benefits accrue from a carefully configured system, well managed implementation and judicious use of the system
2. Ensure an integrative thinking approach pervades the organisation at strategic, tactical and operational levels
3. Build in sufficient flexibility that can adapt to the constantly evolving international strategy.
4. Champion the project with a senior executive.
5. Recruit and train strong employees.

The work of Madapusi and D'Souza (2005) is supported by observations of the case examples, however, much complexity exists beyond their assertions and these need to be resolved for organisations to be successful.

Markus, Tanis, & Van Fenema (2000) advise that for multi-site implementations, organisations should start planning at the strategic level before proceeding to technical and hardware levels. They conclude that, in practice, the scale of the task encourages organisations to tackle the layers independently thereby contributing to failure or partial successes. The two international organisations, Global and Builder, acquired their ERP applications as a direct strategic initiative to standardise processes and information globally. The strategies in the cases of Builder and Global appear to have been created in the manner advocated by Markus et al (2000a), in that business strategy is followed by software configuration, technical platform, and management execution. El Amrani et al (2006) state the definition of the desired organisational vision consists of clearly outlining the future organisation and the direction of people involved. Whilst this is true of the implementation at the Builder and to a lesser extent at Global, it is not the case at Provider and Server and may well account for the situation they find themselves in with regard to upgrades and extensive customisation of the application.

Builder and Global in their second wave of ERP implementations have much greater level senior management involvement. Ke, Wei, Chau & Deng, (2003, p.1124) assert that, "While important to get external knowledge from consultants, the involvement of senior and mid-level managers in the ERP implementation is critical for the organisation to strike a balance of adaption to and customisation of the ERP system." The numerous studies of the critical success factors relating ERP and senior management indicate support invariably to be the most important factor. Brown and Vessey (2003) identify the following five primary success factors:

1. Top management is engaged in the project, not just involved
2. Project leaders are veterans, and team members are decision makers

3. Third parties fill gaps in expertise and transfer their knowledge
4. Change management goes hand-in-hand with project management
5. A satisfying mindset prevails

Boonstrap (2004) found that in many cases stakeholder support was dominant early in a project, becoming dormant over time. This is not seen to be the case in secondary implementations, but it was apparent that senior management support of the replaced applications had waned. It seems that the organisations have now realised the importance of maintaining senior management involvement over an application's operational life.

5.2.1 Interpretation and Findings

It is obvious that all the ERP applications in the case study organisations were purchased for strategic reasons, and that all of the strategies that drove the initial ERP acquisition have endured for the life of the application. It seems that for the case examples the strategies behind ERP initiatives have remained quite constant, with changes to approach being at a tactical level. The acquisition of the software, being strategy driven, indicates that ERP is a strategic tool, however, the way it is subsequently envisaged suggests it can quickly become viewed as 'infrastructure' . This could be because it is relatively inflexible.

The length of time for which organisations maintained a strategic approach to the ERP application differed between the case organisations. Some organisations, such as Server, only maintain senior management focus during the requirement setting or the Markus and Tanis's (2000) 'chartering phase'. Others such as Builder and Global maintain the focus throughout the life of the application. It is telling that Builder and Global did not maintain senior management involvement with their previous applications, and this situation resulted in disparate implementations and problematic maintenance, the ultimate consequence being legacy applications for which the organisations must now maintain continuous senior management involvement. The link between strategy and application after acquisition appears to be more of a governance model, wherein the goals are set and the application is governed to meet those goals. Interestingly, the word 'governance' occurred only once in the interviews and that was by the worldwide coordinator of Builder.

The primary interpretations and findings, for the case examples, concerning the strategy process and its relationship to managing and evaluating ERP are as follow:

    o   Strategic objectives should be defined prior to implementation o Strategic objectives for ERP should create a vision of software and hardware topology prior to implementation

o Strategic ERP objectives appear to remain constant

o To achieve the relevant business outcomes, ERP applications require senior management support throughout their operational life

o ERP requires governance and alignment of incentives to provide business benefits

	Provider SAP	Server Dynamics (AX)	Contractor Dynamics (AX)	Global Oracle	Builder SAP
Impact of Strategy Process on ERP	- Robust formal business strategy process - Strategy driven internal requirements - IT strategy/plan derived from business unit requirements - IT capabilities not part of strategy formulation	- Informal business strategy process - Strategy driven by customer requirements - IT strategy/initiat ives coordinated at low level by users and Development. Manager - IT capabilities not part of strategy formulation	- Lightly formal strategy aided by infrequent external consultant guidance - Poor dissemination of strategy - Strategy driven by demand for growth - IT strategy by CIO's interpretation endorsed by external consultants - IT capabilities not part of strategy formulation	- Formal, well communicate d global strategy - Increasingly less autonomy for regions and countries - Globally centralised IT strategy, gate-keeping IT worldwide - Strategy driven by booming market - IT capabilities not part of strategy formulation but informed by strategy	- Formal centralised strategy extremely well communicate d - Countries have some autonomy but are benchmarked globally - Strategy driven by growth and best price product - Globally centralised IT strategy, gate-keeping IT worldwide - IT capabilities part of strategy formulation

Table 9.   Case study findings about Impact of Strategy Process on ERP construct

5.3   Financial Procedures and Imperatives

Builder, Global and Provider are all financially very strong and this has enabled significant investment in the ERP applications. These organisations appear to have sufficient funds to allow them to sanction any customisation activity, however, the activity is restricted by other impediments: Provider does not have sufficient staff and time; and Builder and Global restrict customisations from concern that they may impact upgrades and standardisation. The Server was not in a strong financial position when it acquired the ERP application but increased debt, even though already highly geared, to take advantage of what it saw as a strategic opportunity. The level of ongoing customisation activity at Server is limited by available funds. Contractor quite probably purchased the ERP so it could divest itself of a division to meet shareholder profit expectations.

The organisations generally find ways to capitalise customisation activity as depreciable fixed assets. This increase in capital is of no major consequence for organisations, such as the Provider, that have high fixed asset values. However, some organisations that have capitalised substantial customisations find that, at the time of a market downturn, the depreciation impacts profitability. Steep changes in technology can also mean the writing down of the asset value of IT. The Capitalising of customisations can then have a major impact on future profits and, in turn, shareholder returns. A good example is the case of the FedEx corporation between 2001 and 2003.

Server does not capitalise customisation activity as all customisations are performed in-house. This is perhaps a reason for the seeming lack of evaluation noticed in this organisation and discussed later.

In all cases, cost was isolated as the major factor in the upgrade decision. The strategies minimising customisations employed by Builder and Global have been put in place to minimise cost of ownership and enable upgrades. Provider and Server simply do not functionally upgrade due to the high cost.

The significant investment required in the ERP application precludes a decision to abandon. Gable et al (2003) found that "the substantial cost and complexity of ERP implementation, and the long implementation periods often needed, increase the costs of switching out of ERP, and reduce the likelihood that organisations will replace their ERP in short or even medium term" (p.82) and that is seen to be the case here.

5.3.1 Interpretation and Findings

It seems that the financial strength of an organisation impacts the potential options available to managers of ERP, and the financial procedures concerning the ability to capitalise customisations or not, seems to impact the evaluation process.

The following are the key findings for the case organisation of the financial procedures and imperatives construct.

- o   Financial strength may impact evaluation decisions, particularly ones concerning customisations
- o   The high cost of upgrades inhibits functional upgrade being undertaken
- o   The level of investment largely precludes abandoning an application

	Provider SAP	Server Dynamics (AX)	Contractor Dynamics (AX)	Global Oracle	Builder SAP
Financial Procedures and Imperatives	- Public company with large asset expenditure - Cash available for budgeted items - Major ongoing investment in ERP - Capitalises customisations -TCO is an increasing problem - Investment precludes change of application	- Highly geared - Limited cash - Internally maintained ERP, cost conscious approach - Customisations not capitalised - Financial position impacts upgrade and maintenance decisions. - Investment precludes change of application	- High growth with low profit - Limited cash - Limited investment in ERP, least cost approach - Capitalises customisations - Wishes to change ERP in the unimplemented divisions, cost being an issue	- Financially very sound - Application acquired at corporate level and allocated - Implementation costed regionally and accrued centrally - Cash rich - Direct ongoing investment in standardisation and upgrades - Capitalises customisations - Investment precludes change of application	- Financially very sound with robust long-term financial planning - Application acquired at corporate level and allocated - Implementation costed regionally and accrued centrally - Cash generative with acquisitions as priority - Major ongoing, strategically driven investment in ERP - Application changed if abs. necessary

Table 10.   Case study findings about Financial Procedures and Imperatives construct

5.4   Upgrades and Their Antecedents

Dowlatshahi (2005, p 3758) found that "the effectiveness of an ERP system design and implementation in the long run is affected by the company's ability to perform the required ERP system maintenance". However, Markus et al (2000a) identified that upgrades are very difficult after making customisations. The organisations they researched lamented the customisations and 'vowed never to modify ERP again'. They decided that most organisations do not upgrade and as a result have legacy systems. Markus and Tanis (2000) concluded it might be more costly to update a poorly documented ERP than a comparable legacy system because the requisite knowledge lies outside the organisation. There can be little doubt from the case organisations as to the relationship between the complexity of upgrades and the level of customisation; even with minimal customisations, as was the case with Global, upgrades are seen as expensive.

Fub et al (2007) found from their studies, citing others by Davenport (2000) and Shang and Seddon (2002), that authors assert pressure to upgrade. For the case examples this was evidenced for both SAP and Oracle; SAP increase upgrade costs for older versions and Oracle restrict support for older versions. These are major factors for organisations undertaking 'technical' upgrades. For the case examples it was evident that these expensive upgrades have little or no functional and organisational benefits and largely just provide an organisation with a later version number and a guarantee of continued support. Upgrades then become a potential risk for the Software Authors as the cost and complexity of 'functional' upgrades has prompted four of the case organisations to replace their systems with the existing applications. A Software Author that could produce a robust product, that was easy to maintain and had a low cost of ownership, would seem to have an opportunity for competitive advantage.

Builder's approach of releasing customisations only when upgrading, is extremely interesting, in that this is obviously similar to how Software Authors release application enhancements. They also have interim releases of service packs to overcome problems between releases. This process is also common practice with engineering software and seems to be a mature approach. If the other organisations did the same, they would be able to upgrade and thoroughly test customisations. Of course the Server would not be able to use its current practice of making customisation while talking to users on the telephone and it might well find this to be a blessing.

5.4.1 Interpretation and Findings

It is apparent from the case organisations that the ability to upgrade is hampered by customisations to the ERP application. The consequence is that the annual maintenance agreements are providing little benefit and that ultimately the inability to upgrade may result in the ERP application's abandonment.

The following are the key findings from the case organisations concerning upgrades and their antecedents:

- o   Functional upgrades are prohibitively expensive
- o   Upgrades may not provide significant business benefits
- o   Customisations render upgrades difficult and perhaps impossible
- o   Authors assert pressure to upgrade by escalating upgrade costs and/or withdrawing support
- o   Maintenance charges may not provide tangible benefits

	Provider SAP	Server Dynamics (AX)	Contractor Dynamics (AX)	Global Oracle	Builder SAP
Upgrades and Their Antecedents	- Managed only 'technical' non-functional upgrades, individual cost being 7.5% of original implementation. - Functional upgrade too expensive due to customisations, and time consuming - Upgrade desired to reverse engineering customisations - Author increases maintenance costs if application not upgraded - Missing functional opportunities through not upgrading	- Cost of upgrades seen as far too expensive - Difficult to upgrade due to customisations overlapping with new functionality - Maintenance ceased and upgrades not taken thus resulting in ERP legacy - Very old applications are not supported by Author - Problem overcome by chasing sunk cost of maintenance agreement and ceasing agreement	- Changing application due to cost of upgrades to develop existing application - Upgrade of old system prevented by excessive cost - Very old applications not supported by Author - Wants to upgrade new system regularly and minimise customisations	Upgrades occur frequently to ensure the system is standardised globally and to get Oracle support - Upgrades are viewed as expensive - Low local benefit indicates a cost benefit analysis desirable prior to deciding to upgrade - Support withdrawn if application is not upgraded to current version - Customisations restricted to enable upgrades	- High cost to upgrade previous ERP prompted acquisition of new ERP - Planned to upgrade bi-annually, release customisations, and have improved processes following upgrades Author to increase maintenance costs if application not upgraded - Customisations minimised to enable upgrades and standard processes

Table 11.   Case study findings on Upgrades and Their Antecedents construct

5.5   Perception of IS

The perception of ERP benefits by the management group was seen in all cases, except the Provider, to be positive. The users' opinions of systems differed between organisations, with Global and Builder particularly having relatively low user satisfaction. Surprisingly the expectation levels by IS personnel seems to be very low and they demonstrate a startling lack of optimism: as indicated by comments such as 'we weren't expecting much", and, we knew that they would "bake and switch" causing problems.

Sedera, Gable, & Chan (2004) identified three ERP stakeholder groups; technical, operational and strategic. They found that these groups were often not agreed in their opinions of ERP. Primarily, they postulated that technical groups tend to emphasise systems quality and strategic groups' look more at holistic organisational impacts. Ifinedo & Nahar (2007) also found that system users and management do not share a coherent vision of ERP systems. Interestingly, Kirsch (2004) decided that sense making of ERP projects changed over time. At the initial stage, sense making was created by both management and technical staff, and during the customisation and ongoing activity by IS managers. These findings preclude generalisation of the perspectives of IT operational and managerial personnel, but further confirms that the perceptions of management, operations and IT personnel are likely to vary. As was seen to be the case in the studied organisations, particularly management and user opinion appears to differ. It was also interesting at Provide that infrequent and frequent users opinion differed.

A contrast on how the application is perceived by users is demonstrated by Global and Builder. The Global project is seen as remote from the region and something that has been imposed upon the organisations; while at Builder, the application is thought of in positive terms, even though it is less user friendly than the previous implementation. This is possibly because of the different strategies employed. The Builder implementation was seen as part of a business initiative to transform the organisation and not an IT project. Builder underwent a process change prior to the implementation whereby the users were forced to work around the original implementation. Additionally, the CEO is seen as very powerful and a champion of the ERP implementation. Amoako-Gyampah (2004, p.180) points out that "it is the shared sense of beliefs regarding IS project benefits that allows organisational participants to find common ground and a shared sense of purpose ... this leads to implementation success". If large gaps exist between managers and end-users, and appropriate steps of reconciliation are not taken, this may lead to implementation failure (Al-Mashari & Zairi, 2000). The Global implementation was also sanctioned by central senior management but the benefits were perhaps not communicated as well and this perhaps contributes to the poor user satisfaction. The manner in which a project is championed, and congruence of stakeholders' views, appears to have long-term impact on perceptions of the application.

5.5.1 Findings and Interpretations

It is apparent that there are a number of stakeholders in an ERP implementation, they have been defined as managers, operation personnel and technical personnel, and these groups may have differing perceptions and opinions concerning the application. Although, all groups seem to agree that ERP is necessary. It is interesting that satisfying one group may in turn cause dissatisfaction for another.

For the case organisations the key findings concerning perception are as follows:

- o The ERP application is perceived as necessary in all organisations
- o The perceptions of ERP may not be consistent between management, operations and technical personnel
- o Technical and operations staff seem to have a lower expectation of ERP than managers
- o Frequent and infrequent users may have different opinions

	Provider SAP	Server Dynamics (AX)	Contractor Dynamics (AX)	Global Oracle	Builder SAP
Perception of IS	- Perspective of ERP not consistent - Management view is 'neutral'; users of the application regularly are happy; infrequent users are less satisfied - Complexity of product blamed for poor acceptance - Perception changing to wanting a vanilla application	- Perception of ERP seen as positive at all levels - Organisation fundamentally relies on ERP	- ERP critical to organisation success - ERP perceived as being sub-optimised	- IS in general is not seen as "core business" - ERP implementation impact is negative on users; and positive on managers. - ERP technology considered to be out of date by IT personnel	- IS is fundamental to business - Users perceive ERP to be inferior to previous implementation - Management acknowledge advantage of standard global application - IT personnel thought the implementation, being business led, was good

Table 12. Case study findings about the Perception of IS construct

5.6 Re-implementations

Wei, Wang, & Ju (2005) consider that misalignment in the Markus and Tannis (2000) onward and upward stage is due to new business requirements not matching an implemented ERP and its underlying information. It would seems appropriate, therefore, for modules to be re-implemented to meet business changes. However, only the Provider has re-implemented a part of the application; Provider re-implemented the finance module due to changes in reporting requirements. The lack of partial re-implementations is seen to be partly due to the seemingly consistent strategies, and also, particularly with the case of Provider, the cost of re-implementing.

Nonetheless, Global and Builder have totally re-implemented or replaced their ERP applications to better control and standardise the organisations' processes and to better monitor organisational performance. This approach to ERP is endorsed by Gossain (2004) who suggests that ERP can become a carrier of institutional logic. Gosain implies further that individuals embedded in an actor network find it difficult to use technology differently to the ways others expect; and that ERP produce greater stability in work practice. He also adds that over time users become institutionalised possibly stifling an organisation. Additionally, he thinks that, in the Markus and Tanis (2000) stages of shakedown, and onwards and upwards, users operate under constrained enactment, whereby the organisation is constrained, and the cognitive processes of members is shaped. Which seems to be the case at both Global and Builder. ERP seems to be ideal for organisations such as these that wish for a high level of control. As was seen in Chapter 2 they may well be less suited to decentralised organisations.

5.6.1 Findings and Interpretations

The implementations studied here are not mature enough to identify whether or not these systems ultimately become constraints on the organisations, but certainly Builder does not expect this to be the case. However, if nothing else, this principle of conveying institutional logic is likely to impact upon objective evaluation of a module by operations personnel.

The following are key findings concerning re-implementation.

- o Partial re-implementation is often desired but seldom undertaken due to disruption and cost.
- o Total re-implementation of ERP or purchase of ERP may be carried out to standardise processes.
- o Institutional logic imposed by an ERP may impact objective evaluation and restrict partial re-implementations.

	Provider SAP	Server Dynamics (AX)	Contractor Dynamics (AX)	Global Oracle	Builder SAP
Re-implementations	- Re-implemented finance to meet changing requirements - Poor implementation blamed on consultants - Implementation is seen to be 'stifling' the business - Plan to re-implement when upgrading	- System setup not seen to be optimal - Consultants advice only an opinion - Will not re-implement to overcome problems	- Cannot re-implement due to reliance on customisations and unsupported application	- Standard system with considered and minimal customisations, so reimplementation will not ever be necessary	- Unsuccessful attempt to re-implement previous ERP to common processes - Implementing SAP so organisations have standard processes

Table 13. Case study findings regarding the re-implementations construct.

5.7 Influences and Consequence of Software Authors and Resellers

All of the companies thought that acquiring an ERP from one of the larger Software Authors was beneficial to the longevity of the application. The two largest case organisation only saw a choice between the two Software Authors SAP and Oracle. The global presence and financial strength of the Software Author is therefore, seen as being a major contributor to ERP selection. It was apparent that all of the organisations thought the author held most of the 'power' in the relationship. Only Global had a strong ongoing relationship with the author, the other organisations not being thought to have any direct relationship.

IS staff seem to have a low opinion of ERP. Both the Provider and Server identified consultancy advice as simply a matter of opinion and not necessarily correct. Banker and Slaughter (2000, p.12) believe that "software engineers do a relatively poor job of making design decisions that have long-range consequences for maintenance". Two reasons for this are given: "cognitive constraints limit the ability of decision makers to consider complicated long-term implications"; and the presence of "inappropriate incentives". Markus et al (2000b) found that, "despite representations during the sales cycle there was widespread lack of knowledge about the details of ERP products.

This is compounded by poor training by Authors and VARs. In all cases the training was deemed inadequate. Training concerned discrete functions, rather than processes, with users finding it hard to appreciate the implications of what they were being trained to do. Research by Chan and Reich (1998, cited Bassellier et al, 2003) found that most companies focus on narrow software-related training, and do not teach more conceptual topics. Lorenzo and Kawalek (2005) also found initial user training to be very poor and part of the "race of going live". As a consequence, the organisation studied by Lorenzo and Kawalek, subsequently introduced a more structured and broad user training with an initial stage of conceptual understanding. This resulted in much better results and higher user satisfaction.

Dowlatshahi (2005, p. 3754) through grounded research into ERP implementation made the following proposition: "organisations must make every attempt to adequately train all ERP users as ERP training can be the most important element in the successful implementation of ERP". Bhattacherjee and Premkumar (2004) point out that Software Authors would be better served if they devoted more resources to creating a positive user experience by investing in user training rather than artificially inflating user expectations. There were often contractual conflicts on pricing and billing arrangements in the case organisations and these disputes may also be reduced with broader education.

The need to improve education was highlighted by Holland and Light (2001), they consider ERP to mature through three levels of post-live maturity of knowledge. They suggest that "after user managers have learnt more about what the software can do, for example, after a year or so, they are often in a much better position to specify what they want to achieve with their software"(p.4). Somers, Nelson, & Ragowsky, (2003), also believe that ERP benefits, due to the learning curve of an ERP, may only be achievable when the implementations are mature applications. Davenport and Brooks (2004, p.18) make the observation that "when it comes to an ES [ERP], too many firms stop short", stating, " ... research reveals that substantial benefits are realised only when an organisation creatively takes the raw components, claims them as its own and directs them to meet its unique business vision". The importance for the system is that ERP itself performs well, "not only in the matters of accuracy, reliability and response time, but how well people in organisation know how to use, maintain and upgrade the ERP systems, and how well the business improves its performance with the ERP system" (Markus et al 2000b, p.246). Better and broader training would accelerate the learning and in-turn improve outcomes. It seems reasonable to conclude that excellent pre-live education would alleviate many of the implementation issues cited in thisbook.

The notion of inbuilt best practice was seen by the case organisations and particularly Global to be a misnomer. The modules and functions seem to be developed to an organisation's requirements and simply marketed as best practice. Kelly, Holland, and Light (1999) also found when conducting case study research that customisations made by organisation were regularly included in the core package. Similarly, Newell, Wagner, and David (2007) researched ERP "best practice" at a furniture manufacturer, the organisation being informed initially that the ERP contained best practice for the organisation. When the organisation pointed out that the process requirements were not being met, the ERP author agreed to develop the application to meet the organisations needs. This they did, duly releasing the application as "best practice" for furniture manufacturers.

Best practice is defined by Dictionary.com(2007) as: a practice which is most appropriate under the circumstances, esp. as considered acceptable or regulated in business; a technique or methodology that, through experience and research, has reliably led to a desired or optimum result. Wagner and Newell (2004) propose that 'best practice' models will be problematic as, by definition, they mandate one epistemological position. They argue that, "in a context where you have diverse user groups, with different work practices and epistemic cultures and with different levels of background experience, a single industry solution is not going to be 'best' from all perspectives"(p.325). They cite an ERP being developed for a university and being sold as best practice on the vendor's web site, even while the vendor was still rapidly customising the technology to meet the university's specific requirements.

Newell et al (2007) are also sceptical that an ERP process is 'best practice' for organisations in different contexts. They conclude that, "while an organisation is thus supposedly implementing best practice when implementing an ES, in reality, an ES implementation is oriented around a set of idealized business processes that often bear very little resemblance to actual day-to-day practice and indeed may inhibit effective practice by oversubscribing what and how work is done" (p.172). Kuldeep and Van Hillegersberg (2000, p.2) identify, "there can be considerable mismatches between actual country, industry and company-specific business practices and the reference models embedded in the ERP systems. While at the abstract level the idea of "universal" best practice may be seductive, at the detailed process level these mismatches create considerable implementation and adaptation problems." Light and Wills (2001) also suggest that the proposed "best practice" models may well not represent best practice for an organisation and will require changing the application.

The notion of best practice seems to be largely a matter of 'first' practice where modules are developed to the needs of an organisation, albeit perhaps a mature organisation, and then sold as best practice. It is not surprising that a vendor seeks best practice from a customer, as a Software Author can not possibly define best practice for all the industries that a product might be sold into. For how could they possibly derive the knowledge? They appear to take a 'practice' and in some cases sanitise it and present it as best practice.

Another potential problem is that Authors constantly add to the functionality, possibly to justify maintenance agreements, and as a result the software becomes increasingly cumbersome, and possibly idiosyncratic. Software Authors should perhaps take note that the organisations studied here, in the main, want to maintain upgrades to keep abreast of technological developments rather than increases in functionality.

5.7.1 Findings and Interpretations

The best practice models proposed by ERP vendors appear to be just 'a' practice. The claim that the processes are best practice seems to create unreasonable expectations for the application and focus an implementation on the application rather than business objectives. The poor training in terms of content and timing further impacts the potential for an optimal implementation.

For the case examples the key findings concerning Software Authors and VARs are:

o   A large financially stable Software Author is an acquisition incentive
o   Software Authors are seen as remote and difficult to influence
o   User training concentrates on discreet functions and this is insufficient for managers and users to conceptualise the application
o   Best practice is a misnomer and is generally "first" practice
o   Upgrades are mainly required for future proofing and not increases in functionality

	Provider SAP	Server Dynamics (AX)	Contractor Dynamics (AX)	Global Oracle	Builder SAP
Influences and Consequence of Software Authors and Resellers	- Author needs to be well respected global org. - Author exerts pressure to upgrade through increasing maintenance costs - 20% cost of application p.a. is seen as a maximum maintenance cost - Consultancy seen as poor - Adding modules increases the maintenance cost and is, therefore, avoided - Training is poor and teaches functions rather than functionality and a process view. - Software Author seen as remote.	- Author needs to be financial strong and viable in the long-term - Support by VAR seen as poor - The author is seen as too distant from the relationship. - The resellers perceived poor performance is impacting Microsoft's image.	-See 'partnering' software author as imperative in delivery of IT - Found with ERP systems that organisational size means that partnering with large ERP author is not possible	- Author flexibility, global footprint, and help with maintenance module pivotal to decision to use software - Oracle asserts pressure to upgrade through withdrawing support	- Global capability of SA important - Technological know how' seen as an advantage - Author increases application cost - Author remote from the implementation

Table 14.   Influences and consequence of software authors and resellers construct case study findings

5.8   Environmental Influences

The industry norms and media do not seem to have an obvious direct influence on acquisition or management of ERP. For example, the CIO of Contractor mentioned recent newspaper reports that discussed a high profile, failed SAP implementation as having no consequence upon the choice of application. This seems somewhat surprising as a $25m investment was to be made and it would seem prudent to at least understand the issues.

The customer seems to be the most powerful external influence and is the major driver for the application in the case of Builder, Global and Server. The Builder application also had to integrate with suppliers but this was not seen as a key factor. It was seen by all the studied organisations that the application should be able to integrate with business partners' applications, but not that the applications needed to be the same as that of a business partner.

5.8.1 Findings and Interpretations

Environmental factors other than customers have surprisingly little impact on the ongoing decision process for ERP. It seems that organisations are largely parochial in their approach to ERP management.

Key findings for the case organisations of environmental influences are as follows:

- o   Customer and, to lesser extent suppliers, influence the technical capability of an ERP but not the actual ERP application
- o   The wider external business environment does not seem to impact the choice of ERP

	Provider SAP	Server Dynamics (AX)	Contractor Dynamics (AX)	Global Oracle	Builder SAP
Environmental Influences	- No apparent power asserted on ERP management and evaluation from external sources	- Specialised industry requires software to be developed - Customer requirements continually impact ERP customisation decisions	- Believe that Australia follows US with regard to IT - Integration with partners seen as important function for ERP - Press information of failed ERP did not cause concern that the product would not be implemented successfully	- Customers were the main driver for commonality - It is not necessary to have the same ERP as partners	- Customers and supplier requirements important in evaluating ERP functions - Transmitting documents via EDI was seen as beneficial

Table 15. Case study findings on the environment influences construct

5.9 Evaluation Procedures

Researcher : "You have mentioned that there are many benefits to common processes but could you please just explain the benefits and whether they are tangible and intangible."

Worldwide coordinator, Builder: " Well, not without inventing"

In all of the cases the budget for the application was established by identifying the cost of possible ERP solutions, rather than a budget being established by an assessment of potential benefits and identification of expenditure commensurate with those benefits. The fit between an ERP package and an organisation's needs was also found by Van Everdingen et al (2000, cited Roseman et al 2004) to be by far the most important criterion when selecting a package and this is seen to be the case here.

The ongoing evaluation processes differs greatly in the case organisations; Server has little or no evaluation process; Contractor has an approval process that does not include financial evaluation; The Provider has numerous processes that appear rigorous, but, the management believed too many ways exist to circumvent the process, and that these render evaluation ineffective; Global have a rigid worldwide process for evaluation, which is aimed at minimising customisations. The decision to sanction a customisation proposal may take up to three years; Builder has what appears a very solid procedure, which is ultimately by a process manager who gate keeps customisations to the process, the intention being to minimise SBU variance.

At the organisations the cost of ERP initiatives is generally policed, whilst benefits are not. Formal benefit analysis, except at Provider, of the acquisition and other initiatives is not undertaken and benefits are largely thought to be impossible to ascertain. The reason is primarily because post implementation benefits are seen to be difficult to attribute directly to a software application. Many of the approaches expounded in IS theory are not used and even the finance personnel paid little attention to NPV and other cost benefit measures. This is consistent with a number of recent studies of ERP. For example, Ashurst and Doherty (2003, pp.3-7), when planning their research, suggested that benefits realisation had three sub-categories: benefits planning, benefits delivery and benefits review. Benefits review was seen to be "an ideal opportunity for organisational learning". While conducting their research they observed the benefits delivery had been focused on technology delivery, there was an absence of focus on organisational benefits. This led them to conclude there to be "insufficient evidence to assess their [ERP] success in benefits terms".

Gunaskekaran et al (2004 cited Esteves, 2005) also found that returned benefits from ERP applications have proved elusive or, at the least, difficult to quantify. Abdinnour-Helm and Lengnick-Hall (2005) found that, if an ERP only rearranges tasks and changes procedures it is unlikely to provide benefits. The perception, according to them, is that ERP provides more benefits to coordination and control processes and less to value creation such as measuring organisational performance and quality assurance. They argue that long-term competitive value from ERP comes from its ability to generate knowledge that a firm can build on. Helpfully, Davenport et al (2004, p.24) suggest that organisations should have a "bifocal" approach to benefits, focusing on short-term cost reduction benefits and long-term competitive benefits. They suggest that "leading organisations will prioritise their benefits and corresponding plans for action to achieve what is most important to them". This is echoed by Parker et al (1988 cited Ndede-Amadi 2004), who explain that an ERP application links to one of two conditions: either it improves the performance of the current organisation; or it improves the outlook for new business opportunities and strategies of the enterprise.

Markus et al (2000b, p.263) found that most organisations did not know if they had achieved benefits; and that many had not prepared business cases to justify ERP in terms of business benefits. They claim that "the lesson is clear: ERP benefits are not automatic. They require human and organisational learning, both of which take time and require focused management attention". Interestingly, they argue for benefits to be measured and someone to be held accountable. Markus et al (2000b) list three items for measuring success of an ERP in the onward and upward phase:

1. Achievement of business results expected for the ERP project, such as reduced IT operating costs and reduced inventory carrying costs.
2. Ongoing improvements in business results after expected results have been achieved
3. Ease in adopting new ERP releases, other new ITs, improved business practices, improved decision making, etc. after the ERP system has achieved stable operations.

Markus & Tanis (2000) explain that the onward and upward stage is difficult to measure formally, but that one possible measure is that of the competence of the IT specialist.

This research questions a dogged approach to cost /benefits analysis. The traditional cost benefits would seem to have a places for assessing automation of activities, but assessing for other less tangible items the time spent appears to outweigh the value of the process. The Global CIO stated "why bother looking?', and the Worldwide Co-ordinator for Builder, when asked if he could identify tangible or intangible benefits, replied, "Well, not without inventing". Ashurst & Doherty (2003) also found that in reality little emphasis was placed on benefit reviews. The benefits may well be impossible to quantify and even the intangibles may arguably be provided by another initiative rather than the ERP. The luminaries, Remenyi and Bannister(2007), along with Money (2007) proposed the following:

> *All formal methodologies and combinations of methodologies bump up against the limits*
> *of physical representations by numbers, two-dimensional diagrams, and the boundaries*
> *of modelling human reason using such tools. It may be that the closest that it is possible*
> *to get to actual workings of the managerial mind in complex situations is to use such*
> *tools as Likert scales, cognitive maps and spider charts. They may be two dimensional,*
> *but at least they are not trapped in the linear world of many other evaluation models*
> *(p.52).*

Gunasekaran, Love, Ahim and Miele(2001) found that organisation are less likely to use traditional tangible methods and are turning to the relationship with strategic, tactical and operational initiatives. Oliver and Romm (2002) contend the greater the expense and strategic importance of an IS, the weaker the role of formal evaluation methods. Jones and Hughes (2001) summarising this change as "IS practitioners and IS Stakeholders in the case study are not concerned with the specifics of IS assessment metrics, detailed benefit measurement formulae, evaluation concepts or cost benefit justification techniques as asserted by traditional positivist approach. They are concern with the success, operation and effectiveness of IS in practice" (p.1999).

Apparently, the prescriptive approach to benefits formerly dominant in IS is now less applicable. Remenyi et al (2007, p.52) explain that "any decision is influenced by a range of factors, some rational, some non-rational, some explicit, others implicit", asserting decisions should take "account of how the world really is rather than simply what the spreadsheet says". They propose that management decisions have the factors Figure 38 depicts: .

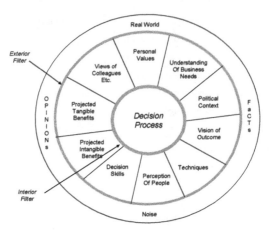

Figure 38.   Decision process model (Remenyi et al, 2007, p. 15)

It seems reasonable that an organisation having sufficient input from senior management, should be empowered to make decisions of the merits of process changes, customisations and upgrades using all of the aspects described by the model of Remenyi et al (2007). It has been accepted that the acquisition may not have a detailed capital expenditure request with a costs benefit analysis and NPV, but it will have an objective. The most crucial aspect of ERP management seems to be identifying and communicating business objectives, and ensuring the personnel responsible for the ERP have the ability and funds commensurate to those objectives.

5.9.1 Findings and Interpretations

The process of evaluation should probably be derived from the strategic driver, if the strategic objective is primarily for cost savings, benefits should reasonably be sought. But if the objective is for less tangible advantage, the search, by definition, may be impossible or at least esoteric. The proposal by Markis and Tanis (2000) that a potential measure of possible benefit could be based on the quality of the ERP specialists involved, this quality should in turn, provide for system and information quality. This would support the model of Delone and McLean (2003).

The key findings covering the evaluation process include:

- o Cost are well understood for ERP initiatives
- o Evaluation is often used to control ERP scope rather than improve financial returns

o   Benefits are difficult to identify and quantify

o   Tangible benefits may be ascertained for discrete and short term gains such as inventory levels

o   Longer term benefits are deliverable from organisational specific information and these are perhaps best evaluated and maintained through identifying, understanding and developing the knowledge of the people managing the application and business functions

	Provider SAP	Server Dynamics (AX)	Contractor Dynamics(AX)	Global Oracle	Builder SAP
Evaluation **Procedures**	- Tangible evaluation of projects over $50,000 with NPV hurdle rate - Below $50,000 just risk assessment - IT budget increased as business cases are approved - Strategic projects meeting strategic objectives of business units are generally approved - Upgrades to hardware and software have highest priority - Tangible benefits considered to be difficult or impossible to identify - Payback projects ranked lowest; business as usual for ranked highest - No calculation for cost of ownership	- Cost rigorously policed - No formal evaluation of application benefits - No sign off of customisations, the 'person who screams the loudest' is addressed first - No standard capital expenditure request	- External review by consultants identified focus of IS - System to support growth - Benefits not quantified - Cost analysis are undertaken - No standard capital expenditure request - CIO puts expenditure proposals linked to the 'strategy document' on CFO desk for automatic signature.	- No tangible or intangible benefits appraisal - Cost negotiated globally - Implementations costed individually - Benefits difficult to identify - Seeking benefits is not considered worthwhile considering time and effort spent	- Created business case with organisational cost savings as basis for IT application - Benefits give largely intangible strategic advantage - Not possible to identify tangible benefits - High level budget becomes detailed on country implementation

Table 16. Case study findings on the evaluation procedures construct.

5.10 Approach to Customisations

There is bound to be an imperfect fit between ERP application and organisation (Rosemann et al, 2004) as it cannot possibly meet all company functionalities, or all specific business requirements, and, therefore, must be adapted (Gattiker & Goodhue, 2005). Markus et al (2000b) explain that organisations know that they are meant to adapt their processes to an application but find it impossible and result to customisations. Klaus et al (2000) go so far as to say that the rich potential for customisation is ERPs distinguishing feature.

Customisations are seen here to be a major enabler of, and restriction to, ERP benefits. Amoako-Gyampah (2004, p.179) observed that "ERP systems are very expensive and, therefore, the decision to adopt these technologies is very likely to come from senior managers". However, as noted by Keen and Digrius (2003), the requirements for customisations are likely to 'bubble-up' from the low level of the organisation: and both of these macro and micro influences have been observed during this investigation. This implies a divergence between acquisition objectives and the ongoing processes. The Contractor case indicates that responding to users, even with evaluation procedures, can lead to almost perpetual customisation activity throughout the life of an ERP. The data collected for this research implies that optimising an application for users significantly increases cost of ownership and jeopardises upgrading. This is confirmed by Light and Wills (2001) who point out, customising ERP source code recreates the problems of legacy applications and may compromise the advantages of ERP.

According to Kelly et al (1999), ERP systems have driven systems customisation to a new phase of maturity, one that has a radically different approach to traditional systems customisation. They explain that the focus of the customisation process shifts from writing software to understanding business process, and that while design skills are still required, there exists a greater need for business content. Soh & Sia (2005) sought to understand the issues behind a decision to identify what to change in an ERP. Breaking the organisational processes down to imposed structures and voluntary structures, they defined imposed structures as those arriving from country and industry regulations, practices and norms; and voluntary structures are those stemming from management decisions based on experience and preferences.

They identify that more necessary voluntary structures arise from:
- Products and services being developed for specific strategic positioning, e.g., niche market segment, cost efficiency focus, or customer intimacy;
- Internal routines being used to create/deliver products and services, e.g., tightly coordinated supply chain, superior customer service;

- o The need for complex and/or flexible pricing, e.g., package pricing; and
- o Internal routines being used to manage strategic resources, e.g., innovative HR schemes.

The less necessary voluntary structures are:
- o User preferences being for ease of use, interface content, and presentation;
- o User preference being for report content and presentation; and
- o User risk tolerance as reflected in control routines or user access.

The approach of resisting customisations by Global and Builder very much restricts the customisation to these less 'necessary' structures. The other organisations appear not to make a distinction concerning necessity.

Banker and Slaughter (2000) said that customisations to areas supporting planning, forecasting and management decision making are considerably more complex and volatile than those that support operational and transactional processing, adding, the more volatile and complex the software; the more structured the approach should be. They concluded that with low complexity and volatility, a less structured approach may be appropriate, but they would never 'advocate ad hoc customisation of software'. Therefore, to invest all customisation with the same level of complexity is probably incorrect, not only in terms of the activity itself, but the potential TCO. The Builder recognised this by restricting customisations to core transactions and adding screen changes to additional tabs. The other case organisations appear not to recognise levels of complexity, particularly in terms of ongoing support and upgrade costs.

Markus et al (2000b) found that during projects many of the customisations made to consultants' recommendations are later found to be unnecessary as the application becomes better understood. Evidence of this fact was noticed at both Provider and Contractor. This poor advice creates a major issue for the ongoing management of the ERP application.

Interestingly, one of the most cited benefit was that the application could be upgraded, and in turn, these expensive applications can be justified because of their longevity. However, for that benefit to be realisable, it is imperative to control the customisations so as to ensure the applications can be configured into future releases. The organisations having ERP the longest, Global, Builder and Provider have recognised this to be the case and have altered, or are altering, their management processes accordingly.

5.10.1 Findings and Interpretations

Customisations of ERP are necessary, and create an overhead for organisations in terms of cost of ownership and ability to upgrade. Customisations must be carefully considered before being made and perhaps only implemented if they are identified as operationally absolutely necessary or strategically imperative.

The following are the key findings for the case organisations concerning customisation of ERP:

- o It is necessary to customise ERP applications
- o Customisations significantly increase cost of ownership
- o As customisations increase, cost of ownership may increase disproportionally
- o Not all aspects of the system have the same complexity, thus cost of ownership varies due to the difficulty in reapplying the customisations to future releases and the likelihood of the underlying function altering
- o A decision on the approach to sanctioning customisations should be made early in the implementation project
- o Organisations come to realise that customisations are problematic only over time
- o The high cost of reapplying customisations prohibits upgrades

	Provider SAP	Server Dynamics (AX)	Contractor Dynamics (AX)	Global Oracle	Builder SAP
Approach to Customisations	- High level of ongoing customisations - Originate at departmental level and below - Differing evaluation techniques based on cost and strategic factors - Respond to "a lot of noise", they does not actually need to be addressed - Find some customisation proposed in implementation unnecessary - Cost of ownership and increasing issue	- System heavily modified and costly to upgrade - Make immediate customisations to system - Find some customisation proposed in implementation unnecessary - Evaluation not imposed	-Original system highly developed - Embargo on any customisations to old system - Customisations to new ERP will be minimised - Evaluation of customisations informal - Recognise customisations are necessary	- Customisations tightly controlled and heavily resisted - Regional requirements are sanctioned globally - Customisation costs are not a major issue - Cost of ownership is a major factor	- Recognised that developing previous ERP caused many problems - Customisation are controlled globally and must be part of global process - Local customisations only sanctioned for legal or specific market requirements - Cost of dev not a major issue - Cost of ownership a major factor - Integrity of core transaction data is protected

Table 17.Case study findings for approach to customisations construct

5.11 Restrictions and Limitations Imposed by ERP

> *Without paying heed to the underlying socio-technical constructs that governed the*
> *symmetrical interaction between corporate norms and technology development (Pasmore*
> *et al 1982; Pan and Scarbourgh 1999; Al-mudimigh et al 2001), many of these*
> *implemented ERP systems have failed to realize their intended purposes (Davenport*
> *19998; Avnet 1999; Buckhout et al 1999; Pan et al 2004) with some even sinking into*
> *catastrophic status (Lim et al., 2004, p. 136)*

The case studies confirm the belief of Markus and Tanis (2000) that it will take an organisation time before obtaining benefits. Lim et al (2004) explain the social changes are a large component of a successful ERP implementation and it is possibly this aspect that causes the benefit hiatus. Interestingly, users in the midst of this disruption and change, according to Abdinnour-Helm and Lengnick-Hall (2005), find that benefits tend to be credited to the "ERP" rather than their efforts. They lament that this tends to erode user acceptance of a system, proposing employee appraisals for frequent users of ERP should include the extent of collaboration with others in the ERP process. They further propose that individual contributions often become overshadowed by corporate objectives, they believe the importance of users should be identified as the core of the process.

Tension existed in many of the organisations in terms of user processes and the application. Observations in all of the case studies confirmed that implementing ERP changed the departmental interfaces and moved organisational bottlenecks. The main reason for this was that data is captured earlier in the processes and needs to be codified by users previously not having the responsibility. This caused a great deal of consternation, particularly at Server, and may well be because ERP renders human agents' actions transparent to the organisation, and in the "sharpening awareness of the effects which one's actions may have on others and indirectly on oneself" (Kalinkos 2004, p.9). In the two organisations resisting user changes, the application is viewed by the users as cumbersome, even though they appear to be aware of the value to the organisation as a whole. The organisations customising the application to meet user requirements appear to have more satisfied users. However, this has placed restrictions on accessing and collating information and upgrading.

This and the previous discussion of training identify that it would be best to become knowledgeable about ERP before finalising processes. Particularly as changing of processes is difficult after they have been configured.

Davenport (2004, p.23) suggests information capability is derived from consistent, timely and accurate information. However, Markus et al (2000b) found that data reporting was a limitation with the implementations they investigated, and this was also the case in all the case studies. The majority of information may be provided by a warehouse and BI tools, but ad hoc reporting and transactional see through information needs to be provided by the ERP database. The transaction orientation of ERP means that data is spread through numerous, normalised, database tables; however, these 'insert' optimised databases are not very suitable for reporting. This is largely due to the data being dispersed across many tables as would be expected with so many functions being held in a normalised database. Organisations, therefore, need to fundamentally address this issue by identifying the primary data needs, not necessarily in terms of OLAP cubes, but unnormalised data repositories.

This limitation has necessitated a data warehouse in two of the organisations. These and the business intelligence add-ons that complement them, appear to be of limited benefit as the case organisations are still having difficulty obtaining reports, particularly ad-hoc reports.

5.11.1 Findings and Interpretations

All of the case organisation identified a period after live that did not produce organisational benefits. Organisation that implement standard processes across business seem to make the application more cumbersome for users. However, applications that are optimised for users become more cumbersome to upgrade and are unable to provide consistent information across SBUs. The reporting of data from the ERP database was seen as problematic by all organisation, and has not been adequately addressed by data warehouse and BI tools.

The following are identified as the key findings of restriction and limitations imposed by ERP from the case organisations:

- o Organisations are disadvantaged for an initial period post-live while becoming familiar with ERP
- o ERP implementations move process 'bottlenecks'
- o Users do not have sufficient understanding of processes
- o User actions and neglect are very apparent to other users

o The more standardised the processes and restricted the customisation, the more 'cumbersome' the ERP

o Process changes are difficult to make post live and implemented processes may restrict an organisation throughout the life of an application

o Reporting of data is difficult and complex

	Provider SAP	Server Dynamics (AX)	Contractor Dynamics (AX)	Global Oracle	Builder SAP
Restrictions and Limitations Imposed by ERP	- ERP will restrict an organisation, unless it is entirely new - It is more difficult to change processes post ERP implementation - Reporting of information is difficult	- Organisation was heavily restricted during the few months after the system was made live - ERP moved organisations' bottlenecks from one department to another - Reporting of information is difficult	- Original system very restrictive, particularly with reporting - Few ERP competitors restricts competitive advantage from ERP	- The system is cumbersome due to lack of customisation	- Low customised standard ERP requires 'work arounds' - Thinking of selling an organisation as it does not fit standard ERP procedures

Table 18.Case study findings on Restrictions and Limitations Imposed by ERP construct .

5.12 Approach to Business Process Analysis

There is a tendency that ERP projects put less emphasis on modelling activities than more traditional information system projects. As many integrated, enterprise-wide software packages like SAP are based on parameterised or standard components, it has been tempting to downplay process analysis and rely on short-circuit evolutionary development methods instead. ... The models serve as communication channels when alternative processes are analysed, they guide the realization of the automatic as well as the manual parts of the information system, they are used to train and inform employees, and they provide documentation that is useful both to other project activities and post-project tasks. (Gulla and Brasethvik, 2000, p. 1).

According to Ndede-Amadi (2004) the main objective of ERP is to enhance control over processes within the organisation. Shang and Seddon (2003) argue that "ERP systems are instruments for improving business processes such as manufacturing, purchasing or distribution. Therefore, ERP implementation and BPR should be closely connected" (Scheer and Habermann 2000, p.58). Davenport et al (2004, p.20) propose, "Organisations improve integration by going through the often-painful process of agreeing on a common way to define key information and perform key business processes".

Markus et al (2000b) found that a problem with ERP implementations is the cross-functional business process as people understand what they do, but not how their work affects others. ERP systems generally use a text based representation of the modules to communicate functionality to managers and users. This means that the description of the functions and detail about data components need to be read and this conceptualised into a comprehensive view of the application (Rolland & Prakash, 2000).

The case organisations had different approaches to process analysis. The Provider did not take a formalised process view until approximately six years after the system was made live. During the implementation they relied on consultants to identify how the system should be configured. However, consultants are usually familiar with only limited parts of the total system, and hardly anybody has a complete understanding of the whole system (Gulla & Brasethvik, 2000). The Provider has now realised that much of the advice received was poor and regrets not having focused on business processes at the time of implementation. It is now desperately trying to focus on processes.

Chapter 5 - Cross Case Analysis and Theory Development

Rosemann (2003) suggests that if process models were not available earlier they can be produced after the system is installed. He proposes the process models to be clustered into three areas:

- o Process-related data are directly linked to business processes and include information about the time, the costs, or the quality of a process.
- o Data related to the resources include information about the utilisation of the involved organisational units, roles and further resources.
- o Objects that are processes, such as orders, invoices, or payments, can be analysed and potential complexity drivers can be identified.

This is difficult for the Provider as the application has been heavily modified for different departments that often had conflicting needs. Provider has found that the more 'powerful' departments have quite optimal functions with those less powerful having sub-optimised ones. The movement away from an optimum solution due to departmental managerial pressures is called by Nandhakumar, Rossi, & Talvinen, (2005), "technology drift". This drift means that configuring optimal processes is now, politically, extremely difficult.

Global and Builder have focused on business processes. Global tries to use the Oracle e-business Suite's processes and only amends these when absolutely necessary. Builder identifies its own 'best practice ' processes, and implements these worldwide through a company standardised SAP application. This approach is the same as that identified by Davenport el al (2004) who found that once an organisation identifies the process flow required it often needs to develop the system accordingly .

> A BPR intervention is not merely the adoption of an ERP system or the business
> processes of an organisation; it implies changes in the way of doing business as well as
> in structure and culture of an organisation: it is changing the way of working of an
> organisation and process-orientated vision that organisation needs to integrate. (El
> Amrani et al, 2006, p. 84).

Swanton and Finley(2007), of AMR Research, strongly advocate the use of business processes to manage ERP and cite both SAP and Oracle e-business suite as products suited to such an approach. Rolland and Prakash (2000) propose the best way to understand an ERP is to map the software and adopted functions. "The map provides a two-way interchange from the ERP package to the organisation and vice-versa" (p.192). Global and Builder have understood this and the Provider is now striving to back track and take a process view. It is not necessary to map the processes to a minute level, but to a level that enables the estimation of the impact of a decision to change a component of ERP on the process. The focus on modules and processes creates a 'matrix' perspective of organisation and ERP as shown in Figure 39.

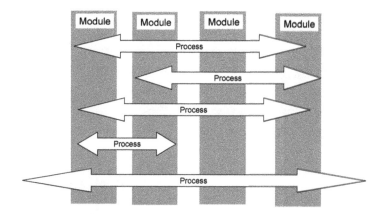

Figure 39. ERP Control Perspective

The procedure recommended by Gulla and Brasethvik (2000) is to map the future business processes to models where the lowest-level processes correspond to transactions in the ERP system. The models describe how the organisation will use the ERP system as well as necessary customisations. They also identify how the new business processes relate to key performance criteria and reporting needs, and how processes can be grouped into areas of responsibility for later job definitions. Only Builder followed such a process.

5.12.1 Interpretations and Findings

The case organisations predominately believe that a process analysis approach to ERP is imperative. This approach is somewhat at odds with the modulur focus of ERP and the knowledge of consultants being concerned with these modules.

The key findings for the case organisations of the construct business process analysis were:
- o Business Process Analysis prior to implementation is important to ERP success
- o ERP has configured, inbuilt processes and organisations have existing and desired processes; both need to be understood and changes to both evaluated
- o Consultants often do not understand the impact of decisions on a process
- o Implemented processes are difficult to change

	Provider SAP	Server Dynamics (AX)	Contractor Dynamics (AX)	Global Oracle	Builder SAP
Approach to Business Process Analysis	- Started to focus on processes 6 years after live due to customisations hampering process - Mapped all processes with aid of SAP pre-sales tool - Now sees business process analysis as fundamental to ERP - Business process analysis now used to identify customisations	- Functions analysed as part of the implementation and these guided customisations - No changes made to processes to align with application - There is no focus on processes post-live	- Process analysis not performed but 'old' system not seen to be supporting an organisation's process	- ERP standard processes implemented which, according to users, have had a negative effect - managers believe it provides vital organisation and customer business wide information	- Worldwide standard best practice process identified by the business - ERP selected for its match with processes - Processes rigidly maintained

Table 19.   Case study findings of the approach to business process analysis construct

5.13 Expected Lifespan of the ERP

> *The substantial switching cost and complexity of ES implementation, and the long implementation period, increase the switching costs of ES reducing the likelihood that organisations will replace ES in the short to medium-term. (Gable, Timbrell, Sauer, and Chan (2002, p. 343).*

The applications were seen by all interviewees as long term investments, the shortest time an application was proposed to last was five to 10 years. A number of respondents suggested that the system would not be changed for 10 to 20 years; some interviewees did not think the system would be changed for 25 years; while yet others judged 'it would last indefinitely'. None of the interviewees are certain of an event or reason that would cause the organisation to change the application.

	Provider SAP	Server Dynamics(AX)	Contractor Dynamics(AX)	Global Oracle	Builder SAP
Expected Lifespan of ERP	- Strategy manager: ERP would last 5 to 10 years - Finance manager: as long as SAP is a major vendor - IT manager: could not foresee a time when the organisation would change from SAP	- The customisation manager: ERP would last not less than 5 to 10 years and would be replaced due to changing requirements - A key user: could not envisage ever changing - The IT manager: expectation the application to last 15 to 25 years; and it might possibly change due to technological advancements	- Finance manager and CIO it "was a 25 year investment"	- The CIO: the system will not be changed in the foreseeable future, but might ultimately be changed due to a move to the hosting of applications	- The worldwide co-ordinator: the ERP would last not less than 10 to 15 years and could not predict why the application would be changed - Finance manager: at least 10 years, but the driver for change might be competitor advantage through IT - The IT manager: as long as 20 years but change might be due to unreasonably pricing

Table 20.   Case study findings on the expected lifespan of ERP

5.14 Towards a Theory

*"No matter how much ES [ERP] functionality has been implemented, getting value from
an ES [ERP] requires ongoing management and attention" (Davenport et al, 2004, p.
24).*

The theory proposed here is based on both the researcher's interpretations of the qualitative data obtained
from the case studies and the relevant existing theory. It is presumed that the theory proposed here will be
relevant to organisations other than the case organisations as it does not prescribe how to manage ERP per
se, but proposes broad issues and considerations for management.

Figure 40 shows the constructs basic to the research as explained in Chapter 2, these are used to position the
following discussion. The constructs illustrated in the conceptual model are threefold: structural constructs
identified at the outset, comprising of external influencers, antecedent influencer, and internal influencers;
and two phases of action constructs – process and outcomes, which characterise the unfolding over time of
the implementation.

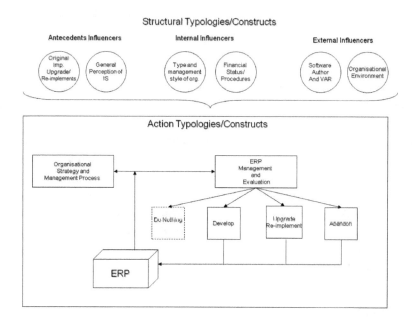

Chapter 5 - Cross Case Analysis and Theory Development

Figure 40.   Conceptual model of structural constructs

Server's insistence on developing the application, and its lack of procedural control, seems to have already resulted in a legacy application. Provider is operating in a smaller geographic region than the other organisations and already has what could be termed, a legacy application. Global and Builder are multi-national organisations and as such operate in a very different environment to Server and Provider; however each has experienced very similar problems with their original ERP. It seems that the need for control is probably not related to organisational size. Although it is perhaps related to organisational type as discussed in Chapter 2.

Builder and Global with their 'second wave' of ERP have created expert teams to manage and understand the application. With their first implementation they had what Wilcocks and Sykes(2003) term a 'technology determinism approach' wherein they devolved responsibility to the technical departments. The move by Builder to create internal business process and technical teams, with the technical team subordinate to the business process team, demonstrates that this issue has been recognised. Builder's approach to identify best practice processes for the organisation seems a sensible and mature one. Global have taken a similar approach, but have, as far as possible, utilised the processes embedded in the Oracle ERP. Both these organisations have maintained tight control of the applications to ensure the ongoing integrity of the processes.

Builder has a centralised management structure whilst Global has more regional autonomy. Ideally the Global ERP would be flexible, allowing for local and organisation wide information to be easily unified, and for upgrades to be readily performed regardless of customisation. For numerous reasons, mainly technical, this is not the case. Therefore, for Global to meet the primary business objective of serving worldwide customers, the ERP must be standardised throughout the organisation. This creates the risk of making the application cumbersome for individual business and stifling their entrepreneurial activities.

Melin (2003) argues that ERP systems create an administrative paradox where they strive for both flexibility and stability. Thisbook proposes that ERP brings with it a number of such dichotomies; customisation and consistent information are at odds; the transaction orientation of ERP is opposed to ad hoc reporting; user satisfaction and stringently controlled customisations conflict; and ERP and a flexible organisation are not a good match. Figure 41 shows some of the dichotomous elements of ERP.

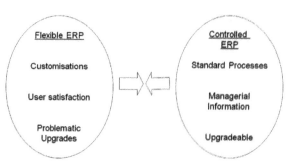

Figure 41.   The ERP dichotomy

Once these conflicts have been recognised the major issue becomes how to manage these conflicting objectives. As Seddon et al (2003) point out, the difficulty with ERP is the decision on the mix required of such important components as configuration, customization and process changes . If, as Davenport (1998) suggests, a purpose of ERP installation is to solve fragmentation of information in a large business, then it seems that standard ERP systems are required in multi-company organisations. However, Abdinnour-Helm and Lengnick-Hall (2005) argue that, with accompanying investment in behaviour and cultural change, ERP can support flexible organisations. It seems necessary to choose either highly standardised processes, which may or may not be based on the embedded 'best practice' models, or, ongoing customisation and accept the consequences of dissimilar implementation and disparate data. It is important that this decision is made early in the implementation process and with due consideration of the implications of the decision.

The ability to address far reaching decisions early in an implementation is seen as a problem due to the lack of knowledge of the process by an organisation's stakeholders. The cases provided evidence that training was inadequate and provided only at the level of parameterisation of modules. It will be imperative to build more appropriate skills through more expansive education, possibly through tertiary education or specialised education. However, it is unlikely to be provided currently in the holistic form deemed essential, by a VAR or Software Author.

In all cases it is clear that consultancy expertise was lacking in the areas of understanding decisions and making sound considered recommendations. After personnel in the case organisations became more familiar with the ERP applications, they recognised that the recommendations made during the implementation phase were not necessarily correct; and unnecessary customisations had been made.

For these reasons it is of paramount importance for an organisation to take ownership and responsibility of the ERP implementation and management through an ERP bureau. A major proposal of this book is that an ERP bureau, similar to instituted at Global and Builder, would be useful in many organisations implementing an ERP. An ERP bureau would ideally be established at the very early stage of the project so that the ERP can be properly managed throughout its life and not suffer from the antecedents of poor implementation demonstrated in some of the case organisations. The organisation taking more ownership during implementation will probably lengthen implementation timeframes but as the applications may last 25 years it is likely to be time well spent. However, the recommendation is that a bureau be formed regardless of the position in the ERP lifecycle and, obviously, this includes post-live.

The postulated ERP bureau would be responsible for the ongoing management of the application. As ERP are generally acquired for strategic initiatives the importance of the rationale for the acquisition needs to be understood and used as a basis for much of the bureau activity. All of the organisations in the case studies had different strategy processes. It is not, therefore, possible, as was claimed in the 1990s with SISP, to be prescriptive of the strategy process for ERP as strategy processes themselves differ in organisations. The important factor is for the strategy or strategic intent to be apparent to the group responsible for ERP. It seems necessary, if business objectives are to be met, that senior management remain involved with the management of the application throughout its operational life. Another matter becoming most apparent was that the original strategy that dictated the ERP acquisition is likely to persist for a long time. This observation means that strategic shift is unlikely to occur and thus require wholesale changes to ERP. Indeed, changes to meet strategic initiatives may be but a 'tilt' of the rudder rather than a change of course.

Markus et al (2000) explain that, what they term 'fragile human capital', is an ongoing problem with ERP management. They cite the difficulty of replacing IT specialists in the project phase with in-house expertise, explaining that in-house knowledge may be restricted to the internal implementation. If this is the case, it seems expertise should be retained or an ongoing relationship with a third party sought. Bannister (2002a) proposed that "at least in some organisations, the rate of development of absorptive capacity is dependent on the nature and quality of general and IS management in an organisation" (p. 156-157). He went onto the suggest that value of IS could be related to the status of the IS personnel and the nature of the relationship between IS and business management. The bureaus having senior management, business management, technical and process experts will ideally create an 'absorptive' capacity and mange the application effectively.

The personnel that constitute the bureau will need sound business knowledge and skills, in-depth understanding of the operation, be educated about ERP and its capabilities, its limitations, and have in-depth education concerning the components of ERP which impact, or potentially impact business processes. This is likely to eradicate invalid decisions being made pre-live by consultants, and the ultimate realisation that an enterprise solution has been configured from a few external consultants' opinions. This is not to say that consultants are not required. It is through a meeting of minds, the consultants need to fundamentally understand the business and the organisations implementation team fundamentally understand the application.

Upgrades are viewed in most cases as being similar to an insurance policy, in that they are made to prevent replacement of an ERP rather than to provide for increases in functionality. However, as demonstrated by the Provider when not upgrading for almost 10 years, the new functionality may ultimately become desirable. Maintenance is generally considered as a cost but for ERP should also be thought of as a benefit exercise (Gable et al, 2003). The benefits of upgrades are mainly through technical improvement in the kernel; examples being recent innovations such as BI tools, RFID recognition and handheld device connectivity. The importance of any proposition concerning upgrades though should be entirely understood before any decision is made. It is apparent that there is conflict between customisation and upgrades. For the case examples it has proven to be extremely difficult to have customisations and to be able to upgrade the application functions. Perhaps the most fundamental decision that the ERP bureau will make is how many of the processes in the ERP can be adopted by the organisation.

The processes in the ERP may be proposed as 'best practice' but in reality they are simply embedded practice, and if they can be implemented with only minimal disruption to the business, then they probably should be. If they cannot, for sound business reasons such as legal and market requirements (as conceived by Builder), a detailed description of the required processes should be made and the processes compared with those being applied. The ERP processes should be changed as little as possible. It should be understood that not all ERP functions have the same level of complexity and that some customisations will have a much higher cost of ownership than others.

Customisation requests and changes of processes should perhaps be evaluated by identifying with the reason for the request. A decision should be made on whether the request is strategic or operational and proceeded as follows: an operational request should only be considered if it is absolutely necessary in terms of legal and market requirements, e.g., it will have a potential major consequence on the organisation if it is not undertaken; and a strategic initiative considered as absolutely necessary if there is a consequence which impacts competitive position or future capabilities. In both instances the cost of ownership should be calculated and Bannister's (2001) 'dis-benefits' understood. The purpose being to identify the total cost of ownership in its broadest sense and to weigh this against the merits of the proposed change.

When customisations are made sufficient documentation should be generated to enable them to be replicated when upgrades are required. When the application is live, and if upgrades are to be taken regularly, it might be good practice to only release new customisations with upgrades, thereby allowing thorough testing and control of releases. Interim customisations would be made for critical problems and be released as 'patches'. Where possible the core transactions of ERP should be maintained and additional information appended to the data tables inline with the practices at Builder.

Builder's approach to adding components of functionality rather than amending existing functionality is believed to reduce cost of ownership. Although more cumbersome for users, the customisations can be more easily isolated and this should significantly reduce the overhead of upgrades. When large customisations are required these should, where possible, form an isolated set of functionality that can be embedded in the application and linked through the database rather than through changes to the existing ERP programs. This approach largely mirrors that of Builder, which is viewed in thisbook as a mature process.

It is impossible to be prescriptive concerning topologies of ERP deployment, but past research has recommended that having as few instances of ERP installations as possible is good practice. This is considered to be a reasonable recommendation, so the proposal is to recognise the technical, geographic and organisational restrictions for a single installation and extrapolate using these restrictions until the minimum number of application installations that can be implemented is identified.

Sammon, Adam, & Carton, (2003) contend data warehousing projects were introduced primarily in an attempt to finally achieve the original benefits expected of ERP that were never realised. The case organisations demonstrate that reporting is difficult even after implementing data warehouses. Importantly, reporting seems to be placed at a lower-level of importance than transactional processes and it is questionable that this is the best approach. Thisbook proposes that the information required from an ERP be understood holistically, in terms of content and use, and in terms of both horizontal and vertical process flows. This necessitates a high level of understanding of the ERP database structure. Figure 42 shows a conceptual model of the ERP environment:

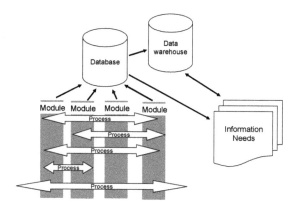

Figure 42.   Conceptualisation of ERP

The existing and vertical and horizontal potential reporting needs will need to be understood and the data requirements to provide them envisaged. The budget for information management should realistically be congruent with the value of the information to the business.

The ERP bureau should then have, as a minimum, the following expertise and knowledge domains:.

- o   strategy processes
- o   strategic intent
- o   organisational needs and intent
- o   organisational information requirements
- o   organisational business processes
- o   the ERP package and embedded processes
- o   IT topologies and configurations
- o   direct and indirect costs with ERP usage
- o   potential dis-benefits of ERP decisions
- o   the oncost of customisations and interfaces to ERP
- o   tangible and intangible benefits with ERP usage
- o   data structures and, horizontal and vertical information needs

The following Figure 43 provides a conceptual model of the inter-facing between proposed ERP bureau expertise and the external factors which may have influence.

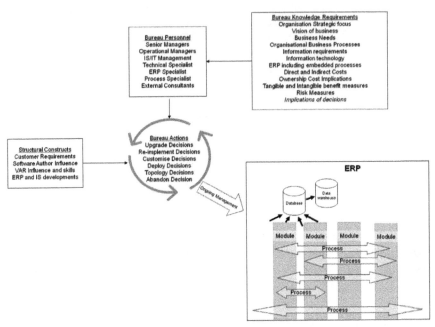

Figure 43.   ERP Management and Evaluation

The ERP bureau should be responsible for all decisions concerning the ERP and it should understand the underlying processes of the ERP and those needed by the organisation. The marrying of the two will be a key process in the management of the ERP. If the ERP has many instances across regions, the IT being a federal approach, it seems reasonable to have a central ERP bureau to support local bureaus that are responsible for the local ERP.

ICT strategies can be broken down into IS, IT and information (IM) strategies (Sabherwal et al, 2001). Plainly an ERP application will require these strategies to exist and be commensurate with each other. The ERP bureau should have an IT, ERP and IM strategy that matches business operations with business objectives. These strategies should be as enduring as possible, with proposed customisations to meet organisational changes considered thoroughly and made only if necessary. The potential of the existing ERP, and the potential from upgrading to later releases, should be continually monitored and senior management advised of the potential business opportunities.

Finally, if an organisation is dissatisfied with the ERP implementation and finds, as the Provider has, that ERP is stifling the business and/or has escalating costs, it is recommended that the organisation recognises the problem has the potential for longevity; resulting ultimately in a great deal of cost to change or re-implement the application. Rather than accepting the increasing legacy nature of ERP the organisation should pro-actively address the situation, by developing a process view of the organisation, and then decide on the most prudent way forward.

In summary, an ERP bureau will vary in size, but should be of sufficient scope to manage the ERP in the host organisation. Thisbook proposes that the ERP bureau should be aware of the following factors:

- ○ *The manner in which the Software Author and VAR exert pressure on the management of ERP through increases in support cost and/or withdrawal of support.*
- ○ *The external factors driving the organisation, and how to respond to these.* The cases had the primary external objective of supporting customers, although the requirement of each in this regard differed.
- ○ *The antecedents of the original implementation and upgrades, and how these may impact the potential of the current ERP.* Questions requiring an answer include: was the strategy flawed; should customisations be reversed; and, what has been learned?
- ○ *The perceptions of, or culture, concerning IS should be understood.* Even though these are difficult to alter, the more that is understood, the better and more conducive the management of the application will be.
- ○ *The current organisational structure and management style.* Existing theory suggests that ERP best fits centralised, highly controlled organisations. If an organisation varies from this, expectations must be tailored to the potential impact of ERP on the organisation.
- ○ *Available funds and the financial status of an organisation.* As these have a major consequence on the options available to the bureau.
- ○ *Long-term tangible benefits can probably not be quantified and the bureau should be empowered to make recommendations based on their knowledge.*
- ○ *Organisational processes and the processes embedded in the ERP need to be understood.* The latter must not be considered 'best practice', organisational processes should derive from considered decisions on the potential for business outcomes and ERP costs over time.
- ○ *The reasons for the application either restricting or enabling the organisation.*

o ***The extent of longevity expected for the application must be gauged.*** As the cases indicate ERP may be installed for decades, the importance of the foregoing must be appreciated with regard to this longevity.

5.15 Conclusion

This chapter has utilised the constructs developed in chapter 2, the research approach and design explained in chapter 3, as well as the information gleaned from the individual cases presented in chapter 4. Findings have been delineated for each of the constructs by analysing the case organisations vis-à-vis the constructs, and utilising existing theory. The chapter has presented the findings as a theoretical framework that might be practically relevant to further organisations.

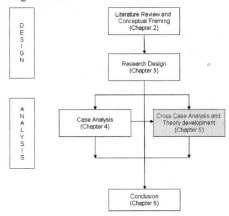

Figure 44. Book design - chapter 5

The remaining chapter, chapter 6, concludes the research by summarising thebook and explaining implications for research and practice.

Chapter 6 - Conclusion

Criticisms that case studies and qualitative studies are not generalizable would be incorrectly ruling out the generalizability of empirical descriptions. (Lee & Baskerville, 2003,p. 222)

This chapter draws a conclusion to the book by discussing the findings to the research questions posed. The chapter begins by summarising the research processes as they relate to the research aims established in Chapter 1. The descriptive case studies and explanative cross case analysis are reviewed and the interpretations and findings highlighted. The potential contribution to theory and limitations are then explained. The chapter concludes with implications for practice and recommendations for future research

6.1 Summary of Research Process

The research aim as stated in Chapter 1 is as follows:

> *The aim of this book is to explore the management and evaluation of operational ERP in organisations in order to develop a theory that will assist practitioners in the administration of ERP and inform academia of the key factors affecting the management processes.*

These broad aims were broken down into the following specific objectives.

1. To understand the process that organisations are incorporating to manage ERP
2. To understand the evaluation processes that are being utilised to maintain and enhance ERP
3. To compare the practices with theory and to outline a theoretical framework for management and evaluation of operational ERP

A wide-ranging literature review incorporating management, organisational structures, ERP and evaluation processes was undertaken and is presented in Chapter 2. It arrived at a conceptual framework of the phenomenon. The constructs shown in Figure 45 were drawn from the conceptual framework and became the basis for data collection in a pilot case study.

Chapter 6 - Conclusion

Figure 45.   Original research constructs

Two further constructs that were identified from the pilot case are explained later in this section.

Chapter 3 examined what is expected of IS research, identifying a call for more practical and relevant research. The philosophical options were discussed vis-a-vis the phenomenon to be investigated, the outcome being that the best approach to this research, for the researcher, was a multi-case qualitative study. The subsequent methodology has been guided by Yin (2003b), the objective being to theorise how it might be possible to manage and evaluate operational ERP. The research could be characterised as a 'soft' positivist study (Kirsch, 2004 cited Seddon and Scheepers 2006), or a transcendental realist study (Miles and Huberman 1994). The research can also simply be viewed as a qualitative study to observe what is happening in a number of organisations, that then draws theoretical conclusions from those findings, and explains how they might prove useful to other organisations.

The methodology and the constructs produced the following questions to guide data collection:

- o What methods are actually employed to manage and evaluate ERP in the case examples?
- o How does the management and evaluation of ERP depend upon the strategic focus of the organisations studied?
- o How have environmental characteristics impacted ERP management decisions and evaluation processes?

Chapter 6 - Conclusion

- o   How do the broad objectives of IT effect management and evaluation methods?
- o   How do ERP enhancements impact upon the frequency and method of evaluation?
- o   What historical, political and industry influences impact upon management and evaluation?

These questions were to design the semi-structured interview guide: it includes the aim of each question and the probes that might be applicable in an interview. A pilot case was undertaken with a public utility organisation labelled Provider. The Provider had been proclaimed in a research publication as being excellent at benefits realisation with ERP implementations. Although thebook revealed the organisation has now revoked these claims, the case is viewed here as an excellent precursor to the study. This case identified two further constructs - business process analysis and management of customisations, these being added as units of analysis to the data collection for subsequent case studies.

Basic comparative information about Provider and the four additional organisations which comprise the five multi-case qualitative research studies of thisbook is summarised in Table 21 below:

Table 21.   Five Case Studies: Industry, Turnover And Cost Of ERP

Organisation	Industry/Type	Revenue $m p.a.	Approximate Cost of Implementation $m	Interviews
Server	Service, Private	50	.5	6
Contractor	Construction, Private	800	35	3
Provider	Utility, Public	3000	40	5
Builder	Aggregates, Private	10000	800	3
Global	Mineral, Private	25000	500-700	5

Chapter 4 describes and analyses the case studies. Each case is examined in accordance with each construct, conclusions are drawn, and a conceptual model of the management and evaluation process presented for each. As proposed by Mishler (1990), passages from the interviews are included to enable the interpretations to be verified or refuted. All of the cases were extremely enlightening and the very frank interviews with respondents have greatly aided thisbook.

Chapter 5 presents a cross-case analysis based on the isolated constructs in order that answers can be formulated for the research questions and conclusions drawn. The analysis aimed to use each of the 10 constructs as the basis of the explanations regarding the management and evaluation of ERP in the five case study organisations. Conclusions were drawn in terms of 'how' and 'why' as deemed appropriate by Gregor (2006) and Yin (2003b) for explanative case analysis. The interpretations and findings are then discussed in a holistic manner to identify an overview of management and evaluation of ERP. The investigation outcomes have been used to deduce a theoretical framework of management and evaluation of ERP.

6.2   Case Study Summary

This research set out to explore the management and evaluation of operational ERP in five organisations in order to better understand the phenomenon and draw conclusions for theory and practice. The individual cases discussed in Chapter 4 provided different approaches to organisational strategy and management, and, as would be expected, each had a different approach to the management and evaluation of its ERP application. The section following summarises individually these practices.

6.2.1 The Case of Provider

Provider has implemented the SAP ERP application, the organisation's mission being to maintain a high quality of product supply by managing the extensive infrastructure needed for product delivery. A robust approach to business strategy is apparent, whereby senior management communicates a rolling five year strategy to business unit managers who in turn interpret the business strategy and identifying how to best support it. This process spurns numerous IS customisation and enhancement requests, allowing the business proposals which emerge, to be amalgamated and become the 'IS strategy'.

Senior business managers are not involved in the IT component of the organisation: and IS/IT managers are not involved in the strategy process. This separation results in disparate and sometimes conflicting requirements. The proposals, depending on the expected cost, are subject to an array of evaluation measures, these range from no evaluation to rigourous cost benefit analysis. The organisation appears to have admirable evaluation procedures for the different value and nature of proposals. However, many 'gaps' exist in the process which allow it to be circumvented, thus largely invalidating the approach.

The ERP was acquired to simplify the IS environment through a strategy of purchase rather than build. The implementation objective has largely failed as the ERP application is integrated with more than 300 other applications, one of which is the business system that was used prior to the application being introduced. The application has been continually customised to such an extent that it is practically impossible to perform a 'functional' upgrade. The organisation cites the many mistakes made during the implementation, the antecedents of which are still having major consequences a decade later. The interviewees lament not taking a 'process view' of the organisation at the time of implementation, now finding some departments to have optimal solutions while others are sub-optimised. This results in processes being slow, disconnected and cumbersome. Senior staff also reflected that the consultancy and education provided at the time of implementation was poor, now realising the consultants were making ill-informed judgements and unnecessary customisations.

Provider has problems obtaining management information due to the complexity of the database and continual customisations. The introduction of a data warehouse has partially alleviated the problem but reporting is still seen as problematic. Customisations are performed by an outsourced body which allows the high ongoing expenditure to be capitalised. As Provider has a very high asset base, the cost of the ERP activity is obscured. Ideally, customisations would be reverse engineered and the application re-implemented. However, the cost, in terms of time and money, has prohibited this being done. Interestingly, the application is still being customised with $5m to be spent in the coming year on further customisations.

The case demonstrated a number of relevant factors: customisation of an ERP and upgrading appeared to be fundamentally opposed; information is difficult to obtain from the extensive database; training and consultancy is not necessarily satisfactory; the departmentally modular approach of ERP applications is somewhat at odds with a process view of an organisation; and implementation antecedents have a long-term impact.

6.2.2 The Case of Server

Server has implemented Dynamics AX from Microsoft across six sites in Australia. The strategy process is seen as 'informal' (Johnson and Scholes 2002) and senior management support for the application existed only when it was in the initial 'chartering' phase (Markus and Tanis, 2000). It is clear the strategy is almost entirely driven by the aim to increase sales to Server's few powerful customers. Server continually attempts to capture data in the ERP application to identify 'reasons for customers to spend' on product maintenance. This collection of data makes the application increasingly complex, data entry arduous and reporting difficult.

Responsibility for implementation of the application has been devolved to a very low level in the organisation, with any employee being able to phone the customisation team with a customisation request. These customisations are initiated without any conscious evaluation; and priorities are set by who 'shouts the loudest'. This seeming lack of control proliferates customisations and prohibits upgrades. Server is finding it difficult to obtain business reports due to the system's complexity and constant changes. As the customisation team is an internal department, the cost is an indirect, payroll overhead, and as such is considered as sunk costs. This may well be a reason for the seeming lack of evaluation and controls.

Server lost confidence in the VAR during implementation and has ceased support, finally terminating the maintenance agreement because of the presumed high cost of applying upgrades. Stopping the maintenance agreement means that Server cannot upgrade resulting in the organisation having what can be termed a legacy ERP application. This mode of operation conflicts with its main objective of purchasing an application from a major vendor so as to ensure the application can be maintained for an extended time.

Numerous researchers contend that senior management involvement is imperative for a successful ERP project (see for example: Akkermans and Helden, 2002; Legare, 2002; McAulay, 2003; Remenyi, 2000; Rosemann, 2001; Somers and Nelson 2001; Kroemmergaard and Rose, 2002; and Shang and Seddon, 2002). Additionally, Baccarini, Salm, and Love (2004) aver that not having senior managerial support constitutes a major risk. Server does not have any control of the application above operational management thereby ensuring the application has become a tactical rather than strategic tool.

6.2.3 The Case of Contractor

Contractor has implemented Dynamic AX from Microsoft in one of its divisions and is in the process of selecting either SAP or Oracle e-business Suite for the remainder of the organisation. The organisation's strategy is to grow, but beyond that directive, strategy dissemination is not apparent. The growth is aimed at the booming mining and construction industry wherein competition is largely based on price.

Since the data collection, Contractor has divested itself of the division that implemented Dynamics AX. Financial accounts show that, without this divestment of the division, the company would not have been profitable; therefore, a possible reason for the acquisition of the application was to accelerate the division's sale. The application that supports the remaining organisation has been customised to such an extent that upgrades cannot be performed, and comprehensive support is no longer provided by the

Software Author. In-house expertise has been released from employment and customisations have ceased, indicating that an organisation with close to $1 billion of revenue is operating with limited support for the major business application. The system does not contain sufficient of the information required to measure costs, or to ascertain project margins that are necessary to inform business quotations; nor is the information in the application easy to access.

The organisation does not utilise cost benefit analysis and acquires IT under what is purported to be an umbrella IT strategy document created almost five years previously. The organisation is thought of as a laggard in terms of IS usage, and this IS usage seems to be restricting the organisation's growth and development.

6.2.4 The Case of Global

Global implemented the ERP Oracle e-business suite throughout the global corporation. The application operates from four 'regional' service centres. The strategy process is centralised and formal, the main priority being the provision of a high grade service to its increasing number of global customers. The ERP acquisition originated from a strategic initiative designed to service these global customers, and to benchmark and compare SBU performance.

The CIO insists IT is not a core component of the business even though almost $1 billion has been spent recently on the ERP application. This application has replaced three relatively recently installed applications around the world. The application is as vanilla as is practical. As a consequence, users find the new application cumbersome, and generally 'prefer the previous ERP implementation' for use in the Asia/Pacific region.

Customisation requests are created in the four regions and passed to a central group for evaluation. In the rare instances that customisations are sanctioned, they are forwarded to the Oracle Corporation to be included in a subsequent version of the application. If Oracle decides not to include the customisations they are made internally. The process from proposal to implementation takes up to three years.

'Technical' upgrades are implemented rapidly as Oracle will not respond to support requests for other than the current version. Interestingly, Oracle is writing a maintenance module for Global which eventually will become the Oracle e-business suite 'best practice' maintenance offering. The major emphasis of the ERP application in this organisation is standardisation of information and ease of upgrade, these being valued much higher than user satisfaction.

6.2.5 The Case of Builder

The Builder, a global organisation, has implemented SAP in some of its regions and aims to 'roll out' the application worldwide. The strategy process used is very formal, originating centrally, but with some regional autonomy in meeting strategic objectives. The application was purchased to standardise worldwide practices so enabling benchmarking and to police the organisation. This has two benefits: worldwide provision of a commodity product which is regionally different in cost and sales values; and transparent individual in-country business performance.

Builder first identified its own best practice processes and then matched them with the ERP application best supporting those processes. In-country customisations are minimised, being only allowed for legal and critical commercial reasons. The application seems to be very well received by the businesses managers and is a fundamental part of the globalisation strategy. The organisation believes the application has been successful because the emphasis is on a business rather than technology initiative. Two central groups are responsible for the ERP - one manages the processes and the other, which is sub-ordinate to the process group, manages the delivery of the technology. The ERP is seen to be enabling the organisational strategy, and Builder has many facets which seem to be a mature approach to ERP management, for example, in the matter the proposal to release customisations with upgrades, so enabling the application to be fully tested and business disruption minimised.

6.3   Cross Case Analysis

The cross case analysis presented in Chapter 5, analysis the cases against each of the constructs and the findings are used to develop a theory framework of management and evaluation of ERP. This section summarises the findings for each of the constructs.

6.3.1   Original Implementation and Its Antecedents

The decisions made when the ERP is implemented may well prevail for the life of the application. For this reason it is extremely important to ensure the ERP meets each organisation's requirements. In the cases studied implementation consultancy was seen to be poor and provided by, 'module jockeys', a term coined by Provider's IT manager, for consultants with expertise in a particular module rather than having a broader knowledge of the application and business in general. The larger case organisations came over time to realise each must take 'ownership' of the application and understand the process flows the organisation requires.

The following are the major impact findings for the original implementation and its antecedents:

o The functional processes implemented when the system is made live are critical as they are likely to prevail indefinitely

o The methods of control and evaluation employed during the original implementation appear to endure

o Customisations should only be sanctioned where absolutely necessary

o Centrally controlled international organisations are more likely to have success from an ERP implementation than decentralised organisations

o Organisations are not learning from others' mistakes, and do not seem to be adopting published, critical success factor guidelines

o ERP management requires alignment of the separate visions of senior management, operations and IT personnel

6.3.2 Impact of Strategy Process on ERP

As ERP applications have a major impact within the many areas of an organisation they automatically take on strategic importance (El Amrani et al, 2006). Of interest is that the strategic objectives for the ERP did not appear to change over time. As explained by Johnson and Scholes (2002), there are many different approaches to both strategy formulation and implementation in an organisation; therefore, it is impossible to be definitive about how the strategy process should relate to the management and evaluation of ERP. However, the strategic objectives, or simply key objectives, need to be identified and well defined.

The most important critical success factor, common to many research studies of ERP, is that ongoing management has senior management support. In all of the cases, senior management supported ERP in the early stages, but in each the length of support time differed. In Builder's case, the CEO was continuously involved, ERP being considered as a strategic weapon; but in Server's case, senior management was only involved in the initial, 'chartering' phase. This research demonstrates the importance of senior managers maintaining involvement with the management of the application if it is to meet business objectives confidently and as completely as possible over time.

The key findings concerning the impact of strategy process on ERP are:

o Strategic objectives of the ERP need to be defined and monitored

o Strategy needs to be interpreted into information needs and a vision for the ERP

- o   ERP objectives are likely to remain quite constant
- o   ERP requires governance and alignment of incentives of technical and operations staff
- o   Senior managers should be involved throughout the life of the ERP

6.3.3 Financial Procedures and Imperatives

In all of the cases the cost of acquiring an application was determined by the price of the ERP products appearing to meet the business requirements, rather than a budget being established against the anticipated monetary benefits of an ERP. The level of investment for both the initial application and the ongoing activities precludes abandonment of the application.

Three of the case organisations are in an extremely strong financial position, enabling them to have major ongoing investments in the applications. Nonetheless, the cost of upgrading extensively customised applications was considered to be prohibitively high, and was one of the major reason for Global and Builder changing to their current ERP. Provider, was also unable to sanction functional upgrades due to cost, even though it is financially healthy.

Contractor and Server are operating under quite severe cash pressures, finding that the financial situation strongly impacts ERP management; and in the case of Server it has influenced the decision to cancel the maintenance agreement. Contractor has divested itself of the division with that has recently implemented ERP, and is delaying the acquisition of a new ERP for the remaining organisation.

The key findings concerning an organisation's financial procedures and imperatives are:

- o   The cost of an ERP application is determined by the market price of applications that 'fit' an organisations requirements
- o   Financial performance impacts ERP management
- o   Financial strength does not overcome the high cost and disruption of upgrades
- o   The level of investment precludes abandoning the applications

6.3.4 Upgrades and Their Antecedents

A 'functional' upgrade is the term used for implementing a new version which includes the customisations made to a previous version. A 'technical' upgrade occurs when the kernel of the application is implemented but the functionality remains static, and the benefits of the new functions in the latest versions are not realised. None of the case organisations had performed 'functional' upgrades because either the upgrades were deemed too time consuming and/or too expensive. This has meant that the functionality that the organisations are buying, at a cost of between 15% and 25% of the value of the application per annum, are not installed by the organisations. Global and Builder have implemented applications to allow upgrades to be made more readily. Builder intends to install new functionality with upgrades in the future but at the time of data collection had not done so.

The benefits of upgrading were seen to be primarily to keep up-to-date with technology rather than for improvements in functions. Organisations tend to stay with the implemented version, with maintenance agreement being considered akin to an insurance policy rather than being of direct value. Software Authors assert pressure to upgrade by either increasing maintenance costs when organisations fall behind maintenance schedules or by ceasing support. This influence results in a technical upgrade whereby the kernel is rolled forward.

The following are the key findings concerning upgrades and their antecedents:

- o Upgrades are expensive and disruptive
- o Oragnisational benefits of upgrading are minimal
- o Customisations make functional upgrades difficult or impossible
- o Software Authors exert pressure to upgrade
- o Maintenance payments provide little tangible benefit
- o Upgrades are mainly required for future proofing and not functionality

6.3.5 Perception of IS

The expectations for the ERP application appear to be very low, particularly when considering the cost of the applications. For example, Global has spent possibly $1 billion on ERP and the CIO believes that "the best we can do is not be noticed". Server's CEO initially thought they had "bought a pup"; and Builder believed that the original implementation of ERP in the UK was perceived as "just another IT project and resented by employees".

The perceptions of stakeholder groups concerning ERP may differ (Ifinedo & Nahar, 2007; Sedera et al,2004; Lim et al, 2004; Kirsch, 2004), this was confirmed in the case studies where the perspectives of ERP were not consistent between business management, users and technical staff. Generally, perhaps surprisingly, management was of the highest opinion; frequent users at Server, were relatively highly satisfied; and users at Provider were satisfied. Both of these applications have been highly customised. Provider recognised that frequent users had a much higher opinion of the application than infrequent users. Global had low user satisfaction; while Builder was considered to have reasonable user satisfaction. The technical staff in the Aisa/Pacific region of Global and at Provider took a very dim view of the technology. The researcher reminds that the above are interpretations only, a model such as technology acceptance model (TAM) was not used.

The organisations consider IS and ERP as fundamental to business operations, but it was apparent that the perception of the IT personnel at Provider, where the application had been installed the longest, had changed from being very positive to very negative. Newell et al (2007) also recognised this phenomenon, coining the phrase 'best for when'.

The following perceptions of IS are identified as being fundamental in the case organisations:

- o IS personnel have low expectations levels for ERP
- o The perception of IS is not consistent between management, and operations and technical personnel
- o Perception may change over time
- o Frequent and infrequent users may have different opinions

6.3.6 Re-implementations

A re-implementation to overcome issues with the original implementation is desired at Provider, but is not being undertaken due to disruption and cost. Provider has re-implemented the finance module to meet changes in financial procedures. The cost of the re-implementation was higher than the original implementation of the module.

Builder wanted to re-implement their original ERP application worldwide prior to abandoning the application, but found the cost and disruption prohibitive. The entire application worldwide has been, or is being, replaced. It seems that re-implementations might be undertaken to meet changing business requirements, or to standardise implementations, but are often not implemented due to high cost or impact on the business.

Key findings concerning application re-implementations are:

- o Re-implementation of ERP or purchase of ERP may be undertaken to standardise processes or reduce customisations
- o Re-implementation is costly and disruptive, and, therefore, is seldom undertaken

6.3.7 Influences and Consequences of Software Authors and Resellers

The case organisations all indicated that a large well established Software Author, such as SAP, had a major influence on the choice of application. Noteworthy is that this research only analysed cases having ERP applications from large well established authors. The Software Authors were seen to be remote from the business and difficult to influence. Only Global has an ongoing relationship; and as Global is one of the largest organisations in the world this is perhaps not surprising.

The notion of 'best practice' was seen to be a misnomer; for instance, Global is having a maintenance module developed to its requirements that will be released as the 'best practice' maintenance module in the Oracle e-business suite. This cannot possibly be 'best practice', simply being a practice. Claims of best practice was also seen to be a fallacy by Kelly et al (1999) and Newell et al (2007).

User training was condemned as poor by all the case organisations, and the knowledge of consultants from the Software Author and VARs limited. The decisions made by consultants were seen as short-sighted and, sometimes, with hindsight, erroneous. The maintenance contracts, now the major income stream for Authors, were found to be very suspect as organisations rarely upgrade. Server has simply cancelled the agreement creating what can be termed a legacy ERP application. If this practice became prevalent Software Authors would quickly be in financial difficulty.

Key findings concerning Software Authors and resellers follow:
- o A large financially stable Software Author is an acquisition incentive
- o Software Authors are seen as remote
- o User training is of discreet functions and not of sufficient scope to conceptualise the application
- o Best practice is a misnomer and it is generally 'first' practice

6.3.8 Environmental Influences

ERP management is influenced by the environment primarily through customers considerations in terms of both satisfaction and revenue. Suppliers were seen as a minor factor in the acquisition of ERP. Other environmental characteristics such as media influence, or industry norms were not thought by the case organisations to have significant impact on the choice of ERP.

Key findings concerning environmental influences are:

- o Customers, and to lesser extent suppliers, influence the functionality required of ERP but not the ERP application per se
- o The external environment other than customer, supplier and Software Author does not seem to significantly impact strategic ERP decisions

6.3.9 Evaluation Procedures

The findings concerning evaluation procedures is one of the most interesting parts of this study. Costs are well understood and quite rigorously policed; but benefits, both tangible and intangible, are generally not identified or sought. ERP is seen as a strategic necessity and if customisations or upgrades are requested they are not measured in traditional cost benefit terms. In the organisations that are standardising processes, the rigorous evaluation is directed towards deciding if the functionality is absolutely necessary, and whether it fits with the desired standard process. Discrete business benefit of the customisation is very much a secondary consideration.

Business processes are so sacrosanct at Builder that alterations are only allowed for legal or market necessities. Builder is considering divesting itself of a very profitable company because it cannot be matched to its standard processes, the Finance Manager stating, "If it [the company] was less profitable it would already have been sold".

Global has a similar process to Builder, having a central team controlling customisations, to ensure that the organisation does not deviate from standard processes, rather than for controlling cost and benefits. Provider does seek to identify cost and benefits for some customisations, interestingly those that are evaluated as being the high return projects are prioritised below strategic and existing software licence requests. Server does not have a cost benefit procedure; Contractor has an informal process.

Key findings concerning evaluation procedures are:

- o Evaluation is largely being used to maintain the integrity of the ERP
- o Costs are identified and controlled
- o Benefits are difficult to identify and quantify

6.3.10 Approach to Customisations

In all the cases customisations were necessary when implementing ERP. The cases indicate that extensive customisation significantly increase cost of ownership and restricts upgrades. Clearly, the case organisations did not appreciate the significant oncost of customisations early in the ERP lifecycle. Global and Builder have addressed this in subsequent implementations; Server, as a consequence, has ceased the maintenance agreement; Contractor is unable to upgrade; and Provider wishes to reverse engineer many of the customisations already made.

Builder and Global evaluation processes restrict customisations and aims to control the cost of ownership and maintain upgrade paths. The other organisations neither take into account nor identify cost of ownership of customisations. The oncost of customisations includes increased support, difficulty in acquiring information and difficulty in upgrading. These may ultimately reduce the life of the application.

The level of complexity of customising the application differs depending on the underlying complexity of the module or function. This complexity impacts cost of ownership and ease of upgrading. Only Builder seems to be aware of this, not allowing core transactions to be altered and adding new fields to additional tabs and tables, thereby maintaining the integrity of the core application. Although, this makes the application more cumbersome for users, it is seen here as a mature approach to managing customisations if upgrades are to be performed. The impact of customisations on the flexibility and cost of ownership of an ERP implies it is extremely important for a decision to customise the application to be made only after taking into account the cost implications over an extended period of time.

Key findings concerning the approach of case organisations to customisation are:

- o Customisations are necessary
- o A considered decision concerning customisation strategy must be made prior to any being sanctioning
- o Customisations increase cost of ownership
- o Cost of ownership varies as not all aspects of the system have the same lvel of complexity
- o Organisations come to realise over time that customisations are problematic

6.3.11 Restrictions and Limitations Imposed by ERP

All of the case organisations recognised a hiatus between making the system live and benefits becoming apparent. During this period the application made business operations more difficult to perform. This is because, generally, data capture happens earlier in an organisation's processes with ERP, causing additional workloads in some departments.

Once an ERP is implemented, change to the processes becomes difficult and costly and can either preclude or slow business change. The major restriction of ERP was identified as obtaining information from the application. All of the organisations identified various problems with reporting, Provider finding this to be the case even after implementing a data warehouse.

The key findings concerning restrictions and limitations imposed by ERP are:

- o A hiatus after live occurs before an organisation achieves normal operations
- o Implementation may move or change organisational bottlenecks
- o Process changes post-live may be difficult
- o Reporting of data is difficult and complex

6.3.12 Approach to Business Process Analysis

Builder, Provider and Global came to realise that business process analysis is critical to ERP applications. Builder and Global did not take a process approach with their first ERP and Provider did not analyse processes during the implementation. All have since realised the importance of business process analysis and that it is critical for both the implementation and evaluation of customisations.

Business process analysis must take into account both the desired processes of the organisation and those embedded in the ERP application. A decision should be made to amend an organisational process or customise the ones embedded in the application. As was identified earlier, consultants often do not understand the process flows of the application and, therefore, it is imperative that an organisation takes ownership of the process analysis, especially when the implemented processes are very difficult to alter.

The key findings concerning the approach to business process analysis are as follows:

- o Business process analysis is a fundamental aspect of understanding ERP
- o ERP has configurable inbuilt processes and organisations have a desired process: both need to be understood, and changes to both evaluated
- o Implemented processes are difficult to change

o   Consultants often do not understand the impact of a decision on business processes

6.3.13 Expected Lifespan of the ERP

The estimated time that the ERP applications will last the case organisations included estimates of '5 to 10 years', "25 years" and "indefinitely". None of the organisations planned to change the application or were sure of events which might transpire that would induce them to change. In summary, they believed the applications would last for the foreseeable future and could not foresee an event or circumstance that would make them abandon the application.

6.4   Towards a Theory

> *As an applied discipline, IS will not achieve legitimacy by the rigour of its method or by its theoretical base, but by being practically useful (Moody & Bowles, 2000, p.351)*

The case organisations believe the training and consultancy provided by VARs and/or Software Authors at the time of implementation is poor. Builder and Global, with their second ERP implementation have taken ownership and the resulting applications are consequently much better aligned with the objectives of the organisations. The major proposal of this book is that organisations take ownership of the applications and establish an 'ERP bureau' which oversees activity throughout the application's life. The proposed bureau needs to be made up of technical, operations and business personnel, as well as senior managers. This is not to say that the bureau must undertake all activity, but it should, as is often the case with outsourcing of IT, oversee third party activity. Importantly, the bureau will be responsible for decisions about, and 'governance' of the application.

The bureau must recognise that it needs to resolve the dichotomies identified in this book; the major dichotomy is that customising an ERP application makes upgrades problematic, even impossible, and continual customisation appears to restrict the ability to obtain management reports, particularly benchmarking and see through reports for multiple business units. However, standard processes with close to vanilla implementations appear to reduce user satisfaction. These factors need to be carefully considered and a decision made based on the nuances of the organisation managing the ERP.

ERP lends itself well to standardised organisational processes but cost, and particularly cost of ownership, is increased substantially with disparate business unit processes and the bureau needs to be aware that ERP are less suited to flexible organisations, being likely to impose control structures that might stifle the organisation.

All of the case organisations identified issues related to reporting. While this is partially alleviated by data warehouses, reporting, particularly ad-hoc reporting, is problematic. Much time is dedicated to managing the transactions associated with ERP but less thought is given to the provision of information. Currently reporting is taken as 'a given' with ERP and organisations are not addressing information needs until late in the implementation cycle or even post-implementation. This causes management frustration and negatively impacts perceptions of the application. Reporting requirements, therefore, need to be identified early and the best approach identified.

In the case study organisations formal evaluation in terms of tangible cost and benefit analysis, utilising such methods as NPV calculations, were not considered to be suitable evaluation tools for many ERP decisions. This was largely due to the benefits being difficult to attribute directly to the ERP. Instead, as Remenyi et al (2007) have shown, the bureau staff will probably need to use more intuition and a number of factors to identify the best choice and decisions. As Remenyi et al (2007, p. 52) point out, decisions should be based on "how the world really is rather than simply what the spreadsheet says". They identify a number of relevant decision-making factors, (see Chapter 5, Figure 38), in terms of evaluation in today's business world. The bureau should be empowered to support business objectives, with expenditure commensurate with the objectives, and how that expenditure is identified will depend on senior managements' faith in the team and the value placed on the objectives. The major evaluation should perhaps be concerned with the abilities of the personnel in the bureau. If the bureau is thought to provide sound expertise, the major issue then centres round communication of business objectives from all levels of the organisation, and the management of ERP against these by the bureau.

The following are 'knowledge elements' derived from the case organisations as relevant for the ERP bureau, and based on the constructs which underpin the study:
- o   Business strategy and objectives
- o   Organisation needs and intent
- o   Organisational information requirements
- o   Organisational business processes
- o   ERP package fit with the organisation's process flows
- o   IT topologies and configurations
- o   Direct and indirect costs

o   Potential negative effects of ERP decisions

o   The oncost of customisations

o   Tangible and intangible benefits of tactical projects

The bureau will need to incorporate sufficient skills to understand these factors and, in turn, make sound decisions concerning the application. A conceptual model of the management and evaluation of ERP by an organisation's bureau is depicted in Figure 46.

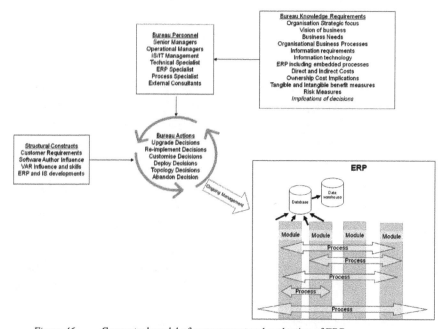

Figure 46.   Conceptual model of management and evaluation of ERP

For efficient, effective operation of ERP thisbook postulates the bureau will need to understand the following factors:

o   How Software Authors and VAR exert pressure to upgrade through either increasing support costs or withdrawing support for older versions of software.

o   External factors that impact the organisation, and how these affect the ERP deliverables, e.g., most of the case organisations' primary focus for ERP is on the customer.

o   The antecedents of the original implementation and upgrades, and how they impact the current ERP, e.g., by querying, was the implementation strategy flawed; should customisations be reversed; and, what has been learned?

o   The perceptions of, or culture, concerning IS. The more comprehensive the understanding, the more conducive management of the application is likely to be.

o   The current organisational structure and management style; there can be little doubt from existing theory, that ERP best fits centralised, highly controlled organisations. If the organisation varies from this, expectations must be tailored to the potential impact of the ERP on it.

o   Available funds and the financial status of the organisation is of major consequence for initial and ongoing management of ERP. With the elusive nature of benefits, ERP decisions may be based on the level of confidence in the capabilities of the personnel in the bureau.

o   Internal sources of department power must be identified and reasoned decisions made, where practical, based on organisational impact rather the power of particular groups.

o   The reasons for the application either restricting or enabling the organisation must be fundamentally understood.

o   The organisational processes will need to be known in their own right, as well as those processes embedded in the ERP.   Implementing the processes embedded in the ERP is the option with the lowest cost of ownership, but these process should not be considered 'best practice'. The impact of these processes on the organisation must be fundamentally understood as well as the potential efficacy of an implementation which is likely to be in place for many years. It may also be less costly and beneficial in terms of information provision, over time, not to optimise user interfaces and implement tactical customisations.

o   The longevity of the proposed application must be estimated and used as a precursor to all of the above factors. If, an organisation intends to utilise the application for 'the foreseeable future' the foregoing considerations become extremely important, especially because major decision reversal with ERP is both costly and time consuming.

The bureau should have a process view of the ERP that goes across the implemented modules, thus creating a matrix view of the application as shown in Figure 46. The organisation's information requirements should be determined and managed as a critical component. In addition to the database, a data warehouse or data mart should be implemented to provide for the information needs of businesses.

Customisations should be made only when absolutely necessary, and after the criteria for necessary customisation has been defined. If an application is in operation and is envisaged to remain in operation for the 'foreseeable future', the customisations already made should be re-evaluated as to their necessity. When customisations are made, procedures should be put in place to incorporate them in future upgrades. Use of Builder's proposed procedure to release customisations only with upgrades is advisable, for this improves testing of customisations, makes the application more stable and minimises disruption. It would be possible to 'patch' the application to overcome bugs between 'releases'.

6.5 Limitations

A fuller explanation of the approach taken to limitations and generalising findings is included in Chapter 3.

"Seen in traditional terms, the reliability and validity of qualitatively derived findings can be seriously in doubt" (Miles and Huberman, 1994, p.4). Yin (2003b) sees the main limitation of case studies as a lack of methodological rigour and difficulty of generalization. The major issue for generalization of qualitative research is that it is sometimes envisaged in the same way as quantitative research where a sample is representative of a wider community (Lee & Baskerville, 2003; Maxwell, 1992; Mishler, 1990; Yin, 2003b) .

Yin (2003b) refers to generalization from case study research as "analytic generalization", suggesting that "if two or more cases are shown to support the same theory, replication may be claimed. The empirical results may be considered yet more potent if two or more cases support the same theory but do not support an equally plausible, rival theory." (p. 32-33). Thebook has established a theoretical proposal and postulates that other similar organisations will find it relevant. A major reason for the focus on relevance is that, over the past five years, IS researchers has been calling for greater relevance of IS theory (see for example Agarwal and Lucas Jr, 2005; Baskerville and Myers,2002; Benbasat and Zmud,2003; Boland Jr and Lyytinen,2004; Boudreau, Gefen, and Straub,2001; Mingers, 2001; Orlikowoski et al., 2001; Orlikowoski and Iacono, 2001 and Vessey, Ramesh, and Glass, 2002).

The research in endeavouring to be of rigorous approach relied extensively on the works of Lee and Baskerville (2003), Maxwell (1992), Mishler (1990) and Yin (2003b). The work of Mishler (1990) provided the greatest guidance by providing the following method to follow:

1. Focus on a piece of "interpretive discourse"
2. Takes text as the basic datum
3. Reconceptualise it as an instance of more abstract and general "type"
4. Provide a method of characterising and coding textual units
5. Specify the structure of the relationship among them
6. Interpret the meaning of the structure within a theoretical framework

This 'internal' validity process helps to validate the rigour of the research but not its 'external' validity (Lee & Baskerville, 2003). The process for external validity has been guided by Lee and Baskerville (2003) where a description of phenomenon is explained and generalised to theory. As Maxwell (1992) points out, when research generalises to a theory, a theory being 'a coherent group of general propositions using principles of explanation for a class of phenomena', the theory may help people make sense of similar events in different circumstances, even if there are then different results. This approach is described succinctly by Seddon and Scheepers (2006) who propose that a phenomenon believed to be true in one setting may be theorised to be true in another. As external validity, or deductive argument, is only as valid as the most controversial premise of the study (Lee & Baskerville, 2003), the theory proposed here identifies factors and influences that need to be gauged by an organisation rather than being a prescriptive set of procedures.

Thisbook strived to emphasise that the type of organisation and the environment it operates within will impact the relevance of the theory to that organisation. Whether this research aids the procedures of organisations when managing ERP, will only be known in the fullness of time.

6.6 Contribution

> *It is no longer true to say that humans create it [society]. Rather we must say: they reproduce or transform it. That is to say, if society is already made, then any concrete human praxis, if you like, act of objectivation, can only modify it; and the totality of such acts sustain or change it. (Bhaskar 1989, pp. xx, Cited Engestrom et al, 1999, pp10).*

Chapter 6 - Conclusion

Thisbook makes an original contribution to knowledge by focusing on an area of limited research. It marshals the disparate relevant theory surrounding the phenomenon, correlates it with the findings from the case organisations and produces a cohesive framework. The framework has particularly been designed to be practically useful to organisations.

The major contributions of thisbook is the unearthing of a number of dilemmas that are instrumental in shaping the approach to managing ERP. They are that (1) due to the strategic importance of ERPs, organisations need to take ownership of the application but are unable to do so due to a lack of knowledge concerning the application, business process and ongoing management and evaluation procedures, (2) ERPs are suited much better to centralised rigidly controlled organisations than decentralised flexible organisations, (3) in larger organisations, standard group wide ERP business processes provides SBU transparency but also reduces user satisfaction, (4) the processes that become embedded in an ERP during implementation are difficult to change and may prevail for the life of the application, and result in abandonment (5) customising an ERP application is necessary but creates difficulties for upgrading the application to later versions, (6) the transaction focus of ERPs makes provision of management reports difficult (7) the longevity of an application is underpinned by the ability to upgrade but upgrades are costly, disruptive to operations and, simply, difficult.

Thisbook makes an original contribution to the literature and theory by addressing these dilemmas through the proposal that organisations should take control of the ERP by establishing an ERP bureau and by specifying a framework of factors that the bureau needs to understand to properly manage an ERP. These include (1) an understanding of the strategic aim of the application (2) an appreciation of the impacts of business factors such as organisation type, strategy process, financial procedures, and financial status (3) an understanding of contextual environmental considerations such as supply chain influencers (4) an understanding of the consequences of the software authors charging procedures (5) the value and application impact of the ERP maintenance agreement (6) an understanding of the impact of customisations on the ability to upgrade (7) knowledge of horizontal and vertical information requirements (8) a recognition that due to the strategic nature of ERP, business drivers and imperatives tend to provide more crucial benefits indicators than traditional cost/benefit justifications.

This provides critical insight into the management and evaluation of operational ERP. As such it has the potential to aid future research and position education about the subject. Perhaps the major contribution to IS theory will not be the findings of this research, but among the proposals for future research, so cementing the broad views proposed here, or indeed, in identifying conflicting theories.

6.6.1 Significance

As outlined in Chapter 1, this study has potential significance for both theory and practice as the subject of management of operational ERP is significantly under researched. Indeed IS theory over the last decade has called for further investigation into the phenomenon of operational ERP (Gable et al, 1997; Davenport, 1998; Markus and Tanis, 2000; Klaus et al, 2000; Chung & Snyder, 2000; Esteves and Pastor, 2001; Dong et al, 2002; Stein et al, 2003; Gable et al 2003, Gosain, 2004; Bendoly and Jacobs, 2005; Sarkis & Sundarraj, 2005; Dowlatshahi, 2005; Esteves and Bohorquez, 2007) and for this type of relevant research (Agarwal and Lucas Jr, 2005; Baskerville and Myers,2002; Benbasat and Zmud,2003; Boland Jr and Lyytinen,2004; Boudreau, Gefen, and Straub,2001; Mingers, 2001; Orlikowoski et al., 2001; Orlikowoski and Iacono, 2001 and Vessey, Ramesh, and Glass, 2002). This book has responded to these calls by investigating the phenomenon and striving within the bounds of due rigour to find relevant practical findings. The approach taken here has been to create findings, from a rigorous process of investigation, and form those findings into a theoretical framework that should prove useful to practitioners and of interest to IS academics.

6.6.2 Future Research

The phenomenon of operational ERP is expanding, whilst the body of research is small. This study, therefore, has the potential to have a major impact on future research. The following are the key areas identified for research:

1. A major issue unearthed by the book has been the important decision to either maintain standard processes or to have ongoing customisations and/or dissimilar processes within a group of organisations. Further research that seeks to understand the following would seem to be useful:
    - the rationale for the two approaches
    - the cost implications of the two approaches
    - user satisfaction with the two approaches
    - the impact upon provision of business objectives in different organisations and different types of organisations with the two approaches

2. The longevity of the Delone and McLean ex-post model of 1992 and 2003 is testament that information systems are seen to depend on user satisfaction. However, the standard processes

adopted by the two major companies explored in thisbook had little regard for user satisfaction. These companies were perhaps the most mature users of ERP as they had replaced comprehensive suites of ERP. Interestingly, the replaced ERP had a far greater emphasis on user satisfaction. Thisbook did not rigorously address user satisfaction, nor accounts of users' cognitive frames of reference with regard to perceived ease of use and usefulness. A study analysing user satisfaction by applying the technology acceptance model (TAM), would provide a better understanding of user satisfaction and in turn systems use.

It is also significant that, for all case examples, the strategic imperative dominated over user considerations. This approach contravenes much of the benefit proposition of the Delone and Mclean model (2003). A potentially interesting study would identify if the Delone and Mclean model is applicable for ERP. It might also be interesting to include a time element that shows the ERP iterating through the Markus and Tannis (2000b) ERP maturity model, after upgrades and customisations, and the resultant impact on user satisfaction.

3. Three of the case organisations fervently believe that the best way to implement and manage an ERP is through business process analysis. Further studies concerning business process analysis and its application with ERP would seem to be very relevant. Particularly for applications other than SAP where a process analysis approach is more unusual e.g. Microsoft ERP applications.

The SAP implementation at Provider was observed to be poor due to a lack of focus on processes. The ramifications of the lack of a process view for organisations implementing ERP would perhaps uncover useful pointers for more effective installations. A very important aspect would be to improve methods of understanding embedded ERP processes and how to match those with required organisational processes. A decision criteria concerning the matching of the ERP and organisational process would potentially have immense value.

4. The case organisations all lamented the ability of the ERP applications to provide management information and reports. This was seen to be the case even after deploying ERP data warehouses and BI tools. An investigation into the level of satisfaction with reporting vis-à-vis the methods of obtaining management information from ERP would be of great interest. Particularly in the area of ad-hoc reporting. Applied research investigating technical methods, such as denormalised materialised views and data marts aimed at business process information that focuses on key data elements dispersed across tables rather than the current preoccupation with

key business indicators would seem a worthwhile study. The research might potentially alleviate one of the major issues identified in thisbook.

5. A key finding was that none of the case organisations had been able to functionally upgrade their ERP application. This was despite paying 15% - 25% of the application cost in annual maintenance fees so that the organisations have access to later versions of the application. This gives rise to a number of potential research projects:

   - a quantitative study aimed at identifying how often organisations perform both technical and functional upgrades.
   - an identification of the factors that inhibit upgrades; seen in thisbook to be complexity of re-implementing customisations, cost of upgrading, disruption to operations and limited benefits of upgrading
   - an investigation into the proposed relationship between cost of upgrades and decisions to abandon an application would seem to have merit. Another potential area of research is a more general study concerning reasons for ERP abandonment.

6. Customisations were seen as necessary by the case organisations and IS theory. They are though something of a necessary evil, as they increase cost of ownership and inhibits upgrades. Investigations into customisation would seem to have much potential. Research aimed at understanding the following seems pertinent:

   - the drivers for customisations
   - the controls and management surrounding customisations both pre and post-live
   - cost, and cost of ownership, of customisations
   - cost vis-à-vis complexity of the functions modified
   - best practice for implementing and technically managing customisations
   - benefit analysis that applies to customisations
   - methods of depreciating and maintaining asset registers for customisations that become capital assets

7. Australian legislation dictates that all IT related expenditure must be fully depreciated in a period of five years. This period seems to be incorrect for an asset that might last organisations, as proposed by the case organisations, 25 years or more. An investigation to ascertain if ERP can be re-valued as an assets (preliminary investigation indicate that it can be) and whether ERP is being re-valued as an asset would be very relevant to practice. Particularly as re-evaluation

could potentially produce a significant one time increase in profit for many organisations. It might also increase awareness of the value of the ERP and the value of maintaining the ERP.

8. The case organisations had very different strategic focus for, and levels of expertise surrounding, ERP. A comparative study to understand the expertise being utilised to manage ERP vis-à-vis the satisfaction of the stakeholder groups, of management, technical and operational, would be of interest.

Amoako-Gyampah (2004) compared managerial and end-user perceptions for SAP R/3 in five case studies, identifying differences in the perception of the two groups. As the perception of ERP in the cases organisations was seen to change over time, it would be interesting to investigate how the perceptions of these two groups might change over an extended period.

9. Brown et al (2000) suggest that a reason to buy ERP is that it costs less than developing applications. This may be the case, but it appears from the case organisation that it remains to be proved. It would be of immense value to theory and practice to properly understand cost of ownership in terms of ERP over an extended period. The application costs, implementation cost, and annual maintenance cost are considerable. If other costs such as customisations, upgrading, applying patches, and support were taken into account the total is likely to be very substantial.

10. The lifespan of ERP make longitudinal studies, long! It seems necessary to strive to understand past events if we are to significantly improve understanding of ERP quickly. Bannister (2002b) called for more IS research into the dimension of history. The approach advocated required past events to be reconstructed from available sources and then interpreted. An historical research approach may accelerate knowledge concerning ERP and create a basis for more targeted research.

11. One of the major finding of this study is that organisations need to take ownership of the ERP application and that this is difficult to achieve due to the lack of knowledge of the application, the implementation process and the ongoing management processes. A study identifying the knowledge requirements of the organisational stakeholders and proposal for education programs would have major implications for theory and practice. Not least for the beleaguered university IS schools.

12.   A study that incorporated much of the foregoing proposals and identified practices around a project life cycle costing process would be of immense value.

These potential subjects for future research are not seen to be exhaustive and it may well be that a reader with a different or broader perspective will identify other aspects that merit research.

6.6.3 Implications for Practice

The implications for practice are many, but none is more important than the confirmation of the potential for an ERP to either inhibit or enable an organisation for an extended period. When an ERP is acquired there will be very few assets that have the potential longevity of the application. However, the decisions that are made in the very early stages of acquisition and implementation are likely to have a major consequence on the ERP lifespan and organisational impact. The primary finding of this study is that organisations should take ownership of their ERP application at the beginning of the implementation lifecycle, for not to do so devolves much of the responsibility for ongoing strategy delivery, operational efficiencies and management information to a third party.

The approach identified here where organisations, particularly when implementing their first ERP, rely on consultants to successfully implement the application and train users is seen to be inadequate and flawed. Universally, training is neither seen as good enough, nor early enough during the implementation process, for stakeholders to be able to make value judgements about the ERP. Some considerable time must elapse, perhaps many years subsequent to the application being made operational before stakeholders, such as those interviewed here, believe they are able to make decisions. At this point many of the organisations have recognised both their senior staff's and consultants' mistakes. However, the cost of re-implementing or replacing the ERP mean that many organisations live with the consequence of these decisions for a prolonged period. Nonetheless, two of the case organisations have replaced ERP at a cost of many hundreds of millions of U.S. dollars to change the emphasis of their ERP applications.

The knowledge lag needs to be addressed by organisations so that they may pro-actively manage the applications. In support of this, there needs to be comprehensive education programs to fill the void, as well as research programs to better identify the knowledge requirements. It is not the aim here to reiterate the conclusions of the study. However, it is likely to be useful to practice if the stakeholders are cognisant of those conclusions when managing ERP. Some of the key factors are as follows:

- an ERP bureau should be established that includes senior management and has personnel with the skills necessary, as defined earlier, to manage the application
- the bureau needs to understand that consultancy advice may be flawed
- the bureau needs be aware of the implications of organisational structure on ERP outcomes and cost of ownership
- the bureau needs to understand the cost of ownership of customisations and the broad implications of customisations upon future opportunities
- the bureau needs to understand the potential of customisations to impact upgrades and as a consequence negate the benefits of having a maintenance agreement
- the bureau needs to have a fundamental understanding of both the processes in the ERP and those desired by the organisation. As well as the consequence of adopting the ERP process or customising them to meet business requirements

If an ERP application is already implemented it is proposed that it might be pertinent for the Bureau to review the application in-terms of its potential contribution to the organisation over its expected lifespan. Remedial action of re-implementing, upgrading, customising or abandoning should be gauged in terms of the key factors identified above and the anticipated life. It is noteworthy that remedial action may extend the ERP lifespan.

The evaluation process for ERP has three core domains; cost of an activity, cost of ownership and benefits. The tangible cost of activity appear to be largely known, nevertheless, there are many indirect costs and potential dis-benefits - negative impacts of say increasing supplier switching costs - that should be understood. Cost of ownership appears to be a major issue that is not understood and organisations need, until further research is undertaken concerning the matter, to create a method to identify with cost of ownership.

The pursuit of tangible benefits in many respects seems to be futile. The benefits are ultimately produced by process or information improvements that are almost impossible to trace back to an application. There is potentially a time lag to benefits and the period of benefits may well be longer than any usual NPV prediction. There are also many potential secondary benefits that are available from ERP that cannot possibly be valued at earlier stages. Therefore, tangible benefit analysis should reasonable be used only for short-term efficiency gains. Investment decisions perhaps need an intangible approach based on a mix of communication of business objectives, the skill set of those involved in the ERP bureau and budgetary funds seems a more pertinent approach. Budgetary funds might be identified by a mixture of benchmarking competitors, potential of strategic business objectives and financial constraints.

6.6.3.1 Implications for Software Author and Value Added Resellers

The Software Authors have been denounced for, poor architecture, the complexity of upgrading applications, asserting pressure to upgrade and being remote from organisations. The Software Authors, however, could potentially cite much mitigation concerning the complexity of a business that strives to produce and maintain a product, that is built with ever changing technology, and aims to be useful to almost any organisation. Nevertheless, there are a number of factors identified in thisbook that could potentially aid Software Authors.

Comments and statements from IT personnel and users illustrate the applications as having a poor reputation. There are a number of possible remedies to this situation: 1. organisations could be helped to take ownership of the implementation and this may take the focus away from the product and rightfully place it upon the implementation and ongoing management of the ERP; 2. tools could be provided that enable organisations and VARs to analyse desired processes against those embedded in the ERP; 3. the misnomer of 'best practice' processes should be abandoned as the implications can only ultimately mean dissatisfaction.

The dichotomy between customisations and upgrades needs to be addressed by Software Authors, particularly as the cost and disruption of upgrades leads many organisations to believe it might be easier to install a new system rather than upgrade. If these applications are to last in organisations for as long as initially envisaged, the upgrade path must be made much smoother. The decision by one of the case organisations to simply cancel the maintenance agreement has far reaching implications. If this were to become a trend then Software Authors, that have in the area of 50% of revenue from maintenance agreement, would be in jeopardy of demise.

VARs are largely responsible for providing consultancy and training, although they should reasonably be aided by the Software Author. The consultancy was seen to be poor by nearly all of the case organisations, with the major complaint being that the consultants are knowledgeable about a single module and do not understand the consequence of what they are doing on other aspects of the application. This has led case organisations to propose that customisations were made when they were not required, and that decisions caused problems in other areas of the application and business. A more expansive training program for consultants would help overcome these issues, as would perhaps a different organisational structure for VAR organisations. One that is more in line with other professional organisations such as accounts and solicitors. Where partnership concepts and mentoring programs are aimed at engendering and fostering knowledge and rewards are given for relationship management rather than tied solely to sales processes.

The education of users was seen to be very poor by all of the case organisations. This should be improved and should not simply be concerned with application features, but education of broad aspects including an understating of decisions in terms of cost and cost of ownership, management of processes and methods of lifecycle project costing. The cost of ownership of customisations in particular should be better communicated. Partnership with tertiary education facilities may help overcome these educational shortfalls.

References

Abdinnour-Helm, S., & Lengnick-Hall, C. (2005). Strategy As A Critical Factor in Applied ERP Success. In *Strategic ERP Extension and Use*. California, USA: Stanford Publishing Press.

Agarwal, R., & Lucas Jr, H. C. (2005). The Information Systems Identity Crisis: Focusing On High-Visibility And High-Impact Research. *MIS Quarterly, 29*(3), 381-398.

Agnell, I., & Smithson, S. (1990). Managing IT: a crisis of confidence? *European Management Journal, 8*(1), 27-36.

Akkermans, H., & Helden, K. V. (2002). Vicious And Virtuous Cycles In ERP Implementation: A Case Study Of Interrelations Between Critical Success Factors. *European journal of Information Systems, 11*, 35-46.

Al-Mashari, M. (2003). Enterprise Resource Planning (ERP) Systems: A Research Agenda. *Industrial Management & Data Systems Journal, 103*(1), 22-27.

Al-Mashari, M., & Zairi, M. (2000). Information and Business Process Equality: The Case of SAP R/3 Implementation. *The Electronic Journal of Information Systems in Developing Countries, 2*(4), 1-15.

Alter, S. (1999). Dimensions of Information Systems Success. *Communications of AIS, 2*(20).

Amoako-Gyampah, K. (2004). ERP Implementation Factors. *Business Process Management Journal, 10*(2), 171-183.

AMR Research. (2005). $17 Billion Expected Future Growth in Enterprise Applications Market [Electronic Version]. Retrieved 14 October 2007 from http://www.amrresearch.com/Content/View.asp?pmillid=18789.

AMR Research. (2006). The Enterprise Applications Global Forecast, 2005–2010 [Electronic Version]. Retrieved 13 October 2007 from http://www.amrresearch.com/Content/View.asp?pmillid=19944.

Andresen, K., & Gronau, N. (2005). Adaptability Concepts For Enterprise Resource Planning Systems-Component Framework. *Paper presented at the Proceedings of the Eleventh Americas Conference in Information Systems*, Omaha, NE, USA.

Applegate, L. M., Austin, R. D., & McFarlan, W. F. (2002). *Corporate Information and Strategy Management*. Burr Ridge: McGraw-Hill/Irwin.

Ash, C. G., & Burn, J. M. (2003). Staged Implementation Of e-business Networks Through ERP: A Case Study Of Siemens (1998-2001). In *Enterprise information systems IV* (pp. 283 - 290). Hingham, MA, USA: Kluwer Academic Publishers.

Ashurst, C., & Doherty, N. F. (2003). Towards The Formulation Of A 'Best practice' Framework For Benefits Realisation In IT Projects. *Electronic Journal of Information Systems, 6*(2), 1-10.

References

Baccarini, D., Salm, G., & Love, P. E. D. (2004). Management Of Risks In Information Tech. Projects. *Industrial Management & Data Systems Journal, 104*(4), 286-295.

Bahn, D. L. (2001). Sustainable Competitive Advantage from Information Technology: Limitations of the Value Chain. In *Strategies Information Technology: Opportunities for Competitive Advantage.* Hershey: Idea Group Publishing.

Banker, R. D., & Slaughter, S. A. (2000). The Moderating Effects Of Structure On Volatility And Complexity In Software Enhancement. *Inform System Research, 11*(3), 219–240.

Bannister, F. (2001). Dismantling the silos: extracting new value from IT investments in public administration. *Information Systems Journal,* 11:65-84.

Bannister, F. (2002a). Sustained delivery of value: the role of leadership in long-term IS effectiveness. Evaluation and Program Planning 25: 151-158.

Bannister, F. (2002b) The Dimension of Time: Historiography in Information Systems Research. *Electronic Journal of Business Research Methods,* Vol. 1 Iss. 1, 1-10.

Bannister, F., & Remenyi, D. (2000). Acts of Faith: instinct, value and IT investment decisions. *Journal of Information Technology, 15,* 231-241.

Bannister, F., McCabe, P., & Remenyi, D. (2001). How Much Did We Really Pay for That? The Awkward Problem of Information Technology Costs. *Electronic Journal of Information Systems Evaluation, 5*(1).

Baskerville, R. L., & Myers, M. D. (2002). Information Systems As A Reference Discipline. *MIS Quarterly, 26*(1), 1-14.

Bassellier, G., Benbasat, I., & Recih, B. H. (2003). The Influence of Business Managers' IT Competence On Championing IT. *Information Systems Research, 14*(4).

Becker, J., & Niehaves, B. (2007). Epistemological Perspectives On IS Research: A Framework For Analysing And Systematizing Epistemological Assumptions. *Information Systems Journal, 17,* 197-214.

Benbasat, I., & Zmud, R. W. (1999). Empirical Research in Information Systems: The Practice of Relevance. *MIS Quarterly, 23*(1), 3-16.

Benbasat, I., & Zmud, R. W. (2003). The Identity Crisis Within The IS Discipline: Defining And Communicating The Discipline's Core Properties. *MIS Quarterly, 27*(2), 193-194.

Bendoly, E., & Jacobs, F. R. (2005). *Strategic ERP Extension and Use.* Stanford, California, USA: Stanford University Press.

Benjamin, R. I., & Levinson, E. (1993). A Framework for Managing IT Enabled Change. *Sloan Management Review,* 23-33.

References

Bernroider, E., & Koch, S. (2001). Differences In Characteristics Of The ERP Systems Selection Process Between Small or Medium and Large Organisations. *Business Process Management Journal, 7, 251-257.*

Bhaskar, R. (1991). *Philosophy and the idea of freedom.* Oxford, UK: Blackwell.

Bhattacherjee, A., & Premkumar, G. (2004). Understanding Changes In Belief And Attitude Toward Information Technology Usage: A Theoretical Model And Longitudinal Test. *MIS Quarterly, 28*(2), 229-254.

Bjornsson, H., & Lundegard, R. (1992). Corporate Competitiveness and Information Technology. *European Management Journal, 10*(3), 341-347.

Boland Jr, R. J., & Lyytinen, K. (2004). Information Systems Research As Design: Identity, Process, and Narrative. In K. T. Bonnie, D.P, Watell, D. (Ed.), *Information systems research : relevant theory & informed practice.* Paris, France: Kluwer Academic Publishings.

Boonstrap, A. (2004). Interpreting an ERP implementation from a stakeholder perspective. *Under Review.*

Boudreau, M., Gefen, D., and Straub, D., & Straub, D. W. (2001). Validation In Information Systems Research: A State-Of-The-Art Assessment. *MIS Quarterly, 25*(1), 1-24.

Broadbent, M., & Weill, P. (1997). Management by Maxim: How Business and IT Managers Can Create IT Infrastructures. *Sloan Management Review, 38*(3), 77-92.

Brown, C., & Vessey, I. (1999). ERP Implementation Approaches: Toward A Contingency Framework. *Paper presented at the International Conference on Information Systems,* Charlotte, North Carolina USA.

Brown, C. V., Vessey, I., & Powell A. (2000). The ERP Purchase Decision: Influential Business and IT Factors. *Paper presented at the Americas Conference on Information Systems* 2000.

Brown, C. V., & Vessey, I. (2003). Managing the next wave of Enterprise Systems: Leveraging lessons from ERP. *MIS Quarterly Executive, 2*(1), 65 -77.

Burn, J., Marshall, P., & Barnett, M. (1999). *E-Business Strategies for Virtual Organisations*: Elsevier.

Burn, R. B. (1994). *Introduction To research Methods.* Melbourne, Australia: Longman Cheshire.

Burrell, G., & Morgan, G. (1979). *Sociological Paradigms and Organisational Analysis.* Aldershot, UK: Ashgate Publishing Ltd.

Carlsson, S. A. (2003). Advancing Information Systems Evaluation (Research): A Critical Realist Approach. *European journal of Information Systems, 6*(2), 11-20.

Carton, F., & Adam, F. (2003). Analysing The Impact Of Enterprise Resource Planning Systems Roll-Outs in Mulit-National Companies. *Electronic Journal of Information Systems, 3, 88-94.*

Chan, F., & Qi, H. (2003). An innovative performance measurement method for supply chain management. *Supply Chain Management: An International Journal, 8*(3), 209-223.

References

Chang, S., Gable, G., Smythe, E., & Timbrell, G. (2000). A Delphi Examination Of Public Sector ERP Implementation Issues. *Paper presented at the International Conference Of Information Systems,* Brisbane, Australia.

Chung, S. H., & Snyder, C. A. (2000). ERP Adoption: A technological Evolution Approach. *International Journal of Agile Management Systems, 2*(1), 24-32.

Ciborra, C. (2002). *The Labyrinths of Information: Challenging the Wisdom of Systems.* Oxford University Press, Oxford.

Clemmons, S., & Simon, S. J. (2001). Control And Coordination In Global ERP Configuration. *Business Process Management Journal, 7*(3), 205-215.

COBIT Framework (nd.) Source COBIT materials. Retrieved 15th September 2005 from *www.isaca.org.*

Columbus IT Partner A/S Annual Report (2002). Columbus IT Partner A/S Annual Report A/S Annual Report 2001/2000). *Retrieved September 2004 from ColumbusIT.com.*

Cresswell, J. W. (1994). *Research Design - Qualitative and Quantative Approaches.* Thousand Oaks, US: Sage Publications.

Crotty, M. (1998). *The Foundation of Social Research: Meaning and Perspective In The Research Process.* St leonards, Australia: Allen & Unwin Ltd.

Cutler, M., & Sterne, J. (2000). *E-Metrics - Business Metrics for the New Economy.*: Netgenesis Corp.

Daellenbach, H. G. (2001). Hard OR, Soft OR, Problem Structuring Methods, Critical Systems Thinking: A Primer. *Paper presented at the ORSNZ Conference Twenty Naught One,* University of Canterbury, Christchurch, NZ.

Davenport, T. H. (1998). Putting the enterprise into the enterprise system. *Harvard Business Review, 76*(4), 121 (111).

Davenport, T., H., & Brooks, J. D. (2004). Enterprise systems and the supply chain. *Journal of Enterprise Information Management, 17*(1), 8-19.

Davenport, T. H., Harris, J. G., & Cantrell, S. (2004). Enterprise systems and ongoing process change. *Business Process Management Journal, 10*(1), 16-26.

De Haes, S. and Van Grembergen,W, (2005). IT Governance Structures, Processes and Relational Mechanisms: Achieving IT/Business Alignment in a Major Belgian Financial Group. *Paper presented at the 38ths" Hawaii International conference on Systems sciences*

Deise, M. V , Nowikow, C., King, P., & Wright, A. (2000). *Executives Guide to E-Business: From Tactics to Strategy.* New York, USA: John Wiley & Sons.

DeLone, W. H., & McLean, E. R. (1992). Information Systems Success: In Search of Independent Variables. *Inform Systems Res., 3*(1), 60-95.

References

DeLone, W. H., & McLean, E. R. (2003). The Delone and McLean Model of Information Systems Success: A Ten-Year Update. *Journal of Management Information Systems, 19*(4), 9-30.

Dennis, A., & Valacich, J. (2001). Conducting Research in Information systems. *Communications of the AIS, 7.*

Denzin, N. K., & Lincoln, Y. S. (2000). *Handbook of Qualitative Research 2nd Ed.* Thousand Oaks: Sage Publications Ltd.

Dobson, P. (2001). The Philosophy Of Critical Realism - An opportunity For Information Systems Research. *Information Systems Frontiers, 3*(2), 199-210.

Dobson, P., Myles, J., & Jackson, P. (2007). Making The Case For Critical Realism: Examining The Implementation Of Automated Performance Management Systems. *Information Resource Management, 20*(2), 138-152

Doolin, B. (1998). Information technology as disciplinary technology: being critical in interpretive research on information systems. *Journal of Information Technology, 13*(4), 301-312.

Doolin, B. (2004). Power And resistance In The Implementation Of A Medical Management Information System. *Inform Systems Journal, 14*, 343-362.

Dong, L., Neufeld, D., Higgins, C. (2002). The Iceberg on the Sea: What do you See? *Eighth Americas Conference on Information Systems.*

Dowlatshahi, S. (2005). Strategic Success factors in Enterprise Resource-Planning Design And Implementation: A Case Study Approach. *International Journal of Production Research, 43*(18).

Earl, M. J. (1989). *Management Strategies for Information Technology.* Hempstead: Prentice Hall International.

Efstathiou, A. (2002). Justification Tools for Enterprise IT Projects. *The Yankee Group - Sourcing Strategies.*

Eisenhardt, K. M. (1989). Building Theories From Case Study Research. *Academy of Management Review, 14*(4), 532 - 550.

El Amrani, R., Rowe, F., & Geffroy-Maronnat, B. (2006). The effects of Enterprise resource Planning Implementation Strategy On Cross-Functionality. *Inform Systems Journal, 16, 79-104.*

El Sawy, O. A. (2001). *Redesigning Enterprise Processes For e-Business*: McGraw Hill.

Engestrom, Y., Miettinen, R., Punamaki, R. (1999). *Perspectives on Activity Theory.* Cambridge: Cambridge University Press.

Enigl, D. C. (2003). Philosophy of Science: Evaluation of Transcendental Realism. from http://home.earthlink.net/~enigl/tr.htm

Eriksen, L. B., Axline, S., Markus, M. L., & Ducker, P. F. (1999). What Happens After 'Going Live' With ERP Systems? Competence Centres Can Support Effective Institutionalization. *Paper presented at the Americas Conference On Information Systems*, Milwaukee, U.S.

References

Eschender, C. (2003). *Prediction 2003: The ERP Market Readies for a Rebound:* Gartner Dataquest.

Esteves, J. M., & Pastor, J. A. (1999). An ERP Life-cycle-based Research Agenda. *Paper presented at the First International workshop in Enterprise Management and Resource* Planning: Methods, Tools and Architectures – EMRPS'99,, Venice, Italy.

Esteves, J., & Pastor, J. (2001). Enterprise Resource Planning Systems Research: An Annotated Bibliography. *Communications of AIS, 7, 1-52.*

Esteves, J. M. (2005). Addressing The Justification of Enterprise Systems Benefits: A Desire And Expectancy Disconfirmation Model. *Paper presented at the Proceedings of the Eleventh Americas Conference On Information Systems,* Omaha, NE, USA.

Esteves, J., & Bohorquez, V. (2007). An Updated ERP Systems Annotated Bibliography: 2001-2005. *Communications of AIS, 19,* 386-446.

Evans, D. E. (2003). *Business Innovation and Disruptive Technology.* New Jersey: Pearson Education.

Farbey, B., Land, F., & Targett, D. (1996). Moving IS Evaluation Forward: Learning Themes And Research Issues. *Journal Of Strategic Information Systems, 8,* 189-207.

Fichman, R. G. (2004). Going Beyond The Dominant Paradigm For Information Technology Innovation Research: Emerging Concepts and Methods. *Journal of the association for Information Systems,* 5(8), 314-355.

Fitzgerald, G. (1998). Evaluating Information Systems Projects: A Multidimensional Approach. *Journal of Information Technology, 13,* 15-27.

Fitzgerald, G., & Howcroft. (1998). Towards Dissolution Of The IS Research Debate: From Polarization To Polarity. *Journal of Information technology, 13*(4), 313-326.

Foucault, M. (1982). The subject and power. In H. Drefus & P. Rabinom (Eds.), *Beyond Structuralism and Hermeutics.* Harvester, NY, USA.

Fub, G., Gmeiner, R., Schiereck, D., & Strahringer, S. (2007). ERP Usage In Banking: An Exploratory Survey Of The World's Largest Banks. *Information Systems Management, 24*(2), 8-22.

Fulford, R. (2003). A Conceptual Model for ASP Adoption. *Seventh Asia Pacific Conference on Information Systems* Paper presented at the Pacific and Asia Conference On Information Systems, Adelaide, Australia.

Fulford, R. and Love, P.E.D. (2004) Propagation of an alternative enterprise service application adoption model. *Industrial Management & Data Systems Journal 104(6),450-456.*

Fulford, R (2006). *Propagation of an initial model for evaluating operational enterprise systems.* 17th Australian Conference of Information Systems, Adelaide.

Gable, G., Van den Heever, R., Scott, J., & Erlank, S. (1997). Large Package Software: The Need For Research. *Paper presented at the Americas Conference On information Systems,* Indianapolis, U.S.

References

Gable, G., Timbrell, G., Sauer, C., & Chan, T. (2002). An Examination Of Barriers To benefits-Realisation From Enterprise Systems In public Service. *Paper presented at the Proceedings of the Xth European Conference on Information Systems*, Gdańsk, Poland.

Gable, G. G., Chan, T., & Tan, W. (2003). Offsetting ERP Risk through Maintaining Standardized Application Software. In G. Shanks, P. Seddon & L. Willcocks (Eds.), *Second-Wave Enterprise Resource Planning Systems*. Cambridge, UK: Cambridge University Press.

Gadamer, H. G. (1976). *Philosophical Hermeneutics translated by King, D.E.* Berkley, USA: University of California Press.

Galliers, R. D. (2003). Change as Crisis or Growth? Toward a Trans-disciplinary View of Information Systems as a Field of Study: A Response to Benbasat and Zmud's Call for Returning to the IT Artifact. *Journal of the Association for Information Systems, 6*(4), 337-361.

Gartner Report (2002). *ERP Market in Turmoil: Market Statistics, 2002 (Executive Summary).* Gartner Inc.

Gattiker, T. F., & Goodhue, D. L. (2005). What Happens After ERP Implementation: Understanding The Impact Of Inter-Dependence And Differentiation On Plant-Level Outcomes. *MIS Quarterly, 29*(3), 559-585.

Giddens, A. (1984). *The Constitution Of Society.* Cambridge, UK: Polity.

Gide, E & Soliman. F. (1999). The use of electronic commerce as a strategic tool in intelligent manufacturing systems. *Proceedings of the 2nd International Conference on Recent Advances in Mechatronics, ICRAM'99* Istanbul, Turkey,24-26 May, 1999".

Gosain, S. (2004). Enterprise Information Systems as Objects and Carriers of Institutional Forces: The New iron Cage? *Journal of the Association for Information Systems, 5*(4), 151-182.

Grant, G. G. (2003). Strategic alignment and enterprise systems implementation: the case of Metalco. *Journal of Information Technology, 18*(3), 159-175.

Gregor, S. (2006). The Nature Of Theory In Information Systems. *MIS Quarterly, 30*(3), 611-642.

Gulla, J. A., & Brasethvik, T. (2000). On the Challenge of Business Modelling in Large Scale Reengineering Projects. *Paper presented at The 4th International Conference of Requirements Engineering*, Schumburg, IL.

Gummeson, E. (1999). *Total relationship Marketing - Rethinking Marketing Management : From 4 P's to 30 R's.* Oxford, UK: Butterworth-Heinman.

Gunasekaran, A., Love, P.E.D., Rahimi, F., Miele, R. (2001). A model for investment justifications in information technology projects. *International Journal of Information Management* 21, 349-364.

Hackney, R., Burn, J., & Dhillon. (2000). Challenging Assumptions For Strategic Information Systems Planning: Theoretical Perspectives. *Communications of the Association of Information Systems, 3.*

References

Hammer, M. (1990). Reengineering Work: Don't Automate, Obliterate. *Harvard Business Review, July-August*, 104-112.

Hasan, H. (1998). *Cultural-Historical Psychology and Activity Theory*. In E. G. a. P. H. H. Hasan (Ed.), *Information Systems and Activity Theory Tools in Context*: Wollongong University Press.

He, X. (2004). The ERP challenge in China: a resource based perspective. *Information Systems Journal, 14*, 153-167.

Heap, S. H., Hollis, M., Lyons, B., Sugden, R., & Weale, A. (1992). The Theory Of Choice: A Critical Guide. Oxford, UK: Blackwell

Heidegger, M. (1962). *Being and Time Translated by John Macquarrie & Edward Robinson*. Blackwell Publishing

Heisenberg, W. (1962). *Physics and Philosophy*. New York: Penguin Science.

Herrmann, P. (2005). Evolution of strategic management: The need for new dominant designs. *International Journal of Management Reviews, 7*(2), 111-130.

Hirscheim, R. A. (1985). Information Systems Epistemology: An Historical Perspective. In E. H. Mumford, R. Fitzberald,R., et al., (Ed.), *Research Methods in Information Systems*. North-Holland, Amsterdam.

Hirschheim, R., & Klein, K. (1994). Realizing Emancipatory Principles in Information Systems Development: The Case for ETHICS. *MIS Quarterly, 18*(1), 83-109.

Holland, C. P., & Light, B. (2001). A Stage Maturity Model for Enterprise Resource Planning Systems Use. *The Database for advances in Information Systems, 32*(2), 34-45.

Hussey, J., & Hussey, J. (1997). *Business Research: A Practical Guide For Undergraduate And Postgraduate Students*. London, UK: McMillian Business Press.

Ifinedo, P., & Nahar, N. (2007). ERP Systems Success: AN Empirical Analysis Of How Two Organisational Stakeholder Groups priotize And Evaluate Relevant Measures. *Enterprise Information Systems, 1*(1), 25-48.

Irani, Z. & Love, P.E.D. (2002) Developing a frame of reference for ex-ante IT/IS investment evaluation. *European Journal of Information Systems* 11: 74 – 82.

Irani, Z., Themistocleus, M., Love, P.E.D. (2003) The impact of enterprise application integration on information system lifecycles. *Information and Management* 41: 177-187.

Ives, B., & Jarvenpaa, S. L. (1991). Applications of Global Information Technology: Key Issues for Management. *MIS Quarterly, 24*(3), 33-49.

Jasperson, J., Carter, P. E., & Zmud, R. W. (2005). A comprehensive conceptualisation of post-adoptive behaviours associated with information technology enabled work systems. *MIS Quarterly, 29*(3), 525-557.

References

Johnson, G., & Scholes, K. (2002). *Exploring Corporate Strategy, 6th Ed.* Edinburgh, UK: Pearson Education.

Johnson, G., Scholes, K. and Whittington (2008). *Exploring Corporate Strategy, 8th Ed.* Edinburgh, UK: Pearson Education.

Jones, S. & Hughes, J. (2001). Understanding IS evaluation as a complex social process: a case study of a UK local authority. *European Journal of Information Systems.* 10: 189-203.

Kallinikos. (2004). Deconstructing information packages - Organisational and behavioural implications of ERP systems. *Information Technology and People, 17*(1), 8-30.

Kanter, J. (1992). *Managing With Information.* New Jersey: Prentice Hall.

Karahanna, E., Straub, D. W., & Chervany, N. L. (1999). Information technology adoption across time: a cross sectional comparison of pre-adoption and post-adoption beliefs. *MIS Quarterly, 23*(2), 182-213.

Kayworth, T. R., Chatterjee, D., & Sambamurthy, V. (2001). Theoretical justification for IT infrastructure investments. *Information Resources Management Journal;, 14*(3), 5-14.

Ke, W., Wei, K. K., Chau, P. K., & Deng, Z. (2003). Organisational Learning In ERP Implementation: An Exploratory Study Of Strategic Renewal. *Paper presented at the North Americas Conference On Information Systems*, Tampa, Florida, US.

Keen, P. G. W. (1981). Value Analysis: Justifying Decision Support Systems. *MIS Quarterly, 5*(1), 1-15.

Keen, J. M., & Digrius, B. (2003). Making Technology Investments Profitable: Wiley.

Kelly, S., Holland, C. P., & Light, B. (1999). Enterprise Resource Planning: A Business Approach To Systems Development. *Paper presented at the Proceedings of 5th Conference on information systems.*

Khoo M.H., and Robey, D. (2007). Deciding to upgrade packaged software: a comprehensive case study of motives, contingencies and dependencies. *European Journal of Information Systems* 16: 555-567.

Kilby, R. J. (2004). Critical Thinking, Epistemic Virtue, And The Significance Of Inclusion: Reflections On Harvey Siegel's Theory Of Rationality. *Educational Theory, 54*(3).

King, J. L., & Schrems, E. L. (1978). Cost-Benefit Analysis in Information Systems Development and Operation. *ACM Computer Survey, 10*(1), 19-34.

Kirsch, L. J. (2004). Deploying Common systems Globally: The Dynamics Of Control. *Information Systems Research, 15*(4), 374–395.

Klaus, H., Rosemann, M., & Gable, G. G. (2000). What is ERP? *Information Systems Frontiers, 2*(2), 141-162.

Klein, H. K., & Myers, M. D. (1999). A Set of Principles for Conducting and Evaluating Interpretive Field Studies in Information Systems. *MISQ, 21*(1), 67-94.

References

Kroemmergaard, P., & Rose, J. (2002). Managerial Competences for ERP Journeys. *Information Systems Frontiers, 4*(2), 199-211.

Kuldeep, K., & Van Hillegersberg, J. (2000). ERP Experiences and Evolution. *Communications of the ACM, 43*(4), 22-26.

Lacity, M. C., & Wilcocks, L. P. (1998). An Empirical Investigation Of Information technology Sourcing Practices: Lessons From Experience. *MIS Quarterly 22(3), 363-409.*

Lawrence, F. B., Jennings, D. F., & Reynolds, B. E. (2005). *ERP in Distribution.* South-Western: Thomson.

Layder, D. (1993). *New Strategies in Social Research.* Oxford, UK: Polity Press.

Lee, A. S. (1991). Integrating Positivist and Interpretivist Approaches To Organisational Research. *Organisational Science, 2*(4), 324-365.

Lee, A. S., & Baskerville, R. L. (2003). Generalizing Generalizability in Information Systems. *Information Systems Research, 14*(3), 221(224).

Legare, T. L. (2002). The Role Of Organisational Factors In realizing ERP Benefits. *Information Systems Management, 19*(4), 21-42.

Light, B., & Wills, K. (2001). ERP And Best Of Breed: A Comparative Analysis. *Business Process Management Journal, 7*(3).

Lim, E. T. K., Pan, S. L., & Tan, C. W. (2004). Managing User Acceptance Towards Enterprise resource Planning (ERP) Systems - Understanding The Dissonance Between User Expectations And Managerial Policies. *European journal of Information Systems, 14*, 135-149.

Lorenzo, O., & Kawalek, P. (2005). Embedding The Enterprise Systems Into The Enterprise: A Model Of Corporate Diffusion. *Communications of the AIS, 15*, 609-641.

Love, P.E.D., Irnai, Z., Standing, C., Lin, C., and Burn, J. (2004) The enigma of evaluation: benefit, costs and risks of IT in Australian small-medium-sized enterprises. *Information & Management 42*: 947-964.

Lucas, H. C. J. (2000). *Information technology for Management, 7th Ed.*: McGraw-Hill Higher Education.

Luttrell, W. (2000). "Good enough" methods for ethnographic research. *Harvard Educational Review, 70*(4), 499-523.

Madapusi, A., & D'Souza, D. (2005). Aligning ERP Systems With International Strategies. *Information Systems Management 22, 7-17.*

Malbert, V. A., Soni, A., & M.A., V. (2001). Enterprise Resource Planning: Common Myths Versus Evolving reality. *Business Horizons, May-June*, 69-76.

Markus, M. L. (1989). Case Selection in A Disconfirmatory Case Study. In C. J.I. & P. R. Lawrence (Eds.), *The Information Systems Research Challenge -- Volume 1: Qualitative Research Methods* (pp. 20-26). Boston, MA, USA: Harvard Business School Publishing Division.

References

Markus, M. L., Axline, S., Petrie, D., & Tanis, C. (2000a). Learning from Adopters' Experiences with ERP: Problems encountered and Success Achieved. *Journal of Information Technology, 15*, pp. 245-265.

Markus, M. L., & Tanis, C. (2000). The Enterprise System Experience - From Adoption to Success. In *Zmud, R.W. (ed.) Framing the Domains of IT Research: Glimpsing the Future Through the Past.* Pinaflex Educational Resources, Cincinatti OH: 173-207.

Markus, M. L., Tanis, C., & Van Fenema, P. C. (2000b). Multisite ERP Implementations. *Communications of the ACM, 43*(4), 42-46.

Marshall, P. (2005). Social Constructionism with a Twist of Pragmatism: A Suitable Cocktail for Information Systems Research. *Paper presented at the 16th Australasian Conference on Information Systems,* Sydney, Australia.

Maxwell, J. (1992). Understanding and Validity in Qualitative Research. *Harvard Educational Review, 62*(3), 279-300.

McAulay. (2003). Transformational leadership: A response To limitations in Conventional Information Systems Evaluation. *Electronic Journal of Information Systems, 1*(2).

McGrath, K. (2005). Doing Critical Research In Information Systems: A Case Of Theory And Practice Not Informing Each Other. *Information Systems Journal, 15*, 85-101.

Mckay, J., & Marshall, P. (2004). *Strategic Management of e-Business.* Brisbane, Australia: Wiley.

McMurray, A. J., Pace, W. R., & Scott, D. (2004). *Research: A Commonsense Approach.* Sydney, Australia: Thomson. Social Science Press.

McNurlin, B. C., & Sprague, R. H. J. (2004). *Information systems management in practice. 6th edition.* Upper Saddle River, NJ: Prentice Hall.

Melin, U. (2003). The ERP System As A Part Of An Organisation's Administrative Paradox. *Paper presented at the European Conference On Information Systems.*

Melville, N., Kraemer, K., & Gurbaxani, V. (2004). Review: Information Technology And Organisational Performance: An Integrative Model Of It Business Value. *MIS Quarterly, 28*(2), 283-322.

Microsoft Open Letter (2003). *Microsoft Letter to Prospective Clients.* Redeemed from Microsoft customer September 2003.

Miles, M. B., & Huberman, A. M. (1994). *Qualitative Data Analysis, 2nd Ed.* Thousand Oaks: Sage Publications Ltd.

Milford, M., & Stewart, G. (2000). Are ERP Implementations Qualitatively Different From Other Large Scale Systems Implementations? *Paper presented at the Americas Conference On Information Systems.*

Mingers, J. (2001). Combining IS Research Methods: Towards a Pluralist Methodology. *Information Systems Research, 12*(3), 240–259.

References

Mintzberg, H. (1979). *The Structuring of Organisations:* Prentice-Hall International.

Mishler, E. G. (1990). Validation in Inquiry-Guided Research: The Role of Exemplars in Narrative Studies. *Harvard Educational Review, 60*(4), 415.

Monk, E., & Wagner, B. (2006). *Concepts In Enterprise Resource Planning.* Boston, Massachusetts, US: Thomson Source Technology.

Monod, E. (2004). Methodological Distinction And Conditions Of Possibilities. *Information and Organisation, 14*, 105-121.

Moody, D. L., & Bowles, S. (2000). Building Links Between IS Research And Professional Practice: Improving The Relevance And Impact Of IS Research. *Paper presented at the 21st International Conference On Information Systems*, Brisbane, Australia.

Morton, N. A., & Hu, Q. (2004). The Relationship Between Organisational Structure and Enterprise Resource Planning Systems: A Structural Contingency Theory Approach. *Paper presented at the Proceedings Of The Tenth Americas Conference On Information Systems*, New York, USA.

Mumford, E. (2003). Information Systems Research and the Quest for Certainty. *Journal of the Association for Information Systems, 4*(4), 197-205.

Murphy, K. E. a. S., S.J. (2002). Intangible benefits valuation in ERP projects. *Information Systems Journal, 12*, 301-320.

Nandhakumar, J., Rossi, M., & Talvinen, J. (2005). The Dynamics Of Contextual Forces Of ERP Implementation. *Journal of Strategic Information Systems, 14*, 221-242.

Navisions Annual Report (2002). Navision Annual report 2001/2002. *Retrieved September 2004 from Microsoft.Com.*

Ndede-Amadi, A. A. (2004). What Strategic Alignment, Process Redesign, Enterprise resource Planning, and e-commerce4 have In Common: Enterprise-Wide Computing. *Business Process Management Journal, 10*(2), 184-199.

Newell, S., Wagner, E. L., & David, G. (2007). Clumsy Information System: A Critical review Of Enterprise Systems. In Desouza (Ed.), *Agile Information Systems: Conceptualization, Construction, and Management*: Butterworth-Heinemann

Olsen, W. (2004). Methodological Triangulation and Realist Research: An Indian Examplar. In B. Carter & C. New (Eds.), *Making Realism Work: Realist Social Theory and Empircal Research.* London and New York: Routledge.

Orlikowski, W. J., & Baroudi, J. J. (1991). Studying Information Technology in Organisations: Research Approaches and Assumptions. *Information System Research, 2*(1), 1-28.

Orlikowski, W. J., & Robey, D. (1991). Information Technology and the Structuring of Oganisations. *Information System Research, 2*(2), 143-169.

References

Orlikowoski, W. J., Barley, S. R., & Robey, D. (2001). Technology And Institutions: What Can Research On Information Technology And Research On Ogranizations Learn From Each Other. *MIS Quarterly, 25*(2), 84-96.

Orlikowoski, W. J., & Iacono, C. S. (2001). Research Commentary: Desperately Seeking the "IT" in IT Research - A Call to Theorizing the IT Artefact. *Information System Research, 12*(2), 121-134.

Osteraker, M. (2001). Phenomenography As A Research Method In Management research [Electronic Version]. *Swedish School of Economics and Business Administration in Vasa.* Retrieved 14 January 2006 from
http://www.ecsocman.edu.ru/images/pubs/2002/12/27/0000034593/phenomenography.pdf.

Paré, G. (2004). Investigating Information Systems with Positivist Case Study Research. *Communications of the Association for Information Systems, 13*, 233-264.

Parker, M. M., Benson, R. J., & Trainor, H. E. (1988). *Information Economics - Linking Business Performance to Information Technology.* Englewood Cliffs (USA). Prentice-Hall.

Patton, M. Q. (1990). *Qualitative Evaluation And Research Methods (2nd ed.).* London, UK: Sage.

Peppard, J., Breu, K. (2003). Beyond Alignment: A Co-evolutionary View of the Information Strategy Process. *Paper presented at the Twenty-Fourth International Conference on Information Systems.*

Peterson, R. R. (2004). Integration Strategies and Tactics for Information Technology Governance. In J. Travers (Ed.), *Strategies for Information Technology Governance.* Hershey, PA.: Idea Group Publishing.

Phelan, P. , Z. B., Frey N. (2002). *Strategic Analysis Report : ERP Improvement and ERP II Deployment — Maximizing Return on Investment.*

Porter, M. E. (1980). *Competitive Strategy: Techniques for Analysing Industries and Competitors.* New York, USA: Free Press.

Porter, M. E. (1988). From Competitive Advantage to Corporate Strategy. *The McKinsy Quarterly,* 35-66.

Poston, R., & Grabski, S. (2000). The Impact Of Enterprise resource Planning Systems On Firm Performance. *Paper presented at the Proceedings of the twenty first international conference on Information systems,* Brisbane, Queensland, Australia

Potter, D. (1987). *Long Range Systems Planning.* Datamation.

Pozzebon, M. (2004). Conducting and Evaluating Critical Interpretive Research. *Paper presented at the IFIP Working Group 8.2 Conference,* Manchester, UK.

Pozzebon, M., & Pinsonneult, A. (2004). The Implementation Of Configurable Information Systems: Negotiations Between Global principles And Local Contexts. *Paper presented at the Twenty-Fifth International Conference On Information Systems, Washington* , D.C. , US.

References

Punch, K. F. (2002). *Developing Effective Research Proposals*. London, Thousand Oaks, New Dehli: Sage Publications.

Ratcliffe, D. (2004). The World of IT Service Management - the Past, Present & Future of ITIL. *Paper presented at the SMF LIG Meeting*, Houston, USA.

Reich, B. H., & Bennasat, I. (2000). Factors That Influence the Social Dimension Of Alignment Between Business And Information Technology Objectives. *MIS Quarterly, 24*(1), 81-113.

Remenyi, D., Sherwood-Smith, M., & White, T. (1997). *Achieving Maximum Value from Information Systems: A Process Approach:* John Wiley & Sons, New York.

Remenyi , D. (2000). The Elusive Nature of Delivering Benefits from IT Investment. *Electronic Journal of Information Systems Evaluation, 3*(1).

Remenyi, D. (2001). *Business Models for e-business*. Henley College of Management.

Remenyi, D., Bannister, F., & Money, A. (2007). *The Effective Measurement and Management of ICT Costs and Benefits*. Oxford, UK: CIMA Publishing.

Rockart, J. F. (1975). Chief executives define their own data needs. *Harvard Business Review, 57*(2), 81-93.

Rolland, C., & Prakash, N. (2000). Bridging the Gap between Organisational Needs and ERP Functionality. *Requirements Engineering, 5*(3), 190-193.

Rorty, R. (1999). *Philosophy and Social Hope*. London: Penguin Books.

Rosemann, M. (2001). Evaluating The Management Of Enterprise Systems With the Balance Scorecard. In *Information technology evaluation methods and management* (pp. 171-184). New York, USA: John Wiley and Son, Inc.

Rosemann, M. (2003). Enterprise Systems Management with Reference Process Models. In G. Shanks, P. Seddon & L. Willcocks (Eds.), *Second-Wave Enterprise Resource Planning Systems*. Cambridge, UK: Cambridge University Press.

Rosemann, M., Vessey, I., & Weber, R. (2004). Alignment In Enterprise Systems Implementations: The Role Of Ontological Distance. *Paper presented at the Proceedings of the Twenty-Fifth International Conference On Information Systems,* Charlottesville, Virginia, USA.

Sammon, D., Adam, F., & Carton, F. (2003). Benefits Realisation Through ERP: The Re-Emergence of Data Warehousing. *Electronic Journal of Information Systems Evaluation, 6*(2).

Sap Annual report (2006). 2006 Annual report. Retrieved September 2007 from www.Sap.Com.

Sarkis, J., & Sundarraj, R P. (2005). Auditing the System in Use: Value Beyond the Baseline. In *Strategic ERP Extensions and Use*. Stanford, California, USA: Stanford University Press.

Scheer, W., & Habermann, F. (2000). Making ERP A Success. *Communications of the ACM, 43*(4), 57-61.

Scott-Morton, M. S. (1991). *The Corporation of the 1990s*. Oxford: University Press.

References

Seddon, P. B., Graeser, V., & Willcocks, L. P. (2002). Measuring IS Organisation effectiveness: An overview and update of senior management perspective. *The DATA BASE for Advances in Information Systems, 33*(2).

Seddon, P., Shanks, G., & Willcocks, L. (2003). Introduction: ERP - The Quiet Revolution? In G. Shanks, P. Seddon & L. Willcocks (Eds.), *Second-Wave Enterprise Resource Planning Systems*. Cambridge, UK: Cambridge University Press.

Seddon, P. B., & Scheepers, R. (2006). Other-Settings Generalization In IS Research. *Paper presented at the Twenty-Seventh International Conference On Information Systems*, Milwaukee, US.

Seddon, P. B., Staples, S., Patnayakuni, R., & Bowtell, M. (1999). Dimensions of Information Systems Success. *Communications of the Association for Information Systems, 20*(2), 2-61.

Sedera, D., Gable, G., & Chan, T. (2004). Measuring Enterprise Systems Success: The Importance Of A Multiple Stakeholder Perspective. *Paper presented at the European Conference On Information Systems.*

Sethi, V., & King, W. (1998). *Organisational Transformation Through Business Process Reengineering: Applying Lessons Learned.* Prentice-Hall.

Shang, S., & Seddon, P. B. (2002). Assessing and managing the benefits of enterprise system: the business manager's perspective. *Information Systems Journal, 12*, 271-299.

Shang, S., & Seddon, P. (2003). A Comprehensive Framework for Assessing and Managing the Benefits of Enterprise Systems: The Business Manager's Perspective. In G. Shanks, P. Seddon & L. Willcocks (Eds.), *Second-Wave Enterprise Resource Planning Systems*. Cambridge, UK: Cambridge University Press.

Shang, S. C. S. (2005). Enterprise Systems in International Business Operations: The Benefits and Problems Of Fit In International Enterprise Systems Implementation. *Paper presented at the Proceedings of the Eleventh Americas Conference on Information Systems*, Omaha, NE, USA.

Sharif, A., Irani, Z., & Love, P. E. D. (2005). Integrating ERP Using EAI: A Model For Post Hoc Evaluation. *European Journal of Information Systems, 14*, 162-174.

Soh, C., & Sia, S. K. (2005). The Challenges Of Implementing "Vanilla" Versions Of Enterprise Systems. *MIS Quarterly Executive, 4*(3), 375-379.

Somers, T. M., & Nelson, K. (2001). The Critical Success Factors Across the Stages of ERP Implementations. *Paper presented at the Hawaii International Conference On Information Systems*, Hawaii, US.

Somers, T. M., Nelson, K., & Ragowsky, A. (2003). Enterprise Resource Planning For The Next Millennium: development Of An Integrative Framework And Implications For Research. *Paper presented at the Americas Conference On Information Systems.*

References

Stake, R. E. (1994). Case Studies in N. K. a. L. Denzin, Y.S. (Ed.), Handbook of Qualitative Research (pp. 236-247). Thousand Oaks, C.A.: Sage.

Staples, D. S., Wong, I., & Seddon, P. B. (2002). Having Expectations Of Information Systems Benefits That Match Received Benefits: does it really matter? *Information and Management, 40*, 115-131.

Stefanou, C.J. (2001). A framework for ex-ante evaluation of ERP software. European Journal of Information Systems. 10 : 205-215.

Stein, A., Hawkings, P., & Foster, S. (2003). ERP Post Implementation: A New Journey. *Paper presented at the 14th Australian Conference On Information Systems*, Perth, Western Australia.

Strassman, P. A. (1997). The Politics Of Information Management : *Policy Guidelines.*

Strong, D. M., Volkoff, O., & Elmes, M. B. (2003). ERP Systems And The Paradox Of Control. *Paper presented at the Ninth Americas Conference on Information Systems*, Tampa, Florida.

Sumner, M. (2005). *Enterprise Resource Planning.* Upper Saddle River, New jersey, US: Pearson, Prentice Hall.

Swanton, B. & Finley, I. (2007). SOA and BPM for Enterprise Applications: A Dose of Reality. *AMR Research Repor May.* AMR Research Inc.

Swift, B. (2001). Making Sense of application service providers, part one: Business computing comes full circle. *Risk Management, 48*(7), 21-24.

Tan, C. W., & Pan, S.L., P. (2002). ERP Success: The Search for A Comprehensive Framework. *Paper presented at the Eight Americas Conference On Information Systems, Dallas, Texas US.*

Tanaszi, M. (2003). *IT Does Matter.* 2005

Tesch, R. (1990). *Qualitative Research: Analysis Types and Software Tools.* New York, London: The Falmer Press.

Themistocleous, M., Irani, Z., & O'Keefe, R. M. (2001). ERP and Application Integration. *Business Process Management Journal, 7*(3), 195-204.

Venkatraman, N. (1994a). IT-Enabled Business Transformation: From Automation to Business Scope redefinition. *Sloan Management Review, Winter 1994*, 73-87.

Vessey, I., Ramesh, V., & Glass, R. L. (2002). Research In Information Systems: An Empirical Study Of Diversity In The Discipline and Its Journals. *Journal of Management Information Systems, 19*(2), 129-174.

Wagner, E. L., & Newell, S. (2004). 'Best' For Whom?: The Tension Between 'Best Practice' ERP Packages And Divers Epistemic Cultures In A University Context. *Journal Of strategic Information Systems, 13*, 305-328.

Walsham, G. (1995). The emergence of interpretivism in IS research. *Information Systems research, 6*(4), 376-394.

References

Walsham, G. (2005). Learning About Being Critical. *Information Systems Journal, 15.*

Ward, J., & Peppard, J. (2002). *Strategic Planning for Information Systems.* Chichester: John Wiley and Sons.

Ward, K. W., Brown, S. A., & Massey, A. P. (2005). Organisational influences on attitudes in mandatory system use environments: a longitudinal study. *International Journal of Business Information Systems, 1*(1/2), 9-30.

Ward, J., Hemingway, C., & Daniel, E. (2005). A Framework For Addressing The Organisational Issues Of Enterprise Systems Implementations. *Journal Of Strategic Information Systems, 14*, 97-119.

Watson, P. (2006). *On-line Analytical Processing OLAP*: Teradata University Network.

Weber, R. (1997). *Ontological Foundations of Information Systems.* Blackburn, Vic., Australia: Coopers and Lybrand.

Wei, H., Wang, E. T. G., & Ju, P. (2005). Understanding Misalignment And Cascading Change of ERP Implementation : A Stage View Of Process Analysis. *European journal of Information Systems, 14*, 324-334.

Weill, P., & Woodham, R. (2002). Don't just Lead, Govern: Implementing Effective IT Governance. *MIT Sloan Management Working Paper.*

Weill, P., & Ross, J. W. (2004). *IT Governance. How Top Performers Manage IT Decision Rights for Superior Results (1st ed.):* Harvard Business School Publishing.

Weitzman, E. A., & Miles, M. B. (1995). *Computer Programs For Qualitative Data Analysis.* Thousand Oaks, California, US: Sage Publications.

Willcocks, L. P., Feeny, D. F., & Islei, G. (1997). *Managing IT as a Strategic Resource.* Maidenhead: McGraw-Hill.

Willcocks, L. P., & Sykes, R. (2003). The Role of the CIO and IT Functions in ERP. In G. Shanks, P. Seddon & L. Willcocks (Eds.), *Second-Wave Enterprise Resource Planning Systems.* Cambridge, UK: Cambridge University Press.

Yin, R. K. (2003a). *Applications of Case Study Research, 2nd Ed.* Thousand Oaks: Sage Publications Ltd.

Yin, R. K. (2003b). *Case Study Research Design and Methods Third Ed.*: Sage Publications.

Zack, M. H. (1999). Developing a Knowledge Strategy. *California Management Review, 41*(3), 125-145.

Zuboff, S. (1988). *In the Age of The Smart Machine.* Oxford: Heinemann Professional Publishers.

Appendix A. Possible factors and permutations of a quantitative survey.

Factor	Rationale	Possible Occurrences
Industry	Australian economics multi-factor productivity analysis industry sectors	17
Organisation size	Small, Medium, Large	3
Organisation Type	Broadly, product or resourced focused	2
Position in the value system	Arbitrarily	4
Profitability	Highly profitable , moderately profitable, breakeven, small loss, large loss	5
Deprecation	Fully, to a large extent, slightly, little (or revalued)	4
Purpose of the system	Broad scope, limited scope, supply chain integration as well as efficiencies and effective focus	6
Age	1 to 15 years in 3 year segments	5
Success	Arbitrarily	4
System Status	Ongoing support, concern over future, system matured	3
Total Possible Permutations		2,937,600

Appendix B. The Foundations of Social Research

Epistemology	Theoretical Perspective	Methodology	Methods
Objectivism	Positivism (and post-	Experimental research	Sampling
Constructionism	positivism)	Survey research	Measurement and scaling
Subjectivism	Interpretivism	Ethnography	Questionnaire
(and their variants)	Symbolic interactionism	Phenomenological	Observation
	Phenomenology	research	Participant
	Hermeneutics	Grounded theory	Non-participant
	Critical inquiry	Heuristic inquiry	Interview
	Feminism	Action Research	Focus group
	Postmodernism	Discourse analysis	Case study
	etc.	Feminist standpoint	Life history
		research	Narrative
		Etc.	Visual ethnographic
			methods
			Statistical analysis
			Data reduction
			Theme identification
			Comparative analysis
			Cognitive mapping
			Interpretative methods
			Document analysis
			Content analysis
			Conversation analysis
			Etc.

Appendix C. Case Study and Construct Analysis

	Provider SAP	Server Dynamics (AX)	Contractor Dynamics (AX)	Global Oracle	Builder SAP
Original Implementation and Its Antecedents	- Main driver Y2K and desire to move away from bespoke software. - Chose the application by comparing functionality and processes. - Identified application cost and established a team to find the required savings: benefits were achieved. - Implementatio n poor due to extent of customisations and lack of	- Main driver over modified out-of-date legacy application. - Cost of application identified from potential applications. -Benefits identified as personnel cost reduction and cost avoidance when growing. - Considerable post-live problems that lasted 7 months. - Viewed as a success. - Customisation of application seen as necessary.	- Main driver extensively modified legacy application. - Implementation justified against the information needs of each division. The division being sold subsequently may indicate an underlying reason. -Implementation considered a success - Business-wide implementation of application in near 'vanilla' form.	- Main driver global standardisation, replacing robust, recently acquired ERP in Australia. - System chosen from a short list of three vendors, the Author considered the most flexible. - Intention was for the application to be as vanilla as possible. - Local opinion is the system is not ideal constituting a backward move. The global perspective is	- Main driver standardised global processes, prior application being modified to sub-unit requirements. - System chosen for match with processes. - Organisation did not identify an overall cost but costs each implementation. - Thought of very favourably by users and management.

	focus on processes			very positive.	
Impact of Strategy Process on ERP	- Robust formal business strategy process - Strategy driven internal requirements - IT strategy/plan derived from business unit requirements - IT capabilities not part of strategy formulation	- Informal business strategy process - Strategy driven by customer requirements - IT strategy/initiatives coordinated at low level by users and Development. Manager - IT capabilities not part of strategy formulation	- Lightly formal strategy aided by infrequent external consultant guidance - Poor dissemination of strategy - Strategy driven by demand for growth - IT strategy by CIO's interpretation endorsed by external consultants - IT capabilities not part of strategy formulation	- Formal, well communicated global strategy - Increasingly less autonomy for regions and countries - Globally centralised IT strategy, gate-keeping IT worldwide - Strategy driven by booming market - IT capabilities not part of strategy formulation but informed by strategy	- Formal centralised strategy extremely well communicated - Countries have some autonomy but are benchmarked globally - Strategy driven by growth and best price product - Globally centralised IT strategy, gate-keeping IT worldwide - IT capabilities part of strategy formulation
Financial Procedures and Imperatives	- Public company with large asset expenditure - Cash available for budgeted items - Major	- Highly geared - Limited cash - Internally maintained ERP, cost conscious approach -	- High growth with low profit - Limited cash - Limited investment in ERP, least cost approach - Capitalises	- Financially very sound - Application acquired at corporate level and allocated - Implementation	- Financially very sound with robust long-term financial planning - Application acquired at corporate level

	ongoing investment in ERP - Capitalises customisations -TCO is an increasing problem - Investment precludes change of application	Customisations not capitalised - Financial position impacts upgrade and maintenance decisions. - Investment precludes change of application	customisations - Wishes to change ERP in the unimplemented divisions, cost being an issue	costed regionally and accrued centrally - Cash rich - Direct ongoing investment in standardisation and upgrades - Capitalises customisations - Investment precludes change of application	and allocated - Implementation costed regionally and accrued centrally - Cash generative with acquisitions as priority - Major ongoing, strategically driven investment in ERP - Capitalises customisations - Application change if absolutely necessary
Upgrades and Their Antecedents	- Managed only 'technical' non-functional upgrades, individual cost being 7.5% of original implementatio n. - Functional	- Cost of upgrades seen as far too expensive - Difficult to upgrade due to customisations overlapping with new functionality - Maintenance	- Changing application due to cost of upgrades to develop existing application - Upgrade of old system prevented by excessive cost - Very old	Upgrades occur frequently to ensure the system is standardised globally and to get Oracle support - Upgrades are viewed as expensive	- High cost to upgrade previous ERP prompted acquisition of new ERP - Planned to upgrade bi-annually, release customisations, and have

	upgrade too expensive due to customisations, and time consuming - Upgrade desired to reverse engineering customisations - Author increases maintenance costs if application not upgraded - Missing functional opportunities through not upgrading	ceased and upgrades not taken thus resulting in ERP legacy - Very old applications are not supported by Author - Problem overcome by chasing sunk cost of maintenance agreement and ceasing agreement	applications not supported by Author - Wants to upgrade new system regularly and minimise customisations	- Low local benefit indicates a cost benefit analysis desirable prior to deciding to upgrade - Support withdrawn if application is not upgraded to current version - Customisations restricted to enable upgrades	improved processes following upgrades Author to increase maintenance costs if application not upgraded - Customisations minimised to enable upgrades and standard processes
Perception of IS	- Perspective of ERP not consistent - Management view is 'neutral'; users of the application regularly are happy; infrequent users are less	- Perception of ERP seen as positive at all levels - Organisation fundamentally relies on ERP	- ERP critical to organisation success - ERP perceived as being sub-optimised	- IS in general is not seen as "core business" - ERP implementation impact is negative on users; and positive on managers. - ERP technology	- IS is fundamental to business - Users perceive ERP to be inferior to previous implementation - Management acknowledge advantage of standard global

				considered to be out of date by IT personnel	application - IT personnel thought the implementation, being business led, was good
satisfied - Complexity of product blamed for poor acceptance - Perception changing to wanting a vanilla application					.
Re-implementations	- Re-implemented finance to meet changing requirements - Poor implementatio n blamed on consultants - implementatio n is seen to be 'stifling' the business - Plan to re-implement when upgrading	- System setup not seen to be optimal - Consultants advice only an opinion - Will not re-implement to overcome problems	- Cannot re-implement due to reliance on customisations and unsupported application	- Standard system with considered and minimal customisations, so reimplementatio n will not ever be necessary	- Unsuccessful attempt to re-implement previous ERP to common processes - Implementing SAP so organisations have standard processes
Influences and Consequence of Software Authors and	- Author needs to be well respected global	- Author needs to be financial strong and viable in the	-See 'partnering' software author as imperative in	- Author flexibility, global footprint, and help with	- Global capability of SAP important - Technological

Resellers	organisation	long-term	delivery of IT	maintenance	' know how'
	- Author exerts	- Support by	- Found with	module pivotal	seen as an
	pressure to	VAR seen as	ERP systems	to decision to	advantage
	upgrade	poor	that	use software	- Author
	through	- The author is	organisational	- Oracle asserts	increases
	increasing	seen as too	size means that	pressure to	application cost
	maintenance	distant from the	partnering with	upgrade through	- Author remote
	costs	relationship.	large ERP	withdrawing	from the
	- 20% cost of	- The resellers	author is not	support	implementation
	application p.a.	perceived poor	possible		
	is seen as a	performance is			
	maximum	impacting			
	maintenance	Microsoft's			
	cost	image.			
	- Consultancy				
	seen as poor				
	- Adding				
	modules				
	increases the				
	maintenance				
	cost and is,				
	therefore,				
	avoided				
	- Training is				
	poor and				
	teaches				
	functions				
	rather than				
	functionality				
	and a process				
	view.				
	- Software				
	Author seen				
	as remote.				

Environmental Influences	- No apparent power asserted on ERP management and evaluation from external sources	- Specialised industry requires software to be developed - Customer requirements continually impact ERP customisation decisions	- Believe that Australia follows US with regard to IT - Integration with partners seen as important function for ERP - Press information of failed ERP did not cause concern that the product would not be implemented successfully	- Customers were the main driver for commonality - It is not necessary to have the same ERP as partners	- Customers and supplier requirements important in evaluating ERP functions - Transmitting documents via EDI was seen as beneficial
Evaluation Procedures	- Tangible evaluation of projects over $50,000 with NPV hurdle rate - Below $50,000 just risk assessment - IT budget increased as business cases are approved	- Cost rigorously policed - No formal evaluation of application benefits - No sign off of customisations, the 'person who screams the loudest' is addressed first - No standard	- External review by consultants identified focus of IS - System to support growth - Benefits not quantified - Cost analysis are undertaken - No standard capital expenditure	- No tangible or intangible benefits appraisal - Cost negotiated globally - Implementations costed individually - Benefits difficult to identify	- Created business case with organisational cost savings as basis for IT application - Benefits give largely intangible strategic advantage - Not possible to identify tangible

		capital	request	- Seeking	benefits
	- Strategic projects meeting strategic objectives of business units are generally approved - Upgrades to hardware and software have highest priority - Tangible benefits considered to be difficult or impossible to identify - Payback projects ranked lowest; business as usual for ranked highest - No calculation for cost of ownership	expenditure request	- CIO puts expenditure proposals linked to the 'strategy document' on CFO desk for automatic signature.	benefits is not considered worthwhile considering time and effort spent	- High level budget becomes detailed on country implementation
Approach to Customisations	- High level of ongoing customisations - Originate at departmental	- System heavily modified and costly to upgrade - Make	-Original system highly developed - Embargo on	- Customisations tightly controlled and heavily resisted	- Recognised that developing previous ERP caused many problems

	level and below - Differing evaluation techniques based on cost and strategic factors - Respond to "a lot of noise", they does not actually need to be addressed - Find some customisation proposed in implementatio n unnecessary - Cost of ownership and increasing issue	immediate customisations to system - Find some customisation proposed in implementation unnecessary - Evaluation not imposed	any customisations to old system - Customisations to new ERP will be minimised - Evaluation of customisations informal - Recognise customisations are necessary	- Regional requirements are sanctioned globally - Customisation costs are not a major issue - Cost of ownership is a major factor	- Customisation are controlled globally and must be part of global process - Local customisations only sanctioned for legal or specific market requirements - Cost of dev not a major issue - Cost of ownership a major factor - Integrity of core transaction data is protected
Restrictions and Limitations Imposed by ERP	- ERP will restrict an organisation, unless it is entirely new - It is more difficult to change processes post ERP implementatio	- Organisation was heavily restricted during the few months after the system was made live - ERP moved organisations' bottlenecks from one department to	- Original system very restrictive, particularly with reporting - Few ERP competitors restricts competitive advantage from ERP	- The system is cumbersome due to lack of customisation	- Low customised standard ERP requires 'work arounds' - Thinking of selling an organisation as it does not fit standard ERP procedures

	n - Reporting of information is difficult	another - Reporting of information is difficult			
Approach to Business Process Analysis	- Started to focus on processes 6 years after live due to customisations hampering process - Mapped all processes with aid of SAP pre-sales tool - Now sees business process analysis as fundamental to ERP - Business process analysis now used to identify customisations	- Functions analysed as part of the implementation and these guided customisations - No changes made to processes to align with application - There is no focus on processes post-live	- Process analysis not performed but 'old' system not seen to be supporting an organisation's process	- ERP standard processes implemented which, according to users, have had a negative effect - managers believe it provides vital organisation and customer business wide information	- Worldwide standard best practice process identified by the business - ERP selected for its match with processes - Processes rigidly maintained
Expected Lifespan of ERP	- Strategy manager: ERP would last 5 to 10 years - Finance	- The Dev. manager: ERP would last not less than 5 to 10 years and would	- Finance manager and CIO it "was a 25 year investment"	- The CIO: the system will not be changed in the foreseeable future, but	- The worldwide co-ordinator: the ERP would last not less than 10 to 15 years and

		manager: as long as SAP is a major vendor - IT manager: could not foresee a time when the organisation would change from SAP	be replaced due to changing requirements - A key user: could not envisage ever changing - The IT manager: expected the application to last 15 to 25 years and might change due to technological advancements		might ultimately be changed due to a move to the hosting of applications	could not predict why the application would be changed - Finance manager: at least 10 years, but the driver for change might be competitor advantage through IT - The IT manager: as long as 20 years but change might be due to the supplier charging unreasonably